Banking, Insurance and Financial Services

Banking, Insurance and Financial Services

Shailendra Sengar

ANMOL PUBLICATIONS PVT. LTD.
NEW DELHI-110 002 (INDIA)

ANMOL PUBLICATIONS PVT. LTD.
H.O.: 4374/4B, Ansari Road, Darya Ganj,
New Delhi-110 002 (India)
Ph.: 23278000, 23261597

B.O.: No. 1015, Ist Main Road, BSK IIIrd Stage
IIIrd Phase, IIIrd Block
Bangalore - 560 085 (India)
Visit us at: www.anmolpublications.com

Banking, Insurance and Financial Services

First Published, 2008

ISBN 978-81-261-3438-0

PRINTED IN INDIA

Printed at Mehra Offset Press, Delhi.

Contents

Preface

This Encyclopaedic Series of Career and Vocational Guidance Covers careers, describing jobs, places of employment, working conditions, qualifications, education and training. This has been developed to aid career and counsellors and job placement coordinators in planning activities for students and potential students about career vocational education programs. It contains a career and vocational guidance model which clarifies what career and vocational guidance services mean and what planners should include in their activities. The model shows an interrelatedness among major thrusts with career development being a central theme of vocational guidance. All of the thrusts depicted in the model represent essential services that should be available to students in career and vocational education programs. The encyclopaedia deals with various sections which correspond to the major thrusts identified in the model: (1) career development; (2) recruitment; (3) guidance and counselling; (4) placement; (5) follow-up and follow-through; and (6) consultation. Each section contains an outline of the perceived needs of the topic, an overview of the topic relative to career and vocational guidance, and some suggested activities and strategies that may be useful in meeting student needs.

It also contains current information about occupations, employment trends, and job searching. Materials on career decision-making, internships, and salaries are also located in each volume. This Series of Encyclopaedia helps students assess their potential for various careers.

Shailendra Sengar

1

Career in Banking Sector

Banking

Significant Points: Wage and salary employment in banking is projected to decline 2 percent over the 2004-14 period, compared to 14 percent growth for wage and salary employment across all industries, as consolidation and automation make banks more efficient.

Office and administrative support workers constitute 2 out of 3 jobs; tellers account for about 1 out of 4 jobs.

Many job opportunities are expected for tellers and other office and administrative support workers because these occupations are large and have high turnover.

Many management positions are filled by promoting experienced, technically skilled professional personnel.

Nature of the Industry: Banks safeguard money and valuables and provide loans, credit and payment services, such as checking accounts, money orders and cashier's checks. Banks also may offer investment and insurance products, which they were once prohibited from selling. As a variety of models for cooperation and integration among finance industries have emerged, some of the traditional distinctions between banks, insurance companies and securities firms have diminished. In spite of these changes, banks continue to maintain and perform their primary role-accepting deposits and lending funds from these deposits.

There are several types of banks, which differ in the number of services they provide and the clientele they serve. Although some of the differences between these types of banks have lessened as they begin to expand the range of products and services they offer, there are still key distinguishing traits. Commercial banks, which dominate this industry, offer a full range of services for individuals, businesses and governments.

These banks come in a wide range of sizes, from large global banks to regional and community banks. Global banks are involved in international lending and foreign currency trading, in addition to the more typical banking services. Regional banks have numerous branches and automated teller machine (ATM) locations throughout a multi-state area that provide banking services to individuals. Banks have become more oriented toward marketing and sales.

As a result, employees need to know about all types of products and services offered by banks. Community banks are based locally and offer more personal attention, which many individuals and small businesses prefer. In recent years, online banks-which provide all services entirely over the Internet-have entered the market, with some success. However, many traditional banks have also expanded to offer online banking and some formerly Internet-only banks are opting to open branches.

Savings banks and savings and loan associations, sometimes called thrift institutions, are the second largest group of depository institutions. They were first established as community-based institutions to finance mortgages for people to buy homes and still cater mostly to the savings and lending needs of individuals.

Credit unions are another kind of depository institution. Most credit unions are formed by people with a common bond, such as those who work for the same company or belong to the same labour union or church. Members pool their savings and, when they need money, they may borrow from the credit union, often at a lower interest rate than that demanded by other financial institutions.

Federal Reserve banks are Government agencies that perform many financial services for the Government. Their chief responsibilities are to regulate the banking industry and to help implement our Nation's monetary policy so our economy can run more efficiently by controlling the Nation's money supply-the total quantity of money in the country, including cash and bank deposits.

For example, during slower periods of economic activity, the Federal Reserve may purchase government securities from commercial banks, giving them more money to lend, thus expanding the economy. Federal Reserve banks also perform a variety of services for other banks. For example, they may make emergency loans to banks that are short of cash and clear checks that are drawn and paid out by different banks.

Interest on loans is the principal source of revenue for most banks, making their various lending departments critical to their success. The commercial lending department loans money to companies to start or expand a business or to purchase inventory and capital equipment.

The consumer lending department handles student loans, credit cards and loans for home improvements, debt consolidation and automobile purchases. Finally, the mortgage lending department loans money to individuals and businesses to purchase real estate.

The money to lend comes primarily from deposits in checking and savings accounts, certificates of deposit, money market accounts and other deposit accounts that consumers and businesses set up with the bank. These deposits often earn interest for the owner and accounts that offer checking provide an easy method for making payments safely without using cash. Deposits in many banks are insured by the Federal Deposit Insurance Corporation, which ensures that depositors will get their money back, up to a stated limit, if a bank should fail.

Technology is having a major impact on the banking industry. For example, many routine bank services that once required a teller, such as making a withdrawal or deposit, are now available through ATMs that allow people to access their accounts 24 hours a day. Also, direct deposit allows companies and governments to electronically transfer payments into various accounts. Further, debit cards, which may also used as

ATM cards, instantaneously deduct money from an account when the card is swiped across a machine at a store's cash register. Electronic banking by phone or computer allows customers to pay bills and transfer money from one account to another. Through these channels, bank customers can also access information such as account balances and statement history. Some banks have begun offering online account aggregation, which makes available in one place detailed and up-to date information on a customer's accounts held at various institutions.

Advancements in technology have also led to improvements in the ways in which banks process information. Use of check imaging, which allows banks to store photographed checks on the computer, is one such example that has been implemented by some banks. Other types of technology have greatly impacted the lending side of banking. For example, the availability and growing use of credit scoring software allows loans to be approved in minutes, rather than days, making lending departments more efficient.

Other fundamental changes are occurring in the industry as banks diversify their services to become more competitive. Many banks now offer their customers financial planning and asset management services, as well as brokerage and insurance services, often through a subsidiary or third party. Others are beginning to provide investment banking services that help companies and governments raise money through the issuance of stocks and bonds, also usually through a subsidiary. As banks respond to deregulation and as competition in this sector grows, the nature of the banking industry will continue to undergo significant change.

Working Conditions: The average workweek for nonsupervisory workers in depository credit intermediation was 35.8 hours in 2004. Supervisory and managerial employees, however, usually work substantially longer hours. About 1 out of 10 employees in 2004, mostly tellers, worked part-time.

Working conditions also vary according to where the employee works. Employees in a typical branch work weekdays, some evenings if the bank is open late and Saturday mornings. Hours may be longer for workers in bank branches located in grocery stores and shopping malls, which are open most evenings and weekends. Branch office jobs, particularly teller positions, require continual communication with customers, repetitive tasks and a high level of attention to security. Tellers also work for long periods in a confined space.

To improve customer service and provide greater access to bank personnel, banks are establishing centralized phone centres, staffed mainly by customer service representatives. Employees of phone centres spend most of their time answering phone calls from customers and must be available to work evening and weekend shifts.

Administrative support employees may work in large processing facilities, in the banks' headquarters, or in other administrative offices. Most support staff work a standard 40-hour week; some may work overtime. Those support staff located in the processing facilities may work evening shifts.

Commercial and mortgage loan officers often work out of the office, visiting clients, checking out loan applications and soliciting new business. Loan officers may be required to travel if a client is out of town, or to work evenings if that is the only time at which a client can meet. Financial service sales representatives also may visit clients in the evenings and on weekends to go over the client's financial needs.

The remaining employees located primarily at the headquarters or other administrative offices usually work in comfortable surroundings and put in a standard workweek. In general, banks are relatively safe places to work. In 2003, the rate of work-related injury and illness per 100 full-time workers was 3.1 in monetary authorities-central bank and 1.3 in depository credit intermediation, lower than the overall rate of 5.0 per 100 employees in the private sector.

Employment: The banking industry employed about 1.8 million wage and salary workers in 2004. About 7 out of 10 jobs were in commercial banks; the remainder were concentrated in savings institutions and credit unions.

Percent Distribution of Employment in Banking by Type of Institution

Industry Segment Establishments	*Employment: Total*	
	100.0	*100.0*
Monetary authorities - Central Bank	0.2	1.2
Depository credit intermediation	99.8	98.8
Commercial banking	69.0	72.2
Savings institutions	15.2	13.8
Credit unions	14.5	11.8
Other depository credit intermediation	1.1	1.0

In 2004, about 83 percent of establishments in banking employed fewer than 20 workers. However, these small establishments, mostly bank branch offices, employed 34 percent of all employees. About 66 percent of the jobs were in establishments with 20 or more workers. Banks are found everywhere in the United States, but most bank employees work in heavily populated States such as New York, California, Illinois, Pennsylvania and Texas.

Occupations in the Industry: Office and administrative support occupations account for 2 out of 3 jobs in the banking industry. Bank tellers, the largest number of workers in banking, provide routine financial services to the public. They handle customers' deposits and withdrawals, change money, sell money orders and traveller's checks and accept payment for loans and utility bills. Increasingly, tellers also are selling bank services to customers. New accounts clerks and customer service representatives answer questions from customers and help them open and close accounts and fill out forms to apply for banking services.

They are knowledgeable about a broad array of bank services and must be able to sell those services to potential clients. Some customer service representatives work in a call or customer contact centre environment, taking phone calls and answering e-mails from customers. In addition to responding to inquiries, these workers also help customers over the phone with routine banking transactions and handle and resolve problems or complaints.

Loan and credit clerks assemble and prepare paperwork, process applications and complete the documentation after a loan or line of credit has been approved. They also verify applications for completeness. Bill and account collectors attempt to collect payments on overdue loans. Many general office clerks and bookkeeping, accounting and auditing clerks are employed to maintain financial records, enter data and process the thousands of deposit slips, checks and other documents that banks handle daily. Banks also employ many secretaries, data entry and information processing workers, receptionists and other office and administrative support workers. Office and administrative support worker supervisors and managers oversee the activities and training of workers in the various administrative support occupations.

Management, business and financial occupations account for about 25 percent of employment in the banking industry. Financial managers direct bank branches and departments, resolve customers' problems, ensure that standards of service are maintained and administer the institutions' operations and investments. Loan officers evaluate loan applications, determine an applicant's ability to pay back a loan and recommend approval of loans. They usually specialize in commercial, consumer, or mortgage lending. When loans become delinquent, loan officers, or loan counsellors, may advise borrowers on the management of their finances or take action to collect outstanding amounts. Loan officers also play a major role in bringing in new business and spend much of their time developing relationships with potential customers.

Trust officers manage a variety of assets that were placed in trust with the bank for other people or organizations; these assets can include pension funds, school endowments, or a company's profit-sharing plan. Sometimes, trust officers act as executors of estates upon a person's death. They also may work as accountants, lawyers and investment managers.

Securities, commodities and financial services sales agents, who make up the majority of sales positions in banks, sell complex banking services. They contact potential customers to explain their services and to ascertain the customer's banking and other financial needs. They also may discuss services such as deposit accounts, lines of credit, sales or inventory financing, certificates of deposit, cash management, or investment services. These sales agents also solicit businesses to participate in consumer credit card programmes. At most small and medium-size banks, however, branch managers and commercial loan officers are responsible for marketing the bank's financial services. This has become a more important task in recent years.

Other occupations used widely by banks to maintain financial records and ensure the bank's compliance with Federal and State regulations are accountants and auditors and lawyers. In addition, computer specialists are needed to maintain and upgrade the bank's computer systems and to implement the bank's entry into the world of electronic banking and paperless transactions.

Employment of Wage and Salary Workers in Banking by Occupation, 2004 and Projected Change, 2004-14. (Employment in Thousands)

Occupation	*Employment, 2004*	*Percent change, 2004-14*	
	Number	*Percent*	
Total, all occupations	1,783	100.0	-1.8
Management, business and financial occupations	432	24.2	-0.1
Top executives	49	2.8	-1.1
General and operations managers	37	2.1	-1.3
Financial managers	78	4.4	0.3
Accountants and auditors	24	1.4	0.3
Credit analysts	14	0.8	-10.3
Financial analysts	19	1.1	19.5
Personal financial advisors	17	0.9	6.8
Financial examiners	5	0.3	-1.8
Loan counsellors	6	0.4	-3.4
Loan officers	106	5.9	-5.7
Professional and related occupations	75	4.2	5.7
Computer support specialists	12	0.6	-0.3
Computer systems analysts	12	0.7	9.6
Sales and related occupations	63	3.5	3.8
Securities, commodities and financial services sales agents	39	2.2	10.3

Contd..

Occupation	*Employment, 2004* *Number*	*Percent*	*Percent change, 2004-14*
Office and administrative support occupations	1,193	66.9	-3.1
First-line supervisors/managers of office and administrative support workers	108	6.0	-9.1
Bill and account collectors	22	1.2	-3.9
Bookkeeping, accounting and auditing clerks	56	3.2	-10.3
Tellers	497	27.9	3.7
Brokerage clerks	7	0.4	-9.4
Credit authorizers, checkers and clerks	12	0.7	-50.2
Customer service representatives	121	6.8	12.9
Loan interviewers and clerks	76	4.3	-14.0
New accounts clerks	88	4.9	-0.3
Information and record clerks, all other	12	0.7	-20.2
Secretaries and assistants	59	3.3	-11.5
Data entry keyers	11	0.6	-23.0
Office clerks, general	43	2.4	-11.3
Office machine operators, except computer	10	0.6	-35.3

Note: May not add to totals due to omission of occupations with small employment

Training and Advancement: Bank tellers and other clerks usually need only a high school education. Most banks seek people who have good basic math and communication skills, enjoy public contact and feel comfortable handling large amounts of money. Through a combination of formal classroom instruction and on-the-job training under the guidance of an experienced worker, tellers learn the procedures, rules and regulations that govern their jobs. Banks are offering more products and spending more on reaching out to their customers. As a result, they will need more creative and talented people to compete in the market place. Banks encourage upward mobility by providing access to higher education and other sources of additional training.

Some banks have their own training programmes which result in teller certification. Experienced tellers qualify for certification by taking required courses and passing examinations. Experienced tellers and clerks may advance to head teller, new accounts clerk, or customer service representative. Outstanding tellers who have had some college or specialized training are sometimes promoted to managerial positions.

Workers in management, business and financial occupations usually have at least a college degree. A bachelor's degree in business administration or a liberal arts degree with business administration courses is suitable preparation, as is a bachelor's degree in any field followed by a master's degree in business administration (MBA). Many management positions are filled by promoting experienced, technically skilled professional personnel-for example, accountants, auditors, budget analysts, credit analysts, or financial analysts-or accounting or related department supervisors in large banks. There are currently no specific licensing requirements for loan counsellors and officers working in banks or credit unions. Training and licensing requirements for loan counsellors and officers who work in mortgage banks or brokerages vary by State. These criteria also may vary depending on whether workers are employed by a mortgage bank or mortgage brokerage.

Various banking-related associations and private schools offer courses and programmes for students interested in lending, as well as for experienced loan officers who want to keep their skills current. The Banking Administration Institute offers the Loan Review Certificate programme for persons who review and approve loans. The Mortgage Bankers Association (MBA) offers the Certified Mortgage Banker (CMB) programme. A candidate who earns the CMB exhibits a deep understanding of the mortgage business. To obtain the CMB, one must have 3 years of experience, earn educational credits and pass an exam. Completion of these courses and programmes generally enhances one's employment and advancement opportunities.

Financial services sales agents usually need a college degree; a major or courses in finance, accounting, economics, marketing, or related fields serve as excellent preparation. Experience in sales also is very helpful. These workers learn on the job under the supervision of bank officers. Sales agents selling securities need to be licensed by the National Association of Securities Dealers and agents selling insurance also must obtain an appropriate license.

Advancement to higher level executive, administrative, managerial and professional positions may be accelerated by taking additional training. Banks often provide opportunities and encourage employees to take classes offered by banking and financial management affiliated organizations or other educational institutions. Classes often deal with a different phase of financial management and banking, such as accounting management, budget management, corporate cash management, financial analysis, international banking and data processing systems procedures and management. Employers also sponsor seminars and conferences and provide textbooks and other educational materials. Many employers pay all or part of the costs for those who successfully complete courses.

In recent years, the banking field has been revolutionized by technological advancements in computer and data processing equipment. Learning how to apply this technology can greatly improve one's skills and advancement opportunities in the banking industry.

Outlook: Wage and salary employment in banking is projected to decline by about 2 percent between 2004 and 2014, compared with the 14 percent growth projected for wage and salary employment across all industries. Employment in the banking industry declined from the 1980s to the 1990s as a result of bank consolidations and technology. In addition, many consumers transferred assets from bank deposits to investment accounts offered by stock brokers and mutual funds. Also, the banking business has faced much more intense competition in the lending business from credit card companies and specialized loan carriers. In recent years, employment in the banking industry has stabilized. These factors are expected to continue but at a slower pace and banks are expected to be better able to compete with non-depository institutions in the future.

The combined effects of technology, deregulation, mergers and population growth will continue to affect total employment growth and the mix of occupations in the banking industry. The decline in some office and administrative support occupations will be offset by growth in some professional and sales occupations. Job opportunities should still be favourable for tellers and other administrative support workers because they make up a large proportion of bank employees and have high turnover.

The consolidation which resulted from bank mergers contributed significantly to employment declines throughout much of the past decade. Merger activity-at a slower pace-is expected to continue over the projection period, dampening employment growth. At the same time, banks have begun to refocus on the branch as a critical means of servicing customers and many banks will open more branch offices in areas in which the population is growing. However, because of widespread automation of many banking services, fewer employees will be hired to staff new branches than in the past.

Advances in technology should continue to have the most significant effect on employment in the banking industry. Demand for computer specialists will grow as more banks make their services available electronically and eliminate much of the paperwork involved in many banking transactions. On the other hand, these changes in technology will reduce the need for some office and administrative support occupations. Employment growth among tellers will be limited as customers increasingly use ATMs, direct deposit, debit cards and telephone and Internet banking to perform routine transactions. Other technological improvements, such as digital imaging and computer networking, are likely to lead to a decrease or change in the nature of employment of the "back-office" clerical workers who process checks and other bank statements. Employment of customer service representatives, however, is expected to increase as banks hire more of these workers to staff phone centres and respond to e-mails.

Deregulation of the banking industry allows banks to offer a variety of financial and insurance products that they were once prohibited from selling. The need to develop, analyze and sell these new services will spur demand for securities and financial services sales representatives, financial analysts and personal financial advisors. Demand for "personal bankers" to advise and manage the assets of wealthy clients, as well as the aging baby-boom generation, also will grow.

However, banks will continue to face considerable competition-particularly in lending-from non-bank establishments, such as consumer credit companies and mortgage brokers. Companies and individuals now are able to obtain loans and credit and raise money through a variety of means other than bank loans. Therefore, some loan officers may be replaced by financial services sales representatives, who sell loans along with other bank services.

Earnings: Earnings of nonsupervisory bank employees involved in depository credit intermediation averaged $494 a week in May 2004, compared with $684 for all workers in finance and insurance industries and $529 for workers throughout the private sector. Relatively low pay in the banking industry reflects the high proportion of low-paying administrative support jobs.

Earnings in the banking industry vary significantly by occupation. Earnings in the largest occupations in banking appear in table.

Median Hourly Earnings of the Largest Occupations in Depository Credit Intermediation, May 2004

Occupation	*Depository credit intermediation*	*All industries*
Financial managers	$31.02	$39.37
Loan officers	21.38	23.48
First-line supervisors/managers of office and administrative support workers	17.78	19.72
Executive secretaries and administrative assistants	16.52	16.81

Con'd...

Occupation	*Depository credit intermediation*	*All industries*
Loan interviewers and clerks	13.13	13.94
New accounts clerks	12.84	12.91
Customer service representatives	12.57	12.99
Bookkeeping, accounting and auditing clerks	12.33	13.74
Office clerks, general	11.21	10.95
Tellers	10.17	10.15

In general, greater responsibilities result in a higher salary. Experience, length of service and, especially, the location and size of the bank also are important. In addition to typical benefits, equity sharing and performance-based pay increasingly are part of compensation packages for some bank employees. As banks encourage employees to become more sales-oriented, incentives are increasingly tied to meeting sales goals and some workers may even receive commissions for sales or referrals. As in other industries, part-time workers do not enjoy the same benefits that full-time workers do.

Very few workers in the banking industry are unionized-only 2 percent are union members or are covered by union contracts, compared with 14 percent of workers throughout private industry.

Careers in Banking

Openings are Available at Various Levels: From bank clerks to probationary officers (PO). The best features of the job are security and good salary, besides the prospects of loans for employees. The good thing for the job-seekers in this field are that demand for trained professionals has increased substantially. The latter is true for private banks, which offer better salaries but correspondingly less job security.

The advertisements for recruitment appear in newspapers as well as Employment News. Recruitments are on the basis of a written test, including a test of reasoning, quantitative aptitude, general awareness, English language and a descriptive test.

The test is qualifying in nature and the marks obtained are not added in the final merit list. Except for the descriptive portion, all other sections contain objective-type questions. In English, the test is aimed at judging the overall comprehension and understanding of the language. The descriptive paper judges the writing skills of the candidates. It is necessary to qualify in all the sections.

Preparation: It is advisable start with the basics. These can be done from class 10 books. After this, start doing section tests, from reasoning, maths, English, etc. Try to get a good score in each section. After that, do full-length tests which contain all the sections, within the stipulated time.

Candidates are also advised to prepare for the interview simultaneously and take care to develop their personality and confidence. After the written examination, the short-listed candidates are called for an interview. General questions are asked to check the candidate's general awareness and relevant issues related to Economics.

For the descriptive paper, the candidate must have a good expression and the word grammatically correct sentences. An important aspect is handwriting. Efforts must be made to improve handwriting, as this could be a major shortcoming in the written paper. Candidates must be aware of current issues in order to write about them.

There are many books and correspondence courses for bank preparatory examinations. There is, however, no substitute for self-study and self-preparation. Regular studies, systematic preparations, self-confidence and regular practice, is all that is required.

At First Banks, Inc., we offer employment opportunities within a wide variety of financial service and support departments. Below you will find a brief description of each of our departments. Search to find jobs available in any area.

Accounting/Legal/Finance: This division provides support to divisions throughout the bank. Legal and regulatory compliance and financial reporting are two examples of the important services provided by this area.

Administrative Support: First Bank recognizes the importance of administrative support and has Administrative Assistant positions in all departments of the bank. These positions are a great career path to enter into the field of banking, often leading to advancement opportunities.

Banking Services: This division is responsible for everything that happens behind the scenes. Learn the banking industry from this perspective or, if experienced, First Bank attracts some of the most talented individuals in the industry with our innovative banking service products. There are many customer service, support and management positions within ATM Services, Collections, Deposit Services, Electronic Banking, International Services, Internet Banking, Telephone Banking and Treasury Management.

Banking Support and Operations: First Bank's Banking Support and Operations division support "the bank" - both our internal and external customers. This division offers exciting careers with Branch Support, Business Analyst, Fraud Prevention, Product Management, Item Processing, Marketing/Advertising/Public Relations and Property Management.

Centralized Credit: First Bank offers exciting careers within our Centralized Credit division, which prepares and provides vital credit data to our various lending departments. Start your credit career in our commercial lending analyst internship programme, or select from other rewarding careers such as a credit officer, credit review officer, credit analyst, collateral analyst, collections and more.

Commercial Lending: Our Lenders, Originators and Administrators work with a comprehensive array of tools to meet customer needs. Our solutions include lines of credit, term loans, commercial real estate loans, asset-based loans and equipment financing. Plus, with the added advantage of our community bank atmosphere, local loan authority and streamlined approval processes, our employees are able to provide the quality service and products customers deserve!

Human Resources: First Bank's Human Resources division provides support by sourcing and recruiting top talent, leading retention efforts, designing compensation/benefit programmes and services and providing corporate training opportunities to First Banks, Inc. employees.

Loan Administration: The Loan Administration group provides support functions for processing personal and business loans. As First Bank grows, so do the opportunities in loan documentation, loan preparation and application processing.

Mortgage: Whether you enjoy being behind the scenes of loan production or out in front selling, explore the fast-paced nature of the mortgage industry and the diverse career opportunities within, such as: mortgage loan production and management positions, underwriting, wholesale representatives and managers, client relationship managers, loan officers and collections, just to name a few.

Retail Banking: Our Tellers, Customer Service Representatives, Financial Services Representatives and Branch Managers posses excellent customer service and sales skills and are the reason customers call us FIRST. If sales and customer service interest you, check out a career opportunity in Personal Banking.

Small Business: Whether our customers are looking to start a small business or need financing, they can expect their experience with First Bank to be outstanding. Become part a dynamic division and explore such career opportunities as a loan officer, business banking officer, business development officer, underwriter, processor, loan administrator, closer and more.

Technical: This division is responsible for the technology needed to support the products and services we offer. Whether your interests include application or project management, programming, networking or information security, we may have the position for you.

Wealth Management: First Bank focuses on providing a broad range of financial services to our customers, whether it's for individuals or businesses. In this dynamic environment apply your expertise as a private banking officer, business development officer, portfolio manager, wealth management advisor, financial consultant and with many more opportunities in this division. There are also many support and operational positions that are essential to the success of this division.

Job Prospects

As the industry is growing there is no dearth of opportunities. In nationalised banks, one can expect regular promotions while in private banks it is performance that is rewarded. But it is not necessary to be a banking professional only to get into banks. As financial services get automated, the industry requires a large number of computer experts. Private computer service contractors are also in great demand. It would be important to have a BE or MCA degree for such jobs.

Bank jobs come with responsibility, as the banker handles other people's money. The person must be service-oriented and like to look after customers. This is where private banks score over nationalised banks.

One reason to be excited about banking as a career is the rapid change taking place. The jobs are becoming comfortable, as the physical environment is pleasing and computerisation has taken the load off tedious jobs. As competition increases, a good banker will certainly be in great demand. It must be remembered that a banking job involves working long hours.

Assess your aptitude before joining a career in banking. The personality required is a mix: for marketing and meeting customers an outgoing personality is required, while for keeping accounts a diligent and persevering attitude is required.

Banking Jobs

Banking Sector holds a wealth of career opportunities for Indian Professionals. Whether one wants to work directly with customers or support those functions that, strive to deliver a superior customer experience. Job opportunities in the national and international banking industry are predicted to be favourable, particularly for Bank tellers and other administrative support jobs because they make up a large proportion of bank employees and workers in these fields often transfer to other occupations or leave the labour force.

Employment in banking is predicted to increase 16 percent between 2005 and 2012. The combined effects of technology and population growth will continue to affect total employment growth and the mix of occupations in the banking industry.

Career Opportunities

Bank personnel are employed at 2 levels:

Clerical: Where the main tasks are to maintain the account books and the documents and attend to customers at the counter.

Managerial: Which involves organizing controlling and supervising banking activities and holding overall charge of one or more departments or branches.

Typical activities for workers in specialized areas are:

Personnel—recruiting and training staff, planning career development of trainees, advising students about careers in banking;

Marketing—designing campaigns to promote new and existing services, researching customers' banking habits to find new opportunities for the bank;

Operations—processing transactions and loans, researching new technology or different working methods to increase the bank's efficiency;

Electronic Services—writing a new section on the bank's website, developing interactive digital TV banking services;

Card Services—authorizing and issuing cards, managing transactions;

Credit and Risk—analyzing loans and deciding whether to approve them.

The various Occupations in the Industry are:

Management, business and financial occupations:

- Chief executives
- General and operations managers
- Marketing and sales managers
- Computer and information systems managers
- Financial managers

- Human resources, training and labour relations specialists
- Management analysts
- Accountants and auditors
- Credit analysts
- Financial analysts
- Personal financial advisors
- Loan counsellors
- Loan officers

Professional and related occupations:

- Computer programmers
- Computer software engineers
- Computer support specialists
- Computer systems analysts

Banking Operations

Financial Services Operations: The Operations team recruits support roles across the whole of the financial services industry from Operations Clerks up to Head of Operations. Specific areas covered include settlements, control, operations risk management, asset servicing, project management, network management, collateral management and prime brokerage. We also cover roles within middle office including trade support, documentation and new product approval.

Fund Management Operations: The team also recruits into fund management operations, middle office and front office support professionals for a diverse client base that includes large institutional asset managers, private wealth management, hedge funds and global custodians. We look at candidates with a minimum of six months' industry experience and recruit all levels up to and including Heads of Operations. We also cover roles such as Fund Administrators, FMAs, trade support, projects and operations line management.

Financial Services Banking

A career in banking is an excellent way to enter the financial services industry because many banking institutions offer significant on-the-job training that allows trainees to rotate among various departments. Consider a job as a bank examiner or teller.

There is a constant demand for accountants in corporate and government environments. There are different accounting specialties as well such as auditors and tax accountants. In addition, accountants who are able to analyze and interpret economic and financial data are in high demand.

Asset management and consumer lending is another major part of banking. Positions in these areas can be found in companies that provide products and services such as:

- credit and related services;
- investment-related services;
- oversight services (accounting, regulatory agencies and data oversight);
- associated marketing services.

Financial planners or financial analysts are involved in wealth management, estate planning, tax planning and retirement planning. By pursuing this career, you have the opportunity to help clients manage their money better to prepare for their children's education and their own retirement.

Personal financial advisors are involved in loan and credit applications. They have a number of duties, including:

- processing applications for personal loans and bank credit cards;
- interview loan applicants;
- collect and analyze financial data;
- steer loan applications through the committee that must approve the loans; and
- set up repayment schedules.

As you can see, there are a number of different roles for anyone interested in banking.

Future with a Banking Career

A career in the banks has always been a sought-after one. Fascination with banking services has never been higher than at present. With the advent of private and foreign banks, the interest of youth in joining banks has only increased further. Another notable factor has also been the pay package which has fattened considerably with the coming of these banks.

Banks have changed their role considerably from being just caretakers of individuals' money to becoming providers of a wide range of services. These financial institutions are going through a sea change to narrow the gap between the lender and the provider and the net has only made the process much smoother.

Banking Executive

Banking executives might work in any of the following areas:

- Clearing, retail and private banking - involving the transfer, borrowing and lending of money (sterling and foreign currency) to private customers, sole traders and partnerships.
- Corporate and commercial banking - dealing with business clients ranging from small start-up companies to major international corporations.
- Investment or merchant banking - involving corporate finance, investment management and dealing in capital markets, usually on a global basis.

Banks work to annual targets for customer numbers and products sold. Marketing and selling the bank's products and services, such as mortgages, loans, share dealing and will writing, is a major part of the job. Banking executives need to know all about these and rival ones offered by competitors, so that they can discuss the benefits fully with customers.

The banking industry has undergone radical change over the last ten years, with many mergers and acquisitions taking place and increased competition from supermarkets, building societies, insurance companies and large retailers to provide financial services to individuals and organisations.

Entry Level: There is such diversity in the banking sector that there are many possible training routes. All banks/financial institutions recruit school leavers and graduates in varying numbers from year to year. However, each institution has its own specific recruitment and training preferences and you should contact individual banks for current details and an application pack.

Most management training schemes require a degree as a starting point. The exact subject is not critically important but study in such fields as economics, finance, business or marketing could prove useful.

For entry to a degree course you would need two to three A level/Advanced Higher/ three to four Higher or equivalent qualifications, together with a minimum of five GCSE/S Grade passes A-C/1-3. The degree would usually last three years, although you might like to consider a sandwich course, which would last four years, including a period of paid work experience.

Making the Grade: Trainee banking executives usually follow a competence-based, on-the-job training programme. If you show the ability and enthusiasm to progress, you can take professional exams and work your way up to a senior position.

You may be encouraged to work towards Associateship of the Chartered Institute of Bankers or, in Scotland, the Chartered Institute of Bankers in Scotland. Scots-qualified bankers, who can demonstrate that they are annually refreshing and updating their banking skills and disciplines, can attain Chartered Banker status.

The Chartered Institute of Bankers, one of the oldest professional bodies in the world, now offers its qualifications through the Institute of Financial Services, its official brand.

Personal Qualities: Since much of your work would be concerned with dealing with a wide variety of people, both colleagues and customers, you would need excellent communication skills, as well as a good head for figures and an understanding of the economic climate. Accuracy and organisational skills would be very important.

As a manager you should be able to inspire confidence and loyalty in your team and also be capable of selling the bank's services effectively. A high degree of computer literacy would be of benefit, as would proficiency in a foreign language. You would generally be expected to maintain a neat, formal appearance.

Looking Ahead: Technology has dramatically changed the face of banking over the past few years and has resulted in such initiatives as telephone and internet banking. If you enter the banking industry, you would almost certainly face the prospect of continuing change. Opportunities look likely to decline at branch level in retail banking but to increase in specialist areas of head office activity.

The vast majority of major UK financial institutions are based within the 'square mile' of the City of London or have moved out to the Docklands area. Edinburgh is another major location as it has a large concentration of capital market expertise in the form of banks, life assurance companies and unit trust and fund managers.

Other areas of concentration for the sector include Glasgow, Leeds, Birmingham, Bristol and Manchester.

A Career in Investment Banking

What is an Investment Bank?

The term "investment bank" does not have a precise definition, but is generally applied to financial houses which, starting from trading as merchants, expanded their role to financing the trading and commercial activities of others, especially in the international market place. For many years, the British houses were known as merchant banks, reflecting their origins.

Investment banks have retained this strong international flavour and often have offices in many other countries, particularly in the major financial centres. While a number of overseas-based investment banks now offer very similar services, some of the best known and longest established firms in the City grew from UK origin.

Typically, an investment banking group nowadays provides worldwide some or all of the following services, either in divisions of the bank or in associated companies within the group:

Corporate Finance and advisory work, normally in connection with new issues of securities for raising finance, takeovers, mergers and acquisitions;

Banking, for governments, institutions and companies;

Treasury dealing for corporate clients in currencies, with financial engineering services to protect them from interest and exchange rate fluctuations;

Investment management, either for corporate pension funds, charities, private clients, either via direct investment for the more wealthy or via unit and investment trusts. In the larger firms, the value of funds under management runs into many billions of pounds; Securities trading, in equities, bonds or derivatives and offering broking and distribution facilities.

Despite the varietv of these services and the consequent complexity of some of the groups, investment banks are still small when compared with the large clearing or commercial banks. Staff numbers of even the largest investment bank are in the low thousands. Success in the investment banking business depends on the ability to provide whatever financial services a client may require and so the people employed need particular qualities of flexibility, innovativeness and client handling skills.

Recruitment: For mainstream banking positions applications are welcomed from graduates in a wide range of disciplines and there is demand for trained specialists with additional qualifications such as in law, accountancy or from a Business School. Opportunities are also available in most firms for those seeking a career in information technology.

For other roles, most investment banks recruit at several different levels. There are vacancies, at certain times, for school leavers at 'A' level or equivalent, although nowadays the opportunities for those without at least A' levels are rather limited. Investment banking can offer an excellent career to the energetic and intelligent school leaver, but with ever increasing competition the need for those with graduate and professional qualifications is increasingly regarded as a minimum.

Relationships within investment banks and with their clients are essentially direct and personal. For this reason the personality of the candidate is of great importance. Imagination, application and readiness to adapt are important aptitudes in any candidate. Fluency in foreign languages is always an asset.

Entry Requirements and Career Structure

Because of the differences in the structure and size of the individual firms, the numbers of staff recruited vary considerably from one to another. For the same reason, the recruiting requirements are by no means identical. The following, however, outlines the prospects for progression of a successful candidate in relation to his or her initial academic qualifications:

With 'A' Levels: Those joining an investment bank with 'A' levels or business studies diplomas will usually start in clerical positions, although there are certainly excellent opportunities for advancement.

With a Degree: The usual minimum entry requirement is an upper second class honours degree or a professional qualification in law or accounting. There is no particular preference for any specific degree subject, although a numerate discipline or subject such as economics, law or business studies can prove to be particularly useful. Graduates will commence as trainees and can progress rapidly to senior managerial appointments, depending on their performance, the potential they show and the results they deliver.

Remuneration: Starting salaries can differ among investment banks and the working day is often long. However, candidates with the necessary skills and abilities can rise quickly to positions carrying considerable responsibility, where they will be rewarded accordingly. Increasingly a major element of remuneration is related to performance or profits and paid as an annual bonus.

Training: Technical training is both 'on the job' and arising from specific training needs highlighted by the requirements of a particular assignment or by annual appraisal. Regulatory compliance training is becoming very important and trainees are likely to have to take examinations to qualify to work with clients. Management training may include specialist external courses where necessary.

Professional Qualifications: An appropriate professional qualification is an advantage. The choice of professional institute will depend upon the area of specialisation, but could be The Chartered Institute of Bankers, The Institute of Chartered Secretaries and Administrators or any of the professional accountancy bodies.

The regulatory framework set up under the Financial Services Authority have special examinations for those dealing with investment or securities business. Studying for such qualifications will require attendance at evening classes and time off for revision is usually allowed. Some firms offer limited day-release facilities and payments are usually made to cover costs of tuition, examinations and text books.

Sales and Related Occupations

Securities, Commodities and Financial Services Sales Agents

Office and administrative support occupations:

- First-line supervisors/managers of office and administrative support workers
- Bill and account collectors
- Bookkeeping, accounting and auditing clerks
- Tellers
- Credit authorizers, checkers and clerks
- Customer service representatives
- Loan interviewers and clerks
- New accounts clerks
- Executive secretaries and administrative assistants
- Secretaries, except legal, medical and executive
- Office clerks, general

Eligibility: International banks actively seek Indian graduates from a wide range of degree subjects. For specialist roles within a bank, graduates in the following disciplines may have an advantage:

- Economics
- Business studies

- Banking and finance
- Financial services
- Computing

A reasonable level of numeracy is important and, with the development of internet banking, an interest in the use of new technology can be useful. However, the most sought after characteristics by these overseas employers, are highly developed communication and people skills.

Investment Banker

Every one of us wants our funds to be in secure hands, in addition to fetching the finest of returns through any type of investment. Not many of us have adequate time to personally go through and comprehend each and every aspect of investing. This situation calls for seeking help from a professional to make the investment decisions for us. An *investment banker* comes handy in such situations, with exposure to various aspects of financial investments.

An investment banker is a person who is either an agent or an underwriter acting as a liaison between the investor and the issuer of new securities such as municipalities and corporations that issue the securities. An investment banker along with other investment bankers forms a syndicate and buys the new securities issued totally and later sells it to either organizations or individuals.

The job of an investment banker is very interesting and with the right kind of knowledge and smartness, investment bankers can reach the road to success.

- The foremost job of an investment banker is to interact with the client and advice him on the various aspects of investing.
- They help organizations in bringing out bonds and securities and selling the same to the general public by acting as mediators in between the organization and the general public.
- They help organizations by working out strategies on takeovers and acquisitions.

- Their proficiency in financial analysis and strong economics background along with strategic skills helps them develop into the best financial guides for their clients by planning and executing prudent financial decisions for them.
- They prepare financial analysis and documents to support both clients and organizations that seek their help.
- They work with institutions that lend money to clients by reforming debt plans, refinancing debts and raising fresh debts.
- They work with clients for equity capital markets by giving them the guidance on how to raise the capital and from where and when.

Investment Banker Training: Two years of MBA, specializing in the stream of finance after completing college is the requirement to be an investment banker. Additional qualification in the field of accountancy and law is an added advantage. Candidates once recruited are given on-the-job training and specialized training in any particular field if they have been recruited specifically.

Holding a professional qualification, such as a specialization from the Chartered Institute of Bankers, The Institute of Chartered Secretaries and Administrators or from any Financial Services Authority can add an edge to the profession of investment banker. These institutes conduct courses and qualifying examinations in investment or securities business. There are firms that encourage their employees to take up such courses during the day by giving them some time off.

- People start their career as trainees and later get absorbed as analysts and stay in that slot for a minimum of three years.
- After gaining sufficient experience, they become fund managers at associate levels.
- They get promoted as vice presidents in another three years time, depending on their skills and contribution.
- Successful investment bankers get to travel extensively around the world for official dealings.

Skills for an Investment Banker

- Strong numerical and analytical skills.
- Consummate oral and written communication skills.
- Keep updated with current market trends
- Skilful negotiator
- Team player
- Maintaining effective operational relations with clients.
- Performance under pressure

Remuneration of an Investment Banker

Remuneration is attractive and as recruits climb the ladder of success into higher categories, they get paid better. Usually the number of hours in work is much more when compared to other fields. Recruits are encouraged by way of bonus that is paid annually *i.e.* remuneration based on the performance of the recruit or profit made by the firm is shared among employees.

Investment banking is a market driven field of work and thus is primarily governed by the market scenario. Few things that influence the prospects of an investment banker are

- Global economy, markets are the key to this job and when markets are suffering so does the job prospect of an investment banker.
- Enviable salaries and smart incentives have stamped a competitive edge to this area of work and thus job seekers in this field are more than the jobs themselves.

Investment Banker Prospects

Investment banking is a market driven field of work and thus is primarily governed by the market scenario. Few things that influence the prospects of an investment banker are

- Global economy, markets are the key to this job and when markets are suffering so does the job prospect of an investment banker.
- Enviable salaries and smart incentives have stamped a competitive edge to this area of work and thus job seekers in this field are more than the jobs themselves.

Loan Officer Training

Loans have the power to convert dreams, wants and desires into reality, be it the dream house or car, travel to favourite destinations or enrolment at prestigious university. *Loan officer*, credit officer, *mortgage officer* - titles may vary. But the job is the same - that of educating customers about loans and assisting in selection of the best loan appropriate for the situation.

Would you like to choose a profession, which involves helping people get money to translate dreams into reality and even overcome difficult situations? Read further....and you will find information related to desired qualification, the job description, training, skills and traits to be a successful loan officer. Find out *how to become a loan officer* and what training is offered. Learn about *work at home loan officer* opportunities.

How to Become a Loan Officer?

The job prospects for loan officers are better for individuals with a bachelor's degree in marketing, finance, business or economics. Familiarity with computer application relevant to the job is also required.

Prior experience in lending or banking and sales experience is preferred but not necessarily required. Those who have not completed college degree should possess several years of work-related experience, on-the-job training and/or vocational training.

Online loan officer training programmes equip prospective candidates with all information pertaining to actual lending and selling of loans. There are online mortgage loan officer training courses that are approved by the Association of Real Estate License Law Officials, which gives prospective candidates an edge. A loan officer has the choice to specialize in commercial lending, consumer or mortgage loans. A loan officer is trained to collect client information and assess his ability to repay a loan.

Licensing for loan officers differs from state to state. There are many courses that provide training for loan officers. Building up good client relationships and effective communication are essential for a successful loan officer. Loan officer training involves understanding all aspects of loan origination as well as completion of loan processing and underwriting. A loan officer must also be trained in marketing skills so as to generate business.

Knowledge: Economics and Accounting, mathematics, administrative and clerical procedures.

Soft Skills: Ability to multi-task, active learning, service orientation, problem solving skills, exceptional people skills, result-oriented, self-motivated, leadership qualities, entrepreneurial spirit, assertive, high energy level are the soft skills which are just as important if not more important compared to prior work experience.

Loan Officer Jobs

Banks, financial institutions, savings institutions, credit unions, trust companies and mortgage brokerage firms employ loan officers. Loan counsellors and officers who find employment in banks or credit unions do not require specific license but those who work in mortgage banks or brokerages have to obtain license as applicable to the place of employment. After gaining substantial years of experience, one can successfully work from home.

The remuneration for those who work as full-time employees of an organization consists of a monthly salary coupled with incentives or commissions that are performance related. Commercial loan officers or mortgage loan officers who work at home earn remuneration for their services in the form of commissions only.

Employment opportunities for loan officers are expected to grow more slowly than average through 2014. The fluctuations in the economy have a direct impact on the demand for competent loan officers. When the interest rates drop, there is a surge for loans as people are willing to borrow money. Whereas, when the interest rates go up, the willingness to borrow money is significantly affected.

Loans are taken for varied reasons and purposes. Individuals or business enterprises in need of financial assistance for a particular period of time seek money from lending institutions. The loan officer helps potential customers apply for loans. Proactively sourcing potential customers or converting leads into active customers, the process starts with understanding client's need or purpose of the loan. Subsequently, the loan officer collects client information that helps to determine appropriate type of loan, probable repayment period and other related matters.

It is the responsibility of the loan officer to clarify any doubts the client may have. Gathering information pertaining to the prospective client can be completed over the phone or at an office. Duly completed application forms will be submitted to the credit analyst for verification and recommendation of loan. The work continues till the client's application for loan is approved. In case, the loan is denied, the loan officer conveys the same to the customer.

Loan counsellors are also called loan collection officers. The job of loan counsellors is almost the same as that of loan officers. Delinquent customers are those who default repayment of loan. In such cases, the loan counsellor contacts the borrowers and structures a suitable method of repayment to avoid default on the loan. If the repayment plan doesn't work out, loan counsellor arranges for maintenance and liquidation of delinquent property. The lending institution uses the collateral to offset pending loan amount.

Mortgage Loan Officer

The primary responsibility of a mortgage loan officer is to assist clients, both homebuyers and commercial enterprises who want to buy real estate or get new loans for existing own property. A competent mortgage loan officer discusses in detail the various options and helps choose the optimal mortgage product to fit client's specific needs. Those who choose the mortgage industry initially start the career as a Federal Housing Administration. Mortgage banking is strictly regulated by a number of federal laws and enforcement agencies, apart from 45 state laws or licensing boards. Hence, prospective mortgage loan officer needs to check with proposed state of employment regarding licensing requirements.

Exposure to aspects of governmental licensing and regulatory compliance requirements will help develop skills necessary to originate, underwrite process and close loans on housing properties. A job that involves a lot of travel, typically, the work involves converting leads to profitable loans; provide advice after understanding client needs, taking applications, conducting preliminary underwriting reviews, submiting loan applications to processing and underwriting for approval. Further, mortgage loan officer will conduct follows-up to ensure that documents required for processing, underwriting and closing are in compliance with company procedures.

Loan Officers

Significant Points: About 9 out of 10 loan officers work for commercial banks, savings institutions, credit unions and related financial institutions.

Loan officer positions generally require a bachelor's degree in finance, economics, or a related field; training or experience in banking, lending, or sales is advantageous. Slower-than-average employment growth is expected despite rising demand for loans, because technology is making for simpler and faster processing and approval of loans. Earnings often fluctuate with the number of loans generated, rising substantially when the economy is good and interest rates are low.

Nature of the Work: For many individuals, taking out a loan may be the only way to afford a house, car, or college education. For businesses, loans likewise are essential to start many companies, purchase inventory, or invest in capital equipment. *Loan officers* facilitate this lending by finding potential clients and assisting them in applying for loans. Loan officers also gather personal information about clients and businesses to ensure that an informed decision is made regarding the creditworthiness of the borrower and the probability of repayment. Loan officers may provide guidance to prospective loan applicants who have problems qualifying for traditional loans. The guidance may include determining the most appropriate type of loan for a particular customer and explaining specific requirements and restrictions associated with the loan.

Loan officers usually specialize in commercial, consumer, or mortgage loans. Commercial or business loans help companies pay for new equipment or expand operations; consumer loans include home equity, automobile and personal loans; mortgage loans are made to purchase real estate or to refinance an existing mortgage. As banks and other financial institutions begin to offer new types of loans and a growing variety of financial services, loan officers will have to keep abreast of these new product lines so that they can meet their customers' needs.

In many instances, loan officers act as salespeople. Commercial loan officers, for example, contact firms to determine their needs for loans. If a firm is seeking new funds, the loan officer will try to persuade the company to obtain the loan from his or her institution. Similarly, mortgage loan officers develop relationships with commercial and residential real estate agencies so that, when an individual or firm buys a property, the real estate agent might recommend contacting a specific loan officer for financing.

Once the initial contact has been made, loan officers guide clients through the process of applying for a loan. The process begins with a formal meeting or telephone call with a prospective client, during which the loan officer obtains basic information about the purpose of the loan and explains the different types of loans and credit terms that are available to the applicant. Loan officers answer questions about the process and sometimes assist clients in filling out the application.

After a client completes the application, the loan officer begins the process of analyzing and verifying the information on the application to determine the client's creditworthiness. Often, loan officers can quickly access the client's credit history by computer and obtain a credit "score," representing a software programme's assessment of the client's creditworthiness. In cases a credit history is not available or in which unusual financial circumstances are present, the loan officer may request additional financial information from the client or, in the case of commercial loans, copies of the company's financial statements. With this information, loan officers who specialize in evaluating a client's creditworthiness—often called loan underwriters—may conduct a financial analysis or other risk assessment. Loan officers include such information and their written comments in a loan file, which is used to analyze whether the prospective loan meets the lending institution's requirements. Loan officers then decide, in consultation with their managers, whether to grant the loan. If the loan is approved, a repayment schedule is arranged with the client.

A loan may be approved that would otherwise be denied if the customer can provide the lender with appropriate collateral—property pledged as security for the repayment of the loan. For example, when lending money for a college education, a bank may insist that borrowers offer their home as collateral. If the borrowers should ever default on the loan, the home would be seized under court order and sold to raise the necessary money.

Some loan officers, referred to as *loan collection officers*, contact borrowers with delinquent loan accounts to help them find a method of repayment in order to avoid their defaulting on the loan. If a repayment plan cannot be developed, the loan collection officer initiates collateral liquidation, in which the lender seizes the collateral used to secure the loan—a home or car, for example—and sells it to repay the loan.

Working Conditions: Working as a loan officer usually involves considerable travel. For example, commercial and mortgage loan officers frequently work away from their offices and rely on laptop computers, cellular telephones and pagers to keep in contact with their employers and clients. Mortgage loan officers often work out of their home or car, visiting offices or homes of clients to complete loan applications. Commercial loan officers sometimes travel to other cities to prepare complex loan agreements. Consumer loan officers, however, are likely to spend most of their time in an office.

Most loan officers work a standard 40-hour week, but many work longer, depending on the number of clients and the demand for loans. Mortgage loan officers can work especially long hours, because they are free to take on as many customers as they choose. Loan officers usually carry a heavy caseload and sometimes cannot accept new clients until they complete current cases. They are especially busy when interest rates are low, a condition that triggers a surge in loan applications.

Training, Other Qualifications and Advancement: Loan officer positions generally require a bachelor's degree in finance, economics, or a related field. Banking, lending, or sales experience is highly valued by employers. Most employers also prefer applicants who are familiar with computers and their applications in banking. Loan officers without college degrees usually advance to their positions from other jobs in an organization after acquiring several years of work experience in various other occupations, such as teller or customer service representative. Personal qualities such as sales ability, good interpersonal and communication skills and a strong desire to succeed also are important qualities for loan officers.

There are currently no specific licensing requirements for loan officers working in banks or credit unions. Training and licensing requirements for loan officers who work in mortgage banks or brokerages vary by State.

Various banking-related associations and private schools offer courses and programmes for students interested in lending, as well as for experienced loan officers who want to keep their skills current. For example, the Bank Administration Institute, an affiliate of the American Banker's Association, offers the Loan Review Certificate Programme for persons who review and approve loans. This programme enhances the quality of reviews and improves the early detection of deteriorating loans, thereby contributing to the safety and soundness of the loan portfolio.

The Certified Mortgage Banker (CMB) designation demonstrates the holder's superior knowledge, understanding and competency in real estate finance. The Mortgage Bankers Association offers three CMB designations: residential, commerce and master's. To obtain the CMB, the candidate must have 3 years of experience, earn educational credits and pass an exam. Completion of these courses and programmes generally enhances one's employment and advancement opportunities.

Persons planning a career as a loan officer should be capable of developing effective working relationships with others, confident in their abilities and highly motivated. For public relations purposes, loan officers must be willing to attend community events as representatives of their employer.

Capable loan officers may advance to larger branches of the firm or to managerial positions, while less capable workers—and those having weak academic preparation—could be assigned to smaller branches and might find promotion difficult without obtaining training to upgrade their skills. Advancement beyond a loan officer position usually includes supervising other loan officers and clerical staff.

Employment: Loan officers held about 291,000 jobs in 2004. About 9 out of 10 loan officers were employed by commercial banks, savings institutions, credit unions and related financial institutions. Loan officers are employed throughout the Nation, but most work in urban and suburban areas. At some banks, particularly in rural areas, the branch or assistant manager often handles the loan application process.

Job Outlook: Employment of loan officers is projected to increase more slowly than average for all occupations through 2014. College graduates and those with banking, lending, or sales experience should have the best job prospects. Employment growth stemming from economic expansion and population increases—factors that generate demand for loans—will be partially offset by increased automation that speeds lending processes and by the growing use of the Internet to apply for and obtain loans. Job opportunities for loan officers are influenced by the volume of applications, which is determined largely interest rates and by the overall level of economic activity. However, besides openings arising from growth, additional job openings will result from the need to replace workers who retire or otherwise leave the occupation permanently.

The use of credit scoring has made the loan evaluation process much simpler than in the past and even unnecessary in some cases. Credit scoring allows loan officers—particularly loan underwriters--to evaluate many more loans in much less time, thus increasing the loan officer's efficiency. In addition, the mortgage application process has become highly automated and standardized, a simplification that has enabled online mortgage loan vendors to offer their services over the Internet. Online vendors accept loan applications from customers over the Internet and determine which lenders have the best interest rates for particular loans. With this knowledge, customers can go directly to the lending institution, thereby bypassing mortgage loan brokers. Shopping for loans on the Internet is expected to become more common in the future, especially for mortgages, thereby reducing demand for loan officers.

Although loans remain a major source of revenue for banks, demand for new loans fluctuates and affects the income and employment opportunities of loan officers. An upswing in the economy or a decline in interest rates often results in a surge in real estate buying and mortgage refinancing, requiring loan officers to work long hours processing applications and inducing lenders to hire additional loan officers, who often are paid by commission on the value of the loans they place.

When the real estate market slows, loan officers often suffer a decline in earnings and may even be subject to layoffs. The same applies to commercial loan officers, whose workloads increase during good economic times as companies seek to invest more in their businesses. In difficult economic conditions, an increase in the number of delinquent loans results in more demand for loan collection officers.

Earnings: Median annual earnings of loan officers were $48,830 in May 2004. The middle 50 percent earned between $35,360 and $69,160. The lowest 10 percent earned less than $27,580 while the top 10 percent earned more than $98,280. Median annual earnings in the industries employing the largest numbers of loan officers in 2004 were as follows:

Federal executive branch and United States Postal Service	$56,900
Accounting, tax preparation, bookkeeping and payroll services	53,870
Management of companies and enterprises	52,260
Local government	47,440
State government	43,400

The form of compensation for loan officers varies. Most are paid a commission that is based on the number of loans they originate. In this way, commissions are used to motivate loan officers to bring in more loans. Some institutions pay only salaries, while others pay their loan officers a salary plus a commission or bonus based on the number of loans originated. Banks and other lenders sometimes offer their loan officers free checking privileges and somewhat lower interest rates on personal loans.

According to a salary survey conducted by Robert Half International, a staffing services firm specializing in accounting and finance, mortgage loan officers earned between $30,000 and $100,000 in 2005, consumer loan officers with 1 to 3 years of experience earned between $30,000 and $35,000 and commercial loan officers with 1 to 3 years of experience made between $45,500 and $70,000.

Commercial loan officers with more than 3 years of experience made between $61,750 and $100,000 and consumer loan officers earned between $25,500 and $50,000. Earnings of loan officers with graduate degrees or professional certifications are higher. Loan officers who are paid on a commission basis usually earn more than those on salary only and those who work for smaller banks generally earn less than those employed by larger institutions.

Ecommerce Consultant

The Internet viewer has a short attention span, barely 46 seconds. In that short time span, you need to capture the viewer's attention and garner sales. It is essential to provide the online customer with a simple secure environment so as to maximize revenues. *Ecommerce consultants* render specialized services to increase the effectiveness of your web site. Strong marketing can be the most important aspect of a *successful ecommerce strategy*, one that is flexible and easy to use. A robust and secure ecommerce environment is also essential for building a loyal customer base. Ecommerce consulting services can help build an ecommerce application and allow you to reap the benefits of an online presence.

How can you Benefit from Ecommerce Consulting Services?

As any ecommerce consultant would advice you, a reliable web hosting service is critical. Your web site must have no down time and must load efficiently. Many a customer would be put off with sites that take ages to load; burdened with extravagant graphics.

If you are looking for services to help you set up your ecommerce web site; you will need technical support and advice to deploy a safe and robust ecommerce application. Ecommerce consulting services include measuring the effectiveness of a marketing campaign with key site metrics such as browse to buy ratio and average basket value and ROI (Return on Investment).

- You can create and launch an advertising programme to effectively market your ecommerce web site. Enhance the online shopping experience to boost sales. After all, your web site is kept alive by its visitors.
- The storefront appearance must work with all browsers and make for easy navigation. The ecommerce design strategy must reflect your web site's uniqueness and inspire trust and confidence.
- Get in place an ecommerce credit card processing package that is secure and simple. Providing multiple payments such as debit cards and electronic cheques also helps. Backend operations are the backbone of your online storefront. You need robust systems for inventory management, reporting and security. They need to provide real time data accurately. You need to use security systems like SSL (Secure Socket Layer). This guarantees that the data provided by your customer will not fall into the hand of a malicious hacker while transferring from his computer to the web server. The ecommerce web site must handle multiple currencies
- You can avail the services of an ecommerce consultant to manage your affiliate marketing programme. An ecommerce consultant can help you understand your customers and target them correctly. Proper records of purchases and shipping information must be maintained.

- Avail the services of ecommerce consulting at the time of launching the site or when you are expanding. It is critical to be aware of your revenue potential, break-even duration and strategies to achieve them.
- An effective ecommerce consultant will help you build a loyal customer base. He can guide you with innovative ways to keep the flow of customers, be it with a marketing campaign to bring new customers or inform old customers about latest updates on the e-store. Loyalty and retention programmes such as adding incentives, price discounts and attractive offers to keep your customers happy go a long way in building up a customer base.
- You need to increase your web presence with effective SEO (Search Engine Optimization). This will get you to the top of search engine page results and bring you more customers.
- Ecommerce consulting services include arranging your products in logical categories to allow customers to search for products easily. Successful ecommerce also hinges on simple catalogues with terms and conditions and privacy policies mentioned clearly. Guarantees and returns policies should be clearly stated. Toll free telephone support is an added help to clarify customer inquires.

Tellers

Significant Points: Most jobs require only a high school diploma; tellers should enjoy public contact, must feel comfortable handling large amounts of money and should be discreet and trustworthy.

About 3 out of 10 tellers work part time.

Most job openings will arise from replacement needs because turnover is high.

Although the job outlook for tellers has improved recently, employment is projected to grow more slowly than average.

Nature of the Work: The teller is the person most people associate with a bank. Tellers make up approximately one-fourth of bank employees and conduct most of a bank's routine transactions. Among the responsibilities of tellers are cashing checks, accepting deposits and loan payments and processing withdrawals. They also may sell savings bonds, accept payment for customers' utility bills and charge cards, process necessary paperwork for certificates of deposit and sell travelers' checks. Some tellers specialize in handling foreign currencies or commercial or business accounts.

Being a teller requires a great deal of attention to detail. Before cashing a check, a teller must verify the date, the name of the bank, the identity of the person who is to receive payment and the legality of the document. A teller also must make sure that the written and numerical amounts agree and that the account has sufficient funds to cover the check. The teller then must carefully count cash to avoid errors. Sometimes a customer withdraws money in the form of a cashier's check, which the teller prepares and verifies. When accepting a deposit, tellers must check the accuracy of the deposit slip before processing the transaction.

Prior to starting their shifts, tellers receive and count an amount of working cash for their drawers. A supervisor—usually the head teller—verifies this amount. Tellers use this cash for payments during the day and are responsible for its safe and accurate handling. Before leaving, tellers count their cash on hand, list the currency-received tickets on a balance sheet, make sure that the accounts balance and sort checks and deposit slips. Over the course of a workday, tellers also may process numerous mail transactions. Some tellers replenish their cash drawers and corroborate deposits and payments to automated teller machines (ATMs).

In most banks, head tellers are responsible for the teller line. They set work schedules, ensure that the proper procedures are adhered to and act as a mentor to less experienced tellers. In addition, head tellers may perform the typical duties of a teller, as needed and may deal with the more difficult customer problems. They may access the vault, ensure that the correct cash balance is in the vault and oversee large cash transactions. Technology continues to play a large role in the job duties of all tellers. In most banks, for example, tellers use computer terminals to record deposits and withdrawals. These terminals often give tellers quick access to detailed information on customer accounts. Tellers can use this information to tailor the bank's services to fit a customer's needs or to recommend an appropriate bank product or service.

As banks begin to offer more and increasingly complex financial services, tellers are being trained to identify sales opportunities.

This task requires them to learn about the various financial products and services the bank offers so that they can briefly explain them to customers and refer interested customers to appropriate specialized sales personnel. In addition, tellers in many banks are being cross-trained to perform some of the functions of customer service representatives.

Working Conditions: Tellers work in an office environment. They may experience eye and muscle strain, backaches, headaches and repetitive motion injuries as a result of using computers on a daily basis. Tellers may have to sit for extended periods while reviewing detailed data.

Many tellers work regular business hours and a standard 40-hour week. A substantial number work just part time. Full-time and part-time tellers may work some evenings and weekends.

Training, Other Qualifications and Advancement: Most tellers are required to have at least a high school diploma. Some have some college training or even a bachelor's degree in business, accounting, or liberal arts. Although a degree is rarely required, graduates may accept teller positions to get into a particular company or to enter the banking field with the hope of eventually being promoted to professional or managerial positions.

Experience working in an office environment or in customer service and particularly cash-handling experience, can be important for tellers. Regardless of experience, employers prefer workers who have good communication skills and who are computer-literate; knowledge of word processing and spreadsheet software also is valuable.

Once hired, tellers usually receive on-the-job training. Under the guidance of a supervisor or other senior worker, new employees learn company procedures. Some formal classroom training also may be necessary, such as training in specific computer software.

Tellers should enjoy contact with the public. They must have a strong aptitude for numbers and feel comfortable handling large amounts of money. They should be discreet and trustworthy, because they frequently come in contact with confidential material. Tellers also must be careful, orderly and detail-oriented in order to avoid making errors and to recognize errors made by others.

Tellers can prepare for better jobs by taking courses offered throughout the country by banking and financial institutes, colleges and universities and private training institutions.

Tellers usually advance by taking on more duties in the same occupation or by being promoted to head teller or to another supervisory job. Many banks and other employers fill supervisory and managerial positions by promoting individuals from within their organizations, so outstanding tellers who acquire additional skills, experience and training improve their advancement opportunities.

Employment: Tellers held about 558,000 jobs in 2004. The overwhelming majority worked in commercial banks, savings institutions, or credit unions. The remainder worked in a variety of other finance and other industries. About 3 out of 10 worked part time.

Job Outlook: Employment prospects for tellers have improved recently. Employment is projected to grow, but more slowly than average for all occupations through 2014. Banks are looking at their branch offices as places to attract customers for the increasing number and variety of financial products the banks sell. As recently as a few years ago, banks were closing branch offices and discouraging the use of tellers in an effort to cut costs, but in a turnaround, banks are now opening branch offices in more locations. They also are keeping them open longer during the day and on weekends, a practice that is expected to increase opportunities for tellers, particularly those who work part time. Most job openings will arise from replacement needs because turnover is high—a characteristic typical of large occupations that normally require little formal education and offer relatively low pay. Tellers who have excellent customer service skills, are knowledgeable about a variety of financial services and can sell those services will be in greater demand in the future.

Despite the improved outlook, automation and technology will continue to reduce the need for tellers who perform only routine transactions. For example, ATMs and the increased use of direct deposit of paychecks and benefit checks have reduced the need for bank customers to interact with tellers for routine transactions. In addition, electronic banking is spreading rapidly throughout the banking industry. This type of banking, conducted over the telephone or the Internet, also will reduce the number of tellers over the long run.

Employment of tellers also is being affected by the increasing use of 24-hour telephone centres by many large banks. These centres allow a customer to interact with a bank representative at a distant location, either by telephone or by video terminal. Such centres usually are staffed by customer service representatives, who can handle a wider variety of transactions than tellers can, including applications for loans and credit cards.

Earnings: Salaries of tellers may vary with their experience and with the region of the country, size of city and type and size of establishment. Median annual earnings of tellers were $21,120 in May 2004. The middle 50 percent earned between $18,320 and $23,900 a year. The lowest 10 percent earned less than $15,850 and the highest 10 percent earned more than $28,100 a year. As in other occupations, part-time tellers may not enjoy the same benefits—such as vacations, health and life insurance and pensions—as full-time workers.

Cashiers

Significant Points: Cashiers are trained on the job; this occupation provides opportunities for many young people with no previous work experience. Nearly one-half of all cashiers work part time.

Despite projected slower-than-average employment growth, good employment opportunities are expected because of the large number of workers who leave this occupation each year.

Many cashiers start at minimum wage.

Nature of the Work: Supermarkets, department stores, gasoline service stations, movie theaters, restaurants and many other businesses employ cashiers to register the sale of their merchandise. Most cashiers total bills, receive money, make change, fill out charge forms and give receipts.

Although specific job duties vary by employer, cashiers usually are assigned to a register at the beginning of their shifts and are given drawers containing a specific amount of money with which to start—their "tills." They must count their tills to ensure that they contain the correct amount of money and adequate supplies of change. Cashiers also handle returns and exchanges. They must ensure that returned merchandise is in good condition and determine where and when it was purchased and what type of payment was used.

After entering charges for all items and subtracting the value of any coupons or special discounts, cashiers total the customer's bill and take payment. Acceptable forms of payment include cash, personal checks, credit cards and debit cards. Cashiers must know the store's policies and procedures for each type of payment the store accepts. For checks and charges, they may request additional identification from the customer or call in for an authorization. They must verify the age of customers purchasing alcohol or tobacco. When the sale is complete, cashiers issue a receipt to the customer and return the appropriate change. They may also wrap or bag the purchase.

At the end of their shifts, they once again count the drawers' contents and compare the totals with sales data. An occasional shortage of small amounts may be overlooked but, in many establishments, repeated shortages are grounds for dismissal. In addition to counting the contents of their drawers at the end of their shifts, cashiers usually separate and total charge forms, return slips, coupons and any other non-cash items. Most cashiers now use scanners and computers, but some establishments still require price and product information to be entered manually. In a store with scanners, a cashier passes a product's Universal Product Code over the scanning device, which transmits the code number to a computer. The computer identifies the item and its price. In other establishments, cashiers manually enter codes into computers and descriptions of the items and their prices appear on the screen.

Depending on the type of establishment, cashiers may have other duties as well. In many supermarkets, for example, cashiers weigh produce and bulk food, as well as return unwanted items to the shelves. In convenience stores, cashiers may be required to know how to use a variety of machines other than cash registers and how to furnish money orders and sell lottery tickets. Operating ticket-dispensing machines and answering customers' questions are common duties for cashiers who work at movie theaters and ticket agencies. In casinos, *gaming change persons* and *booth cashiers* exchange coins and tokens and may issue pay-offs. They may also operate a booth in the slot-machine area and furnish change persons with a money bank at the start of the shift, or count and audit money in drawers.

Working Conditions: Nearly one-half of all cashiers work part time. Hours of work often vary depending on the needs of the employer. Generally, cashiers are expected to work weekends, evenings and holidays to accommodate customers' needs. However, many employers offer flexible schedules. Because the holiday season is the busiest time for most retailers, many employers restrict the use of vacation time from Thanksgiving through the beginning of January.

Most cashiers work indoors, usually standing in booths or behind counters. In addition, they often are unable to leave their workstations without supervisory approval because they are responsible for large sums of money. The work of cashiers can be very repetitious, but improvements in workstation design are being made to combat problems caused by repetitive motion. In addition, the work can sometimes be dangerous; cashiers' risk from robberies and homicides is much higher than that of the total workforce, although more safety precautions are being taken to help deter robbers.

Gaming change persons and booth cashiers can expect a safer work environment than cashiers in other industries. However, casinos are not without their hazards such as exposure to fumes from cigarettes, cigars and pipes and noise from slot machines.

Training, Other Qualifications and Advancement: Cashier jobs tend to be entry-level positions requiring little or no previous work experience. Although there are no specific educational requirements, employers filling full-time jobs often prefer applicants with high school diplomas. Gaming change persons and booth cashiers are required to obtain a license and background check from their State's gaming board and must meet a certain age requirement, usually set at 21 years old.

Nearly all cashiers are trained on the job. In small businesses, an experienced worker often trains beginners. The trainee spends the first day observing the operation and becoming familiar with the store's equipment, policies and procedures. After this, trainees are assigned to a register—frequently under the supervision of an experienced worker. In larger businesses, trainees spend several days in classes before being placed at cash registers. Topics typically covered in class include a description of the industry and the company, store policies and procedures, equipment operation and security.

Training for experienced workers is not common, except when new equipment is introduced or when procedures change. In these cases, the employer or a representative of the equipment manufacturer trains workers on the job.

Persons who want to become cashiers should be able to do repetitious work accurately. They also need basic mathematics skills and good manual dexterity. Because cashiers deal constantly with the public, they should be neat in appearance and able to deal tactfully and pleasantly with customers. In addition, some businesses prefer to hire persons who can operate specialized equipment or who have business experience, such as typing, selling, or handling money. Advancement opportunities for cashiers vary. For those working part time, promotion may be to a full-time position. Others advance to head cashier or cash-office clerk. In addition, this job offers a good opportunity to learn about an employer's business and can serve as a steppingstone to a more responsible position.

Employment: Cashiers held about 3.5 million jobs in 2004. Of these, 29,000 were employed as gaming change persons and booth cashiers. Although cashiers are employed in almost every industry, 27 percent of all jobs were in food and beverage stores. Gasoline stations, department stores, other retail establishments and restaurants also employed large numbers of these workers. Outside of retail establishments, many cashiers worked in amusement, gambling and recreation industries, local government and personal and laundry services. Because cashiers are needed in businesses and organizations of all types and sizes, job opportunities are found throughout the country.

Job Outlook: Opportunities for full-time and part-time cashier jobs should continue to be good, because of employment growth and the need to replace the large number of workers who transfer to other occupations or leave the labour force. There is substantial movement into and out of the occupation because education and training requirements are minimal and the predominance of part-time jobs is attractive to people seeking a short-term source of income rather than a full-time career. Historically, workers under the age of 25 have filled many of the openings in this occupation—in 2004, almost fifty percent of all cashiers were 24 years of age or younger. Some establishments have begun hiring elderly and disabled persons to fill some of their job openings.

Cashier employment is expected to grow more slowly than average for all occupations through the year 2014. The rising popularity of purchasing goods online may reduce the employment growth of cashiers, although many customers still prefer the traditional method of purchasing goods at stores. Also, the growing use of self-service check-out systems in retail trade, especially at grocery stores, should have an adverse effect on employment of cashiers. These self-checkout systems may outnumber checkouts with clerks in the future in many establishments. The impact on employment growth of cashiers will largely depend on the public's acceptance of the new self-service technology.

Job opportunities may vary from year to year, because the strength of the economy affects demand for cashiers. Companies tend to hire more persons for such jobs when the economy is strong. Seasonal demand for cashiers also causes fluctuations in employment.

Opportunities will be strong for gaming cashiers as more States legalize casinos and gaming becomes more popular. An increasing number of gaming venues and high turnover in this occupation will generate many job openings. However, many casinos are finding ways to use less cash in their operations, particularly the slot machines, which now generate tickets that can be accepted by other slot machines.

Earnings: Many cashiers start at the Federal minimum wage, which was $5.15 an hour in 2005. Some State laws set the minimum wage higher and establishments must pay at least that amount. Wages tend to be higher in areas in which there is intense competition for workers.

Median hourly earnings of cashiers, except gaming in May 2004 were $7.81. The middle 50 percent earned between $6.72 and $9.10 an hour. The lowest 10 percent earned less than $5.91 and the highest 10 percent earned more than $11.30 an hour. Median hourly earnings in the industries employing the largest numbers of cashiers in May 2004 were:

Grocery stores	$7.90
Department stores	7.89
Other general merchandise stores	7.85
Health and personal care stores	7.68
Gasoline stations	7.54

Median hourly earnings for gaming cashiers in May 2004 were $9.87. The middle 50 percent earned between $8.23 and $11.74 an hour. The lowest 10 percent earned less than $7.07 and the highest 10 percent earned more than $13.51 an hour.

Benefits for full-time cashiers tend to be better than those for cashiers working part time. In addition to typical benefits, those working in retail establishments often receive discounts on purchases and cashiers in restaurants may receive free or low-cost meals. Some employers also offer employee stock-option plans and education-reimbursement plans.

Counter and Rental Clerks

Significant Points: Jobs primarily are entry level and require little or no experience and minimal formal education.

Faster-than-average employment growth is expected as businesses strive to improve customer service.

Part-time employment opportunities should be plentiful.

Nature of the Work: Whether renting videos, air compressors, or moving vans or dropping off clothes to be drycleaned or appliances to be serviced, customers rely on counter and rental clerks to handle their transactions efficiently.

Although the specific duties of these workers vary by establishment, counter and rental clerks answer questions involving product availability, cost and rental provisions. Counter and rental clerks also take orders, calculate fees, receive payments and accept returned merchandise.

Regardless of where they work, counter and rental clerks must be knowledgeable about the company's goods and services, policies and procedures. Depending on the type of establishment, counter and rental clerks use their special knowledge to give advice on a wide variety of products and services, ranging from hydraulic tools to shoe repair. For example, in the car rental industry, these workers inform customers about the features of different types of automobiles and about daily and weekly rental costs. They also ensure that customers meet age and other requirements for renting cars and they indicate when and in what condition the cars must be returned. Those in the equipment rental industry have similar duties but also must know how to operate and care for the machinery rented. In drycleaning establishments, counter clerks inform customers when items will be ready and about the effects, if any, of the chemicals used on garments. In video rental stores, counter clerks advise customers about the use of video and game players and the length of a rental, scan returned movies and games, restock shelves, handle money and log daily reports.

When taking orders, counter and rental clerks use various types of equipment. In some establishments, they write out tickets and order forms, although most use computers or barcode scanners. Most of these computer systems are user friendly, require very little data entry and are customized for each firm. Scanners read the product code and display a description of the item on a computer screen. However, clerks must ensure that the data on the screen pertain to the product.

Working Conditions: Firms employing counter and rental clerks usually operate nights and weekends for the convenience of their customers. As a result, many employers offer flexible schedules. Some counter and rental clerks work 40-hour weeks, but about half are on part-time schedules—usually during rush periods, such as weekends, evenings and holidays.

Working conditions usually are pleasant; most stores and service establishments are clean, well lighted and temperature controlled. However, clerks are on their feet much of the time and may be confined behind a small counter area or may be required to move, lift, or carry heavy machinery or other equipment. The job requires constant interaction with the public and can be stressful, especially during busy periods.

Training, Other Qualifications and Advancement: Most counter and rental clerk jobs are entry-level positions that require little or no experience and minimal formal education. However, many employers prefer workers with at least a high school diploma.

In most companies, counter and rental clerks are trained on the job, sometimes through the use of videos, brochures and pamphlets. Clerks usually learn how to operate a firm's equipment and become familiar with the firm's policies and procedures under the observation of a more experienced worker. However, some employers have formal classroom training programmes lasting from a few hours to a few weeks. Topics covered in this training include the nature of the industry, the company and its policies and procedures, operation of equipment, sales techniques and customer service. Counter and rental clerks also must become familiar with the different products and services rented or provided by their company to give customers the best possible service.

Counter and rental clerks should enjoy working with people and should have the ability to deal tactfully with difficult customers. They also should be able to handle several tasks at once, while continuing to provide friendly service. In addition, good oral and written communication skills are essential.

Advancement opportunities depend on the size and type of company. Many establishments that employ counter or rental clerks tend to be small businesses, making advancement difficult. In larger establishments, however, jobs such as counter and rental clerks offer good opportunities for workers to learn about their company's products and business practices. These jobs can lead to more responsible positions. It is common in many establishments to promote counter and rental clerks to event planner, assistant manager, or salesperson. Workers may choose to pursue related positions, such as mechanic, or even establish their own business. In certain industries, such as equipment repair, counter and rental jobs may be an additional or alternative source of income for workers who are unemployed or semiretired. For example, retired mechanics could prove invaluable at tool rental centres because of their knowledge of and familiarity with, tools.

Employment: Counter and rental clerks held 451,000 jobs in 2004. About 23 percent of clerks worked in consumer goods rental, which includes video rental stores. Other large employers included drycleaning and laundry services; automotive equipment rental and leasing services; automobile dealers; amusement, gambling and recreation industries; and grocery stores.

Counter and rental clerks are employed throughout the country, but are concentrated in metropolitan areas, where personal services and renting and leasing services are in greater demand.

Job Outlook: Employment of counter and rental clerks is expected to increase faster than average for all occupations through the year 2014, as all types of businesses strive to improve customer service by hiring more clerks. In addition, some industries employing counter and rental clerks—for example, rental and leasing services and amusement and recreation industries—are expected to grow rapidly. Nevertheless, most job openings will arise from the need to replace experienced workers who transfer to other occupations or leave the labour force. Part-time employment opportunities are expected to be plentiful.

Earnings: Counter and rental clerks typically start at the minimum wage, which, in establishments covered by Federal law, was $5.15 an hour in 2004. In some States, the law sets the minimum wage higher and establishments must pay at least that amount. Wages also tend to be higher in areas where there is intense competition for workers. In addition to wages, some counter and rental clerks receive commissions, based on the number of contracts they complete or services they sell.

Median hourly earnings of counter and rental clerks in May 2004 were $8.79. The middle 50 percent earned between $7.21 and $11.99 an hour. The lowest 10 percent earned less than $6.15 an hour and the highest 10 percent earned more than $16.79 an hour. Median hourly earnings in the industries employing the largest number of counter and rental clerks in May 2004 were as follows:

Automobile dealers	$17.87
Automotive equipment rental and leasing	10.42
Lessors of real estate	9.92
Consumer goods rental	7.78
Drycleaning and laundry services	7.62

Full-time workers typically receive health and life insurance, paid vacation and sick leave. Benefits for counter and rental clerks who work part time or work for independent stores tend to be significantly less than for those who work full time. Many companies offer discounts to both full-time and part-time employees on the goods or services they provide.

2

Career in Financial Sector

Careers in the Financial Services

As soon as you leave school and often earlier, banks send attractive offers to persuade you to pen an account with them; devoted grandparents have often already opened savings accounts, or invested money for you in a national savings certificates or premium bonds. If you go to university you'll will have to take out a loan to pay your fees - and in the current student climate it will be hard to avoid having an overdraft; and once you're earning, you may start making larger investments, saving for the future with an ISA (individual savings account) or take out a mortgage to help you buy your first home.

All of these activities - bank accounts for paying in your cheques, loans, savings, investments and mortgage—are everyday examples of financial services "products".

Financial Services is the industry that encompasses a wide range of activities to do with personal, industrial and commercial finance. There's much more to it than your High Street Clearing Bank, although that's probably the face of financial services with which you're most familiar. But supermarkets like Tescos, Safeways and ASDA now offer banking services, allowing you to make deposits and draw out funds. Marks and Spencer has offered pensions, savings and investments for several years. Insurance companies are moving into banking, just as banks move into insurance. And in the financial centres of the world, like the City of London or Wall Street in New York fortunes are made and lost in the stockmarkets.

It's very difficult now to draw a line around any sector in the financial services industry and list the services typical organisations in that sector will provide.

Broadly, in the financial services industry you have:

Commercial banks and building societies - dealing with transmission of money, loans, mortgages, pensions, insurance, foreign currency, trade finance, stocks and shares ... and a wide range of other investment and lending services.

Supermarkets, airlines, large motor car companies etc. - retail financial products such as mortgages, pensions, tax efficient savings accounts, ordinary savings and current accounts.

Investment banks - dealing with corporate finance and engineering such as mergers, acquisitions and takeovers; capital market activity such as bonds and equities (shares); stock market analysis; fund and portfolio management, derivatives including foreign exchange hedging Insurance companies.

Insurance and re-insurance - providing financial protection against risk for the cost of a premium .

Independent financial advisers - helping people plan for their financial future.

Broking firms - buying and selling stocks and shares.

Unit and investment trust companies - financial organisations concerned with earning money for their investors through techniques such as portfolio management.

The financial services sector is an exciting industry in which to work. Technology is changing it out of all recognition. Can you believe that just 30 years ago there were no credit cards in the UK? And no ATMs (cash point machines) either? Now most people pay by debit or credit cards, undertake financial transactions by telephone—or even through the Internet on their PC—and many papers forecast that it won't be long before electronic money on a plastic card, such as Mondex or VisaCash, replaces the coins and notes in your pocket (so what will we all do about pocket money then?).

A Career for Life!: In the old days young people entering a bank or insurance company worked their way up from the bottom and probably stayed with that organisation all their working lives. Those were the days when banks were expanding and recruiting heavily. Banks do still recruit, but the numbers are smaller the hours are more variable (with many organisations opening on Saturday and Sunday) - and there's certainly not a job for life anymore! On the plus side, there's much more opportunity to move around and there are plenty of openings in other parts of the financial services industry. As an example, financial advisers and planners whether working in a bank, building society, insurance company, estate agent, or independently - are increasingly in demand to help people plan their financial futures.

If you have the right qualifications you can move from a general area into a specialist financial area - and there are plenty of openings for IT, personnel and marketing specialists too! That's not to say you don't have to work hard once you've obtained the qualifications, of course!

Most employers will look for one or more of the following, depending on the sector an entry level you're aiming for:

Good GCSEs (5 at c and Above), including maths and English and A levels

Certificate in Financial Services Practice (an Institute of Financial Services Qualification)

Certificate for Financial Advisers (if that's the area you're interested in)

Degree - perhaps in a business or financial subject.

National Vocational Qualifications - such as customer services, relevant to all sectors

Other relevant professional qualification

Building a Career in Financial Services

There has probably never been such a challenging time to start a career in financial services. Finance is big business, operating at a local level, nationally and on a global scale - and all at the same time. Competition is fierce. Many non-traditional players have entered the market (*i.e.* supermarkets, high street retailers and online banking) and there has been a stream of mergers and de-mutualisations.

More than ever, being financially literate and making good financial decisions is an important part of daily life; from those early decisions about how to spend - or save - through to decisions about pensions and easing your life after retirement. It's likely that you'll have a bank account by the time you've left school and if you go to university, you'll probably leave with a loan and an overdraft. Once you're earning, you may start making larger investments, for example, by taking out a mortgage to help you buy your first home.

A Career for Life—Not any More: In the past young people entering a bank or a financial services organisation worked their way up from the bottom and probably stayed with that organisation all their working lives. Those were the days when the financial services industry was expanding and recruiting heavily. They do still recruit, but the numbers are smaller - and it's unlikely that there will be a job for life.

Nevertheless, the diversity of jobs on offer is increasing. They vary from opportunities in retail banks - which might include dealing with standing orders and cheques, or working as a cashier, or a business adviser or in a relationship managerial role - through to trading and sales, fund management and analysis in investment banks. And today there is much more opportunity to move around. With the right qualifications you can move from a general area into a specialist financial area- for example, there are plenty of openings for IT, personnel and marketing specialists.

Financial Analysis: A Calculated Choice

Today, in an era of global business, global markets and global competition, a career in finance offers a host of opportunities. With markets tumbling up and down, there is increasing scope for bulls and bears in the many financial activities such as finance management, financial analysis, foreign exchange and capital market services, leasing and hire purchase, commodity markets and a range of non-banking services that can provide excitement to those interested in a career in finance. Moreover, as Indian industry looks progressively outward for investment, there has been an increasing demand for specialists in the field of financial services.

Among the various specialisations, that of the Chartered Financial Analyst (CFA) has gained in importance as it covers some of the core areas of finance - corporate finance, financial services and investment management.

The CFA while providing training in financial accounting, focuses more on financial management and analysis, helping business optimise returns on financial resources. The CFA programme looks at areas of corporate finance, financial services like venture capital, leasing and hire purchase, project planning and so on, as well as international finance and investment management.

Areas of Work: The CFAs can work in a range of functions, from managers of specialised services to general managers. The area of expertise includes: Corporate Finance, which deals with management accounting and financial management; Investment Management, which includes aspects of economics, quantitative techniques, economic legislation and security evaluation; and Financial Services, which covers project planning, merchant banking services, portfolio management, venture capital, leasing, hire purchase, new issue management, credit rating and other allied areas.

Eligibility: The CFA training develops in the student an analytical bent of mind which is a prerequisite for effective evaluation of the various alternatives in money management.

The Institute of Chartered Financial Analysts of India (ICFAI) head-quartered in Hyderabad, conducts a certified Financial Analysts Course. This is a three-year postgraduate programme conducted as a distance education course with contact classes conducted in major cities in the country. You must be a graduate in any discipline with at least 50 per cent marks and a minimum of 18 years of age. Admission is based on an admission test, which focuses primarily on verbal and quantitative reasoning abilities and tests the aptitude of a candidate for professional studies in financial studies. The course also includes practical training which enables students pick up some practical experience in the fields of corporate finance, investment management and financial services.

You can also take up the CFA course as a regular full-time programme at some business schools like Narsee Monjee Institute of Management, Mumbai, S.P. Jain Institute of Management and Research, Mumbai, International Management Institute, New Delhi, BITS, Pilani and Xavier Institute of Management, Bhubaneshwar.

Professionals and executives who complete the CFA programme in order to update their knowledge and enhance their expertise, have a distinct advantage.

Placement Prospects: On completing the ICFA course most students receive offers for challenging professional positions. Openings for CFAs are available in banking, insurance, corporate sectors, finance and leasing companies.

In the corporate sector, CFAs can work as financial analysts, fund managers, or as executives in charge of resource mobilisation and investment.

CFAs can work in banks and financial institution as appraisal executives, specialists in leasing, hire purchasing, portfolio management and merchant banking.

With some years of experience, CFAs can also work on their own as financial consultants and investment advisors.

The Reserve Bank of India (RBI), International Development Bank of India (IDBI), Unit Trust of India (UTI), Industrial Finance Corporation of India (IFCI) and several other corporate organisations take on CFAs.

So, if you love working with numbers and long to be in the buzz of financial activities, the CFA course could be a good option to pursue.

The Institute of Financial Services

The Institute of Financial Services is ideally placed to take advantage of these changing times. Drawing on the technical expertise of its parent organisation, The Chartered Institute of Bankers (CIB), the Institute has developed a wide range of professional, vocational and academic qualifications and entered into a number of partnerships with employers, academic institutions and professional bodies. Amongst these are: UMIST (University of Manchester Institute of Science and Technology); University of Kent at Canterbury; and the Chartered Institute of Marketing.

Some of the qualifications available from the Institute are:

- The Certificate in Financial Services Practice which is particularly relevant for those looking to enter in a front office or customer service role.
- As part of the degree route students can study for the Diploma in Financial Services Management, designed to 'fast-track' their management career, it also forms the foundation level of the Institute's Associateship and BSc (Hons) in Financial Services from UMIST.
- For those who want to work in the field of financial advice, the Certificate for Financial Advisers is one of the qualifications that must be achieved if an adviser is to practice unsupervised. In addition, if they are interested in giving mortgage advice, the Certificate in Mortgage Advice and Practice is a comprehensive qualification for mortgage advisers and intermediaries, which has been accredited by the Mortgage Code Compliance Board.

Most of the students who study with the Institute study part time. This means they are mostly in full-time employment and many employers will offer financial support for relevant qualifications - either by paying fees or offering loans with little or no interest. This is not necessarily a new idea but it is one that must become more appealing to many more school leavers as they contemplate the price they have to pay in achieving their degrees.

Independent Financial Adviser

Independent Financial Advisers give advice to individuals and businesses about products such as pensions, life insurance, mortgages, savings and financial protection policies. They are called independent because they can advise about policies and schemes from a range of companies - they are not tied to dealing only with one.

Work Activities: Independent financial advisers (IFAs) provide financial advice to suit the needs of their clients (ranging from individuals to large companies). They also make arrangements for that advice to be carried out if the client wishes. Clients may be seeking investment advice for the short, medium or long term.

The products that IFAs deal with are known broadly as personal investment products. These include things like mortgages, life insurance, pensions, savings accounts, protection policies (for example, income protection and personal health insurance) and stock market investment schemes. New products are being designed all the time, so IFAs need to keep up-to-date. Some IFAs specialise in one kind of product.

When the IFA first meets a client, they discuss the client's current situation and their financial needs. For example, a person may be self-employed and need to make financial plans to provide an income in case they are ill. Another may want to set up a health protection policy to cover their family for private medical care.

The IFA then researches the financial market for appropriate products and recommends different options to the client. The client might then ask the IFA to act on the recommendations (for example by making arrangements for a policy to be set up) or to do further research.

IFAs are legally required to keep a separate file on each client, where notes of every meeting and copies of all correspondence must be kept. They must also keep a sub-set of files for each product they advise on and those bought by the client. For most products recommended the IFA must write a detailed explanation of the reasons behind their choice.

Personal Qualities and Skills: As an IFA you will need to be numerate and have excellent communication skills. Clients need advice at all stages of life, including events like redundancy and bereavement, so you will need to be sensitive to the pressures that people face.

When doing research and writing up reports you will need to be methodical and thorough. The ability to make strategic decisions is essential.

Familiarity with information technology is important.

Pay and Opportunities: The pay rates given below are approximate. Independent financial advisers (IFAs) earn in the range of £16,500 - £18,500 a year, rising to around £30,000 - £40,000. Higher earners can make around £63,000 a year. Earnings may include commission and may depend on the amount of business an IFA can generate.

IFAs' working hours can be erratic. Most divide their working hours between daytime office work and visiting potential clients in the early evening and sometimes at weekends.

Employment throughout the UK is with firms of independent financial advisers and some insurance brokers and pension consultants. Many IFAs are self-employed.

The following information is sourced from government statistics. The government's definition of types of job is slightly different to that used in this programme. For this type of job, the most relevant Government-defined occupation is 'Finance and investment analysts/advisers'.

In 2001 there were 10,400 people working as 'Finance and investment analysts/advisers' in Scotland. 48 in every 10,000 employees working in Scotland were employed as 'Finance and investment analysts/advisers'.

Entry Routes and Training: Training is provided by individual companies and follows the guidelines set down by the Financial Services Authority. The training covers knowledge of the financial industry and its products as well as skills in dealing with clients. It is divided into three stages and leads to the Financial Planning Certificate. You cannot become an IFA without this qualification, or an equivalent such as the Certificate for Financial Advisers (CeFA).

Even when qualified, you will have to do a considerable amount of study each year as part of your continuing professional development. You will have to keep a full record of your personal training to show that you are keeping up-to-date with developments in the financial services industry and financial products market.

Independent financial advisers must be registered with the Financial Services Authority.

Qualifications: It is usual to become an Independent Financial Adviser with a degree or professional qualification, though it is possible to enter with fewer qualifications - depending on your employer. For entry to a degree in Financial Services the usual requirement is 3/4 Highers (A-C) plus Standard Grades (1-3) in at least 1 other subject. Subjects should include English and Maths.

Adult Opportunities: Many entrants have a background in other areas of financial work. This could be as a bank officer or customer adviser in a building society.

A clean current driving licence is an advantage.

The Institute of Financial Services (IFS) offers a range of professional qualifications including the Certificate for Financial Advisers (CeFA) and the Chartered Insurance Institute (CII) offers qualifications in Financial Administration, Mortgage Advice and Financial Planning. All are available by distance learning.

- 20% of people in occupations such as independent financial adviser are self-employed.
- 9% work part-time.
- 13% have flexible hours.

Financial Analyst

A unique opportunity for a talented individual to join a fast growing property investment company and gain exposure to all aspects of the investment process. Principal responsibilities will include financial analysis of commercial property investment opportunities, preparation of financial models, cash flow forecasts and IRR calculations. You will liaise regularly with banks and work in close conjunction with the investment surveyor and asset manager to ensure benchmark returns are achieved.

Who We're Looking For:

- o ACA qualified or equivalent.
- o Educated to degree level, preferably in engineering or mathematics and from a top tier university.
- o A highly analytical, creative mind with an ability to conceptualise complex transactions and understand the qualitative impact of key variables. We will be looking for "lateral" thinking abilities.
- o A good understanding of bond/financial mathematics and excellent spread sheet skills. Knowledge of interest rate hedging instruments (swaps and options) would also be an advantage as well as "risk-adjusted" return calculations.
- o An ability to quickly grasp the essential requirements of a given task and to take initiative to seek missing information or perform further research without recourse to the supervising principal.
- o Personable, able to work within a team and interact effectively with external advisers, developers and banks. Strong negotiating skills will be an advantage.
- o Some experience of property would be an advantage although this is not essential.

About our Client: Our client is a specialist in commercial property investment and funding. The successful candidate will be joining a leading provider of capital to the UK commercial property market and be given the opportunity to assist in structuring investment funds that deliver returns of 15%-20% pa or more.

Lead Financial Analyst

A progressive and challenging role has become available working for one of the UK's leading FS organisations, focusing on the design ,development and maintenance of highly complex forecasting models and the analysis of results to identify actual performance against forecast, this role offers an excellent platform for you to develop a long term career working for a market leader.

Who We're Looking for?: We are looking for individuals with a proven background in creating forecasting models and the analysis of results to identify potential risk area's. You will need a strong commercial awareness and be able to conceive strategy's to resolve complex business problems. A high level of Excel skills is required and previous experience of a statistical package would be an advantage.

About our Client: Barclaycard Business was established in 2003 as a result of the merger of two businesses by Barclay's Bank plc and is VISA largest European commercial card issuer, providing processing services for over a third of UK retailers.

Barclaycard Business is entirely dedicated to supporting businesses, providing their customer base with simple, cost-effective management of general business expenditure, as well as travel and entertainment spend and day-to-day staff expenses. Almost 4500 people are employed at Barclaycard's Northampton site covering 4 strategic business units. These are Barclaycard Business, Barclaycard UK Consumer Finance, Partnerships & Joint Ventures and Barclaycard International.

What's an Offer?: Barclaycards employees are just as important as its customers and that's why as well as a competitive salary, you will receive an extensive benefits package based on a variety of schemes. These include reward schemes offering free gifts, staff bank accounts offering benefits such as commission free currency and discounted insurance, flexible working hours and private healthcare.

Coupled with this, a wide range of learning opportunities will be available to you including use of Barclay's award winning University and a significant study package.

Corporate Finance Analyst

The Corporate Finance Analyst will provide financial, business and operational support in acquisition evaluation and modelling and will manage the full due diligence process.

Key responsibilities will include:

- o Performing industry research to highlight opportunities within the company's existing business or expansion into new business verticals or geographic markets.

- Analysing and evaluating the selected companies to be potentially acquired on a financial and transactional perspective - developing detailed financial models and valuation scenarios.
- Coordinating and implementing due diligence for potential transactions from a business and finance standpoint and formulating the required recommendations.
- Participating as a team member in transaction negotiations and legal documentation and attending meetings with target companies.
- Supporting the Corporate Finance & Investor Relations Director in the development of the company's acquisition strategy, as well as participating in overall business and operational related assignments and projects.
- Supporting the Corporate Finance & Investor Relations Director in presentations to the Board of Directors and may also undertake presentations on certain models.

Who We're Looking for?: You will have gained broad professional experience in finance preferably within an international and fast-moving environment, including in practice or banking. Strong modelling and database building skills in Excel, as well as an excellent knowledge of PowerPoint, will also be important.

The successful candidate will have excellent communication skills and a strong command of English. The role will also suit a self starter capable of taking a proactive approach and undertaking whole projects with minimal supervision. Awareness of market developments, particularly in financial software environments and a vision for where the market is going in the future is essential.

About our Client: A leading global banking software company with a firm foundation and strong financials. The company's core processing products encompass all banking segments; Private, Wholesale, Universal and Retail from small to large scale banks. With a global presence through 39 offices in 5 continents and an international client base of 500+ financial Institutions, the business works together with strategic alliance and key business partners.

The company has revenues in excess of $165 million and in June 2001 the business became a public company listed on the SWX Swiss Exchange. The company has three principle assets: its products; its people; and its clients. With a strong business model and value system, the company is committed to pursuing growth through aggressive client addition as well as continuing to improve its service model to support its existing clients.

European Operations Financial Analyst

This role reports to the European Operations Controller based in the UK. The Analyst is responsible for the financial analysis of monthly actual results, forecasting and planning for the business units Investment Accounting Services and Securities Data Management. A key focus is the ability to collaborate with business managers of the business unit to ensure appropriate development of meaningful, valued added MIS and the regular examination, explanation and implication of business results. Additional emphasis is placed on understanding the impact of investment decisions and providing independent, forward-looking analysis. The position will also be required to support future growth initiatives, efficiency projects and the cost allocation modelling of the Bank.

Principal Responsibilities

1 Development of close working relationships with revenue and expense managers to ensure their needs are served and their key deliverables are met via cost centre reporting and analysis and monthly consolidated management information.

2. The candidate must have the ability to manipulate, analyse and present clearly the monthly movements of revenue and expense results and variations from estimates, budget and prior month.

3. Balance Sheet controls, responsibility for analysing, reconciling and controlling the accounts within remit of responsibility.

4. Assist and support the London Corporate Reporting team during the month end cycle.

5. Assist in the forecasting & annual budgeting cycle. The need to maintain and produce accurate schedules, causal track and reconciliation is key.
6. Assist and support the reporting, identifying deliverables and recording the costs and benefits of initiatives and efficiency projects.
7. As part of a Management Reporting team, must be flexible to support and respond to ad hoc reporting and small-scale development work on as-needed basis.
8. Assist in the analysis of the Allocated P&L illustrating the profitability of the business unit. Providing meaningful analysis of variances to support the quarterly business review meetings.

Who we're looking for CIMA/ACCA qualified accountants preferred.

Previous exposure to analytical accounting positions - in particular supporting an Operations area managing the budgeting, forecasting and production of variance analysis.

Chartered Financial Analyst (CFA)

The Institute of Chartered Financial Analysts of India (ICFAI), a non-profit organisation, which was established in 1984, with the objective of imparting high-quality training in finance and management to students, working executives and professionals in India. ICFAI launched the Chartered Financial Analyst (CFA) Programme in 1985 and since then has been instrumental in developing a new cadre of finance professionals in India.

ICFAI functions under the overall guidance of the Board of Governors comprising leading consultants, senior IAS Officers, bankers and corporate executives. The Academic Council of ICFAI comprises of practitioners and distinguished academicians from IIMs and other leading educational institutions. ICFAI is credited with a team of qualified and experienced professional staff and faculty members.

Eligibility: Any graduate in any discipline from a recognized university is eligible to seek admission to the

Programme, which is made on the basis of an admission test. The students appearing in the final year examination of graduation are also eligible. However, MBAs, Post Graduate Diploma Holders in Management, CAs, CWAs, CSs, CAIIBs, first class graduates/postgraduates and senior executives with ten years of service in the public sector or the private sector may seek exemption from the admission test.

The admission test aims at testing the aptitude of the candidates for professional studies in financial analysis. Hence the test places emphasis on the test of quantitative reasoning. The admission test is held four times in a year *i.e.* in the months of January, April, July and October at 24 centres spread all over the country The candidates who are successful in the admission test and those who are exempted from passing the admission test are enrolled for the Programme.

Job Prospects: Upon successful completion of the programme the candidates are awarded the degree and designation of Chartered Financial Analysts. ICFAI being closely associated with such institutes all over the world including the USA, Japan, Norway, France, Singapore etc., the successful candidates may seek careers not only in India but also abroad.

At present over 150 CFAs have found placements in several banks, financial institutions and corporate sector. In these fields, the CFAs occupy the key position with lucrative salary and perks like Appraisal Executives, Fund Managers, Investment Managers, Financial Analysts, Manager Hire Purchase, Manager Portfolio Management, Financial Consultants, Investment Advisors etc., Plethora of mutual Funds and hire purchase companies during the recent years have increased the employment opportunities for CFAs manifold.

Where to Apply?: ICFAI and its affiliates offer the following Educational Programmes on a distance-learning mode in the areas of:

Finance

Accounting

Insurance

Management

1. The CFA Programme (The Chartered Financial Analyst Programme).

The Chartered Financial Analyst (CFA) Programme was launched in 1985 with an innovative course design and curriculum. Over the years, the CFA Programme received overwhelming response from a cross section of candidates. The CFA Charter awarded by ICFAI is widely recognized as the symbol of professional excellence in finance .The CFA Programme is well recognized by leading employers in India. The Government of India (AICTE) accorded recognition to the CFA Programme as a Postgraduate Diploma in Financial Analysis. Currently there are over 1850 CFAs who successfully completed the CFA Programme of ICFAI and received the prestigious CFA Charter. The CFAs are well placed in the corporate sector, banks, financial institutions, Insurance companies, mutual funds and the financial services sector. Thus ICFAI has been instrumental in developing a new cadre of finance professionals in India.

The CFA Programme of ICFAI is widely recognized as the hallmark of excellence in Financial Management and Analysis. The CFA Programme is a comprehensive professional programme in financial analysis as applicable to Corporate Finance & Control, Investment Analysis & Portfolio Management, International Finance & Risk Management and Financial Services & Banking. It is offered in two modes.

a) The Regular CFA Programme

   Duration: 3 years

   Eligibility: Graduates in any discipline

b) The Accelerated CFA Programme

   Duration: 2 years

   Eligibility: for First Class Graduates, Postgraduates, Working Executives and Professionals like CA/CWA/CS/MBA/CAIIB.

2. CPA Programme (The Certified Public Accountant Programme): The Institute of Chartered Financial Analysts of India (ICFAI) has set up the Society of Certified Public Accountants (SCPA) a non-profit society

to develop and regulate the profession of Certified Public Accountants in India on sound ethical lines through rigorous standards of certification, membership, professional practice and continuing education. The National Institute of Certified Public Accountants (NICPA) is a constituent of SCPA and offers the " Certified Public Accountant" (CPA) Programme .The CPA Programme is based on the state of the art theory and contemporary practice and covers all major allied areas of accountancy so as to enable the students and practitioners face challenges and seize the opportunities of the future.

Eligibility: Graduates (from any stream)

3. C-RIM Programme (The Certified Risk & Insurance Manager Programme): The Institute of Certified Risk & Insurance Managers (ICRIM) has been set up by the Institute of Chartered Financial Analysts of India (ICFAI), a non-profit society for the development of the Profession of Risk & Insurance Managers. ICRIM offers the "Certified Risk & Insurance Manager" (C-RIM) Programme which is a comprehensive professional programme covering all major areas in Risk & Insurance Management.

   Eligibility: Graduates (from any discipline)

4. The CTM Programme (The Certified Treasury Manager Programme): (One year): The Association of Certified Treasury Managers (ACTM), India (an affiliate of ICFAI), in association with the Association of Chartered Treasury Managers (ACTM), USA, offers the professional certification programme in Treasury, Forex and Risk Management titled the "Certified Treasury Manager" (CTM).

   It is widely appreciated as the leading professional course in treasury and forex management. This programme is designed keeping in mind the significant developments that have taken place in the Treasury and Forex Management. It is offered to Treasury & Forex Professionals, Risk Managers, Postgraduates and other Professionals like CA/CWA/CS/MBA/CAIIB and students of these courses.

Eligibility: CFA, CA, CWA, CS, MBA, M.Com and Final Level Students of these courses (Provided they are graduates), Post Graduates, Students of PG Courses and Working Executives.

5. The CIB Programme (The Certified Investment Banker Programme) (One year): The Society of Certified Investment Bankers (SCIB) is set up by ICFAI for the development and regulation of the profession of Certified Investment Bankers. .SCIB offers a certification programme titled the "Certified Investment Banker (CIB)". The programme is offered to Investment Bankers, Postgraduates and other Professionals like CA/CWA/CS/MBA/CAIIB and students of these courses.

   Eligibility: CFA, CA, CWA, CS, MBA, M.Com and Final Level Students of these courses (provided they are graduates). Post Graduates, Students of PG Courses and Working Executives.

6. The CPM Programme (The Certified Portfolio Manager Programme) - Leading to the International CIIA Qualification from ACIIA, London: The CPM Programme is offered by The Council for Portfolio Management & Research (CPMR), an affiliate of ICFAI. It is a focused programme covering indepth all the relevant areas of Portfolio Management and Investment Analysis. It is offered to Equity Research Analysts, Executives in Mutual Funds & Stock Broking Firms, Postgraduates and other Professionals like CA/CWA/CS/MBA/CAIIB and students of these courses.

   Eligibility: CFA, CA, CWA, CS, MBA, M.Com and Final Level Students of these courses (Provided they are graduates). Post Graduates, Students of PG Courses and Working Executives.

7. MBA Programme & Global Strategic Management (GSM) Programmes: The Icfaian Council for Open and Distance Education (ICODE) an ICFAI Affiliate in collaboration with Transworld University, USA provides Professional education for executive positions through its high quality MBA & GSM Programmes .The MBA Programme offers

specialization in Finance, Marketing, International Business& Human Resource

Management: The GSM Programme focuses on International Business and management of MNCs.

8. Foundation Courses (CFA/MBA/CPA/C-RIM):

   ICFAI and its affiliates offers the following Foundation Courses:

   (a) *CFA Foundation Course:* ICFAI has designed the foundation course keeping in view of the degree college students who are interested in pursuing professional certification programme such as CFA Programme. The CFA Foundation Course covers topics on Financial Accounting, Micro-Economics and Macro-Economics.

   (b) CPA Foundation Course is designed for the benefit of CPA aspirants to plan and commence the studies right from the undergraduate level. The CPA Foundation course will enable college students to acquire a strong foundation in management and accountancy, so that they can confidently work towards acquiring the CPA designation and build careers in accounting.

   (c) C-RIM Foundation Course is designed for the benefit of C-RIM aspirants to plan and commence the studies right from the undergraduate level. The C-RIM Foundation course will enable college students to acquire a b foundation in Insurance related subjects, so that they can confidently work towards acquiring the C-RIM designation and build careers in Insurance.

   (d) MBA Foundation Course is designed for the benefit of MBA aspirants to plan and commence the studies right from the undergraduate level. The MBA Foundation course will enable college students to acquire a b foundation in Management related subjects, so that they can confidently work towards acquiring the MBA qualification.

Eligibility for Foundation Courses: All the Degree and Engineering college students (any discipline) are eligible to enrol into the Foundation Course.

Progression to Professional Certification Programmes: On successful completion of the above foundation courses, the candidates can enrol into the respective programme and pursue these programmes along with their Graduation.

Financial Management

"A career more bullish than stock-broking and healthier than medicine," claims a recent advertisement. Discounting the exaggeration, with the Indian financial services market opening up, Financial Planning is an attractive emerging career option in the years to come.

The management of the finances of a business/organisation in order to achieve financial objectives is the basic objective of financial management.

Taking a commercial business as the most common organisational structure, the key objectives of financial management would be to create wealth for the business, generate cash and provide an adequate return on investment bearing in mind the risks that the business is taking and the resources invested.

Financial Planning is one of the key elements of financial management.

The Work: Put simply, financial planning is the process of establishing personal financial goals – and a plan for fulfilling them. The objective of financial planning is to ensure that the right amount of money is available in the right hands at the right point of time in future to achieve the financial goals. This ongoing process involves taking stock of all existing resources, developing a plan to utilise them and systematically implementing the plan in order to achieve short and long-term results. The plan must be monitored and reviewed periodically so that adjustments can be made, if necessary, to ensure that it continues to move towards the client's financial goals.

Financial planning helps people make advance provision for financial needs that may arise in future.

In addition to education, estate and retirement planning, financial planning also addresses other areas like cash management, investment management, income tax planning, charitable planning, business planning, stock broking and debt and risk management. You can draw parallels between the family doctor and a financial planner. The family doctor takes care of your physical health and the financial planner takes care of your financial health, ensuring orderly and systematic achievement of your financial goals.

One of the greatest challenges for the financial planner is the need to provide a comprehensive plan that will allow the client to achieve the greatest number of financial objectives possible, even including those that the client may not have considered. Often, the role of the planner is to "protect" the client from focusing on short-term goals at the expense of long-term objectives and needs.

In contrast to other financial specialists who limit their focus to a particular area of their client's financial life, *e.g.*, insurance, securities or taxation, the financial planner takes a 'big picture' approach to address a host of financial issues within the context of the client's overall situation.

Financial Planners often choose to establish their own financial planning practice either by themselves or together with other planners. In the US, for instance, about 40 per cent of financial planners are self-employed practitioners. Others work for banks, financial planning organisations, life insurance companies, accounting firms, large stockbrokers and large companies to look after employee's benefits.

Employment Opportunities: There are many factors driving the emergence of financial planners. For one, money decisions have become more complicated. Secondly, India now has a continuously growing number of people with savings to invest.

The corrosive effect of inflation on savings lying idle, the bewildering number of investment avenues and the varying risks of each, combined with rising aspirations will continue to fuel the need for such financial "doctors".

Increasingly, a large number of individual investors – small as well as high net-worth–are seeking the services of these "investment doctors" to write their personal balance sheets. The demand for these planners also springs from a variety of social factors – increasing life expectancy, non-permanent jobs and growing ambition to study and travel abroad. Many progressive corporates are also beginning to offer financial planning to their employees as an add-on bonus. In fact, every family today requires financial planning to prepare for the future.

Financial planning then is a dynamic growth profession in which strong careers can be established.

What it Takes?: To become a successful financial planner, you must have strong interpersonal and communication skills in addition to excellent grounding in financial analysis. Being able to listen, asking appropriate questions and sensitively assisting the clients in clarifying their goals are all keys to success. You must also have the ability to communicate somewhat complex financial concepts and strategies to clients in non-technical, easy-to-understand terms.

On the technical side, strong attention to detail is required as you analyse all types of financial options, including their tax implications and legal restrictions. Financial computing skills are recommended for performing the mathematical calculations quickly and accurately.

The required technical skill-sets include awareness of various categories of assets and financial products, understanding of portfolio management principles and economic cycles and their impact on financial markets, knowledge of laws pertaining to ownership of assets, estate planning, etc. and income tax laws.

Finally, to become a successful financial planner you must be able to work well in cooperation with a range of other financial specialists to meet your clients' needs.

It has been noticed that those with a background in accountancy, law, insurance, investments, finance or taxation stand a better chance at being successful financial planners.

What you'll Make?: This industry offers exciting future prospects. Financial planners are among the higher paid professionals abroad. The annual income for financial planners depends on a variety of factors, including expertise, experience, the type and number of clients served, fees charged and even geographic location.

The planner could charge on an hourly basis for consultation or receive commission from the sale of financial products you agree to purchase in order to implement financial planning recommendations. Some financial planners also work on a salary and bonus basis for financial services firms.

While financial planning is a great career option, it is no catwalk. Since it is a relatively new concept, the professional's biggest challenge lies in convincing people that they would gain by paying for advice on personal finance.

Currently, people are used to free advice – from insurance agents or CAs, for example. While young professionals are somewhat more open, the typically cautious investors in the 50+ age bracket tend to be scared of venturing into new investment avenues. Also, we are not typically in the habit of planning that far ahead.

Where to Study?: So far as financial planning is concerned, the regulators in India have not prescribed any specific qualifications. In other countries, CFP (Certified Financial Planner) is a recognised qualification and is based on written tests and relevant experience.

The Chartered Financial Planner (CFP) course is presently offered in India by two authorised education providers of the Association of Financial Planners (AFP) in technical collaboration with the Financial Planning Association of Australia Ltd. (FPA). The 2-year distance-learning programme covers topics such as insurance planning and risk management, retirement planning, tax and estate planning, employee benefits, wealth creation, budgeting, cash flow management, debt management and financial plan construction.

Alternatively, an MBA/CFA/CA/Insurance specialisation singly or in combination, would also give you a broad understanding of the various investment instruments and options and their implications.

Financial Managers

Significant Points: About 3 out of 10 work in finance and insurance industries.

A bachelor's degree in finance, accounting, or a related field is the minimum academic preparation, but many employers increasingly seek graduates with a master's degree in business administration, economics, finance, or risk management.

Experience may be more important than formal education for some financial manager positions—most notably, branch managers in banks.

Jobseekers are likely to face competition.

Nature of the Work: Almost every firm, government agency and other type of organization has one or more financial managers who oversee the preparation of financial reports, direct investment activities and implement cash management strategies. Because computers are increasingly used to record and organize data, many financial managers are spending more time developing strategies and implementing the long-term goals of their organization.

The duties of financial managers vary with their specific titles, which include controller, treasurer or finance officer, credit manager, cash manager and risk and insurance manager. *Controllers* direct the preparation of financial reports that summarize and forecast the organization's financial position, such as income statements, balance sheets and analyses of future earnings or expenses.

Controllers also are in charge of preparing special reports required by regulatory authorities. Often, controllers oversee the accounting, audit and budget departments. *Treasurers* and *finance officers* direct the organization's financial goals, objectives and budgets. They oversee the investment of funds, manage associated risks, supervise cash management activities, execute capital-raising strategies to support a firm's expansion and deal with mergers and acquisitions. *Credit managers* oversee the firm's issuance of credit, establishing credit-rating criteria, determining credit ceilings and monitoring the collections of past-due accounts. Managers specializing in international finance develop financial and accounting systems for the banking transactions of multinational organizations.

Cash managers monitor and control the flow of cash receipts and disbursements to meet the business and investment needs of the firm. For example, cash flow projections are needed to determine whether loans must be obtained to meet cash requirements or whether surplus cash should be invested in interest-bearing instruments.

Risk and *insurance managers* oversee programmes to minimize risks and losses that might arise from financial transactions and business operations undertaken by the institution. They also manage the organization's insurance budget.

Financial institutions, such as commercial banks, savings and loan associations, credit unions and mortgage and finance companies, employ additional financial managers who oversee various functions, such as lending, trusts, mortgages and investments, or programmes, including sales, operations, or electronic financial services.

These managers may be required to solicit business, authorize loans and direct the investment of funds, always adhering to Federal and State laws and regulations.

Branch managers of financial institutions administer and manage all of the functions of a branch office, which may include hiring personnel, approving loans and lines of credit, establishing a rapport with the community to attract business and assisting customers with account problems. The trend is for branch mangers to become more oriented toward sales and marketing. It is important that they have substantial knowledge about all types of products that the bank sells. Financial managers who work for financial institutions must keep abreast of the rapidly growing array of financial services and products.

In addition to carrying out the preceding general duties, all financial managers perform tasks unique to their organization or industry. For example, government financial managers must be experts on the government appropriations and budgeting processes, whereas health care financial managers must be knowledgeable about issues surrounding health care financing. Moreover, financial managers must be aware of special tax laws and regulations that affect their industry.

Financial managers play an increasingly important role in mergers and consolidations and in global expansion and related financing. These areas require extensive, specialized knowledge on the part of the financial manager to reduce risks and maximize profit. Financial managers increasingly are hired on a temporary basis to advise senior managers on these and other matters. In fact, some small firms contract out all their accounting and financial functions to companies that provide such services.

The role of the financial manager, particularly in business, is changing in response to technological advances that have significantly reduced the amount of time it takes to produce financial reports. Financial managers now perform more data analysis and use it to offer senior managers ideas on how to maximize profits. They often work on teams, acting as business advisors to top management. Financial managers need to keep abreast of the latest computer technology in order to increase the efficiency of their firm's financial operations.

Working Conditions: Working in comfortable offices, often close to top managers and to departments that develop the financial data those managers need, financial managers typically have direct access to state-of-the-art computer systems and information services. They commonly work long hours, often up to 50 or 60 per week. Financial managers generally are required to attend meetings of financial and economic associations and may travel to visit subsidiary firms or to meet customers.

Training, Other Qualifications and Advancement: A bachelor's degree in finance, accounting, economics, or business administration is the minimum academic preparation for financial managers. However, many employers now seek graduates with a master's degree, preferably in business administration, economics, finance, or risk management. These academic programmes develop analytical skills and provide knowledge of the latest financial analysis methods and technology.

Experience may be more important than formal education for some financial manager positions—most notably, branch managers in banks. Banks typically fill branch manager positions by promoting experienced loan officers and other professionals who excel at their jobs. Other financial managers may enter the profession through formal management training programmes offered by the company. The American Institute of Banking, which is affiliated with the American Bankers Association, sponsors educational and training programmes for bank officers through a wide range of banking schools and educational conferences.

Continuing education is vital to financial managers, who must cope with the growing complexity of global trade, changes in Federal and State laws and regulations and the proliferation of new and complex financial instruments. Firms often provide opportunities for workers to broaden their knowledge and skills by encouraging them to take graduate courses at colleges and universities or attend conferences related to their specialty. Financial management, banking and credit union associations, often in cooperation with colleges and universities, sponsor numerous national and local training programmes. Persons enrolled prepare extensively at home and then attend sessions on subjects such as accounting management, budget management, corporate cash management, financial analysis, international banking and information systems. Many firms pay all or part of the costs for employees who successfully complete courses. Although experience, ability and leadership are emphasized for promotion, advancement may be accelerated by this type of special study.

In some cases, financial managers also may broaden their skills and exhibit their competency by attaining professional certification. Many different associations offer professional certification programmes. For example, the CFA Institute confers the Chartered Financial Analyst designation on investment professionals who have a bachelor's degree, pass three sequential examinations and meet work experience requirements. The Association for Financial Professionals (AFP) confers the Certified Cash Manager credential to those who pass a computer-based exam and have a minimum of 2 years of relevant experience. The Institute of Management Accountants offers a Certified in Financial Management designation to members with a bachelor's degree, with at least 2 years of work experience and who pass the institute's four-part examination and fulfil continuing education requirements. Also, financial managers who specialize in accounting may earn the Certified Public Accountant (CPA) or Certified Management Accountant (CMA) designation.

Candidates for financial management positions need a broad range of skills. Interpersonal skills are important because these jobs involve managing people and working as part of a team to solve problems. Financial managers must have excellent communication skills to explain complex financial data. Because financial managers work extensively with various departments in their firm, a broad overview of the business is essential.

Financial managers should be creative thinkers and problem-solvers, applying their analytical skills to business. They must be comfortable with the latest computer technology. Financial operations are increasingly being affected by the global economy, so financial managers must have knowledge of international finance. Proficiency in a foreign language also may be important.

Because financial management is critical to efficient business operations, well-trained, experienced financial managers who display a strong grasp of the operations of various departments within their organization are prime candidates for promotion to top management positions. Some financial managers transfer to closely related positions in other industries. Those with extensive experience and access to sufficient capital may start their own consulting firms.

Employment: Financial managers held about 528,000 jobs in 2004. Although they can be found in every industry, approximately 3 out of 10 are employed by finance and insurance establishments, such as banks, savings institutions, finance companies, credit unions, insurance carriers and securities dealers. About 1 in 10 works for Federal, State, or local government.

Job Outlook: Employment of financial managers is expected to grow about as fast as average for all occupations through 2014. The increasing need for financial expertise as a result of regulatory reforms and the expansion of the economy will drive job growth over the next decade. As the economy expands, both the growth of established companies and the creation of new businesses will spur demand for financial managers. However, mergers, acquisitions and corporate downsizing are likely to restrict the employment growth to some extent.

As in other managerial occupations, jobseekers are likely to face competition, because the number of job openings is expected to be less than the number of applicants. Candidates with expertise in accounting and finance—particularly those with a master's degree—should enjoy the best job prospects. Strong computer skills and knowledge of international finance are important; so are excellent communication skills, because financial management jobs involve working on strategic planning teams. In addition, a good knowledge of compliance procedures is essential because of the many regulatory changes instituted in recent years.

Over the short term, employment growth in this occupation may slow or even reverse due to economic downturns, during which companies are more likely to close departments or even go out of business—decreasing the need for financial managers.

The banking industry will continue to consolidate, although at a slower rate than in previous years. In spite of this trend, employment of bank branch managers is expected to increase, because banks are refocusing on the importance of their existing branches and are creating new branches to service a growing population. As banks expand the range of products and services they offer to include insurance and investment products, branch managers with knowledge in these areas will be needed. As a result, candidates who are licensed to sell insurance or securities will have the most favourable prospects.

The long-run prospects for financial managers in the securities and commodities industry should be favourable, because more people will be needed to handle increasingly complex financial transactions and manage a growing amount of investments. Financial managers also will be needed to handle mergers and acquisitions, raise capital and assess global financial transactions. Risk managers, who assess risks for insurance and investment purposes, also will be in demand.

Some companies may hire financial managers on a temporary basis, to see the organization through a short-term crisis or to offer suggestions for boosting profits. Other companies may contract out all accounting and financial operations. Even in these cases, however, financial managers may be needed to oversee the contracts.

Computer technology has reduced the amount of time and the staff required to produce financial reports. As a result, forecasting earnings, profits and costs and generating ideas and creative ways to increase profitability will become a major role of corporate financial managers over the next decade. Financial managers who are familiar with computer software that can assist them in this role will be needed.

Earnings: Median annual earnings of financial managers were $81,880 in May 2004. The middle 50 percent earned between $59,490 and $112,320. Median annual earnings in the industries employing the largest numbers of financial managers in 2004 were as follows:

Securities and commodity contracts intermediation and brokerage	$129,770
Management of companies and enterprises	97,730
Non-depository credit intermediation	88,870
Local government	67,260
Depository credit intermediation	64,530

According to a 2005 survey by Robert Half International, a staffing services firm specializing in accounting and finance professionals, directors of finance earned between $78,500 and $178,250 and corporate controllers earned between $61,250 and $147,250.

A 2004 survey of manufacturing firms conducted by Abbot, Langer and Associates, Inc., a human resources management consulting firm, reported the following median annual incomes: chief corporate financial officers, $130,000; corporate controllers,

$86,150; cost accounting managers, $67,161; and general accounting managers, $64,100.

Large organizations often pay more than small ones and salary levels also can depend on the type of industry and location. Many financial managers in both public and private industry receive additional compensation in the form of bonuses, which, like salaries, vary substantially by size of firm. Deferred compensation in the form of stock options is becoming more common, especially for senior-level executives.

Economists

Significant Points: Slower than average job growth is expected as firms increasingly employ workers to perform more specialized tasks with titles that reflect the specific duties of the job rather than the general title of economist.

Job seekers with a background in economics should have good opportunities, although some of these opportunities will be in related occupations.

Candidates who hold a master's or Ph.D. degree in economics will have the best employment prospects and advancement opportunities.

Quantitative skills are important in all economics specialties.

Nature of the Work: Economists study how society distributes scarce resources, such as land, labour, raw materials and machinery, to produce goods and services. They conduct research, collect and analyze data, monitor economic trends and develop forecasts. They research issues such as energy costs, inflation, interest rates, exchange rates, business cycles, taxes, or employment levels.

Economists devise methods and procedures for obtaining the data they need. For example, sampling techniques may be used to conduct a survey and various mathematical modelling techniques may be used to develop forecasts. Preparing reports, including tables and charts, on research results is an important part of an economist's job. Presenting economic and statistical concepts in a clear and meaningful way is particularly important for economists whose research is directed toward making policies for an organization. Some economists also might perform economic analysis for the media.

Many economists specialize in a particular area of economics, although general knowledge of basic economic principles is useful in each area. *Microeconomists* study the supply and demand decisions of individuals and firms, such as how profits can be maximized and how much of a good or service consumers will demand at a certain price. *Industrial economists* or *organizational economists* study the market structure of particular industries in terms of the number of competitors within those industries and examine the market decisions of competitive firms and monopolies.

These economists also may be concerned with antitrust policy and its impact on market structure. *Macroeconomists* study historical trends in the whole economy and forecast future trends in areas such as unemployment, inflation, economic growth, productivity and investment. Closely related to macroeconomists are *monetary economists* or *financial economists*, who study the money and banking system and the effects of changing interest rates. *International economists* study international financial markets, exchange rates and the effects of various trade policies such as tariffs. *Labour economists* or *demographic economists* study the supply and demand for labour and the determination of wages.

These economists also try to explain the reasons for unemployment and the effects of changing demographic trends, such as an aging population and increasing immigration, on labour markets. *Public finance economists* are involved primarily in studying the role of the government in the economy and the effects of tax cuts, budget deficits and welfare policies. *Econometricians* investigate all areas of economics and use mathematical techniques such as calculus, game theory and regression analysis to formulate economic models that help to explain economic relationships and that are used to develop forecasts related to the nature and length of business cycles, the effects of a specific rate of inflation on the economy, the effects of tax legislation on unemployment levels and other economic phenomena.

Many economists have applied these fundamental areas of economics to specific applications such as health, education, agriculture, urban and regional economics, law, history, energy and the environment.

Most economists are concerned with practical applications of economic policy and work for a variety of organizations. Economists working for corporations are involved primarily in microeconomic issues, such as forecasting consumer demand and sales of the firm's products. Some analyze their competitors' growth and market share and advise their company on how to handle the competition. Others monitor legislation passed by Congress, such as environmental and worker safety regulations and assess its impact on their business. Corporations with many international branches or subsidiaries might employ economists to monitor the economic situations in countries where they do business or to provide a risk assessment of a country into which the company might expand.

Economists working in economic consulting or research firms may perform the same tasks as economists working for corporations. Economists in consulting firms also perform much of the macroeconomic analysis and forecasting that is conducted in the United States. These economists collect data on various indicators, maintain databases, analyze historical trends and develop models to forecast growth, inflation, unemployment, or interest rates. Their analyses and forecasts are frequently published in newspapers and journal articles.

Another large employer of economists is the government. Economists in the Federal Government administer most of the surveys and collect the majority of the economic data characterizing the United States. For example, economists in the US Department of Commerce collect and analyze data on the production, distribution and consumption of commodities produced in the United States and overseas, while economists employed by the US Department of Labour collect and analyze data on the domestic economy, including data on prices, wages, employment, productivity and safety and health. Economists who work for government agencies also assess economic conditions in the United States or abroad in order to estimate the economic effects of specific changes in legislation or public policy. Government economists advise policy makers in areas such as telecommunications deregulation, Social Security revamping, the effects of tax cuts on the budget deficit and the effectiveness of imposing tariffs on imported steel. An economist working in State or local government might analyze data on the growth of school-age or prison populations and on employment and unemployment rates, in order to project future spending needs.

Working Conditions: Economists have structured work schedules. They often work alone, writing reports, preparing statistical charts and using computers, but they also may be an integral part of a research team. Most work under pressure of deadlines and tight schedules, which may require overtime. Their routine may be interrupted by special requests for data and by the need to attend meetings or conferences. Frequent travel may be necessary.

Training, Other Qualifications and Advancement: A master's or Ph.D. degree in economics is required for many private-sector economist jobs and for advancement to more responsible positions. Economics includes numerous specialties at the graduate level, such as advanced economic theory, econometrics, international economics and labour economics. Students should select graduate schools that are strong in specialties in which they are interested. Undergraduate economics majors can choose from a variety of courses, ranging from microeconomics, macroeconomics and econometrics to more philosophical courses, such as the history of economic thought. Because of the importance of quantitative skills to economists, courses in mathematics, statistics, econometrics, sampling theory and survey design and computer science are extremely helpful. Some schools help graduate students find internships or part-time employment in government agencies, economic consulting or research firms, or financial institutions prior to graduation.

In the Federal Government, candidates for entry-level economist positions must have a bachelor's degree with a minimum of 21 semester hours of economics and 3 hours of statistics, accounting, or calculus. Whether working in government, industry, research organizations, or consulting firms, economists with a bachelor's degree usually qualify for most entry-level positions as a research assistant, for administrative or management trainee positions, or for various sales jobs.

A master's degree usually is required to qualify for more responsible research and administrative positions. Many businesses, research and consulting firms and government agencies seek individuals who have strong computer and quantitative skills and can perform complex research. A Ph.D. is necessary for top economist positions in many organizations. Many corporation and government executives have a strong background in economics.

A master's degree usually is the minimum requirement for a job as an instructor in a junior or community college. In most colleges and universities, however, a Ph.D. is necessary for appointment as an instructor. A Ph.D. and extensive publications in academic journals are required for a professorship, tenure and promotion.

Aspiring economists should gain experience gathering and analyzing data, conducting interviews or surveys and writing reports on their findings while in college. This experience can prove invaluable later in obtaining a full-time position in the field, because much of the economist's work, especially in the beginning, may centre on these duties. With experience, economists eventually are assigned their own research projects. Related job experience, such as work as a stock or bond trader, might be advantageous.

Those considering careers as economists should be able to pay attention to details, because much time is spent on precise data analysis. Patience and persistence are necessary qualities, given that economists must spend long hours on independent study and problem solving. Good communication skills also are useful, as economists must be able to present their findings, both orally and in writing, in a clear, concise manner.

Employment: Economists held about 13,000 jobs in 2004. Government employed 58 percent of economists, in a wide range of government agencies, with 34 percent in Federal government and 24 percent in State and local government. The US Departments of Labour, Agriculture and State are the largest Federal employers of economists. The remaining jobs were spread throughout private industry, particularly in scientific research and development services and management, scientific and technical consulting services. A number of economists combine a full-time job in government, academia, or business with part-time or consulting work in another setting.

Employment of economists is concentrated in large cities. Some work abroad for companies with major international operations, for US Government agencies and for international organizations, such as the World Bank, International Monetary Fund and United Nations.

In addition to the previously mentioned jobs, economists hold faculty positions in colleges and universities. Economics faculties have flexible work schedules and may divide their time among teaching, research, consulting and administration.

Job Outlook: Employment of economists is expected to grow more slowly than average for all occupations through 2014. Employment growth should be the fastest in private industry, especially in management, scientific and technical consulting services. Rising demand for economic analysis in virtually every industry should stem from the growing complexity of the global economy, the effects of competition on businesses and increased reliance on quantitative methods for analyzing and forecasting business, sales and other economic trends.

Some corporations choose to hire economic consultants to fill these needs, rather than keeping an economist on staff. This practice should result in more economists being employed in consulting services. However, job growth will be limited as firms increasingly employ workers to perform more specialized tasks with titles that reflect the specific duties of the job instead of the general title of economist. In addition, few new jobs are expected in government, but the need to replace experienced workers who transfer to other occupations or who retire or leave the labour force for other reasons will lead to job openings for economists across all industries in which they are employed. Individuals with a background in economics should have job opportunities, although some of these opportunities will be in related occupations.

As firms increasingly employ workers to perform more specialized tasks, the best opportunities for individuals with backgrounds in economics are expected to be in positions that have titles other than economist. Some examples of job titles often held by those with an economics background are financial analyst, market analyst, public policy consultant, researcher or research assistant and econometrician.

A master's or Ph.D. degree, coupled with a strong background in economic theory, mathematics, statistics and econometrics, provides the basis for acquiring any specialty within the economics field. Economists who are skilled in quantitative techniques and their application to economic modelling and forecasting and who also have good communications skills, should have the best job opportunities. Like those in many other disciplines, however, Ph.D. holders are likely to face keen competition for tenured teaching positions in colleges and universities.

Bachelor's degree holders may face competition for the limited number of economist positions for which they qualify. However, they will qualify for a number of other positions in which they can take advantage of their economic knowledge by conducting research, developing surveys, or analyzing data. Many graduates with bachelor's degrees will find jobs in industry and business as management or sales trainees or as administrative assistants. Bachelor's degree holders with good quantitative skills and a strong background in mathematics, statistics, survey design and computer science also may be hired by private firms as researchers. Some will find jobs in government.

Candidates who meet State certification requirements may become high school economics teachers. The demand for secondary school economics teachers is expected to grow, as economics becomes an increasingly important and popular course.

Earnings: Median annual wage and salary earnings of economists were $72,780 in May 2004. The middle 50 percent earned between $53,650 and $96,240. The lowest 10 percent earned less than $41,040 and the highest 10 percent earned more than $129,170.

The Federal Government recognizes education and experience in certifying applicants for entry-level positions. The starting salary for economists having a bachelor's degree was about $24,667 a year in 2005; however, those with superior academic records could begin at $30,567. Those having a master's degree could qualify for positions at an annual salary of $37,390. Those with a Ph.D. could begin at $45,239, while some individuals with experience and an advanced degree could start at $54,221. Starting salaries were slightly higher in selected geographical areas where the prevailing local pay was higher. The average annual salary for economists employed by the Federal Government was $89,441 a year in 2005.

Financial Analysts and Personal Financial Advisors

Significant Points: A college degree and good interpersonal skills are among the most important qualifications for these workers.

Although both occupations will benefit from an increase in investing by individuals, personal financial advisors will benefit more.

Financial analysts and personal financial advisors who have earned a professional designation are expected to have the best opportunities; competition is anticipated to be keen for highly lucrative positions in investment banking.

About 4 out of 10 personal financial advisors are self-employed.

Nature of the Work: Financial analysts and personal financial advisors provide analysis and guidance to businesses and individuals to help them with their investment decisions. Both types of specialists gather financial information, analyze it and make recommendations to their clients. However, their job duties differ because of the type of investment information they provide and the clients for whom they work. *Financial* *analysts* assess the economic performance of companies and industries for firms and institutions with money to invest. *Personal financial advisors* generally assess the financial needs of individuals, offering them a wide range of options.

Financial analysts, also called *securities analysts* and *investment analysts*, work for banks, insurance companies, mutual and pension funds, securities firms and other businesses, helping these companies or their clients make investment decisions. Financial analysts read company financial statements and analyze commodity prices, sales, costs, expenses and tax rates in order to determine a company's value and to project its future earnings.

They often meet with company officials to gain a better insight into the firm's prospects and to determine its managerial effectiveness. Usually, financial analysts study an entire industry, assessing current trends in business practices, products and industry competition. They must keep abreast of new regulations or policies that may affect the industry, as well as monitor the economy to determine its effect on earnings.

Financial analysts use spreadsheet and statistical software packages to analyze financial data, spot trends and develop forecasts. On the basis of their results, they write reports and make presentations, usually making recommendations to buy or sell a particular investment or security. Senior analysts may even be the ones who decide to buy or sell if they are responsible for managing the company's or client's assets. Other analysts use the data they find to measure the financial risks associated with making a particular investment decision.

Financial analysts in investment banking departments of securities or banking firms often work in teams, analyzing the future prospects of companies that want to sell shares to the public for the first time.

They also ensure that the forms and written materials necessary for compliance with Securities and Exchange Commission regulations are accurate and complete. They may make presentations to prospective investors about the merits of investing in the new company. Financial analysts also work in mergers and acquisitions departments, preparing analyses on the costs and benefits of a proposed merger or takeover.

Some financial analysts, called *ratings analysts*, evaluate the ability of companies or governments that issue bonds to repay their debts. On the basis of their evaluation, a management team assigns a rating to a company's or government's bonds. Other financial analysts perform budget, cost and credit analysis as part of their responsibilities.

Personal financial advisors, also called *financial planners* or *financial consultants*, use their knowledge of investments, tax laws and insurance to recommend financial options to individuals in accordance with the individual's short-term and long-term goals. Some of the issues that planners address are retirement and estate planning, funding for college and general investment options. While most planners offer advice on a wide range of topics, some specialize in areas such as retirement and estate planning or risk management.

An advisor's work begins with a consultation with the client, from whom the advisor obtains information on the client's finances and financial goals. The advisor then develops a comprehensive financial plan that identifies problem areas, makes recommendations for improvement and selects appropriate investments compatible with the client's goals, attitude toward risk and expectation or need for a return on the investment.

Sometimes this plan is written, but more often it is in the form of verbal advice. Financial advisors usually meet with established clients at least once a year to update them on potential investments and to determine whether the clients have been through any life changes—such as marriage, disability, or retirement—that might affect their financial goals. Financial advisors also answer questions from clients regarding changes in benefit plans or the consequences of a change in their jobs or careers.

A large part of the success of financial planners depends on their ability to educate their clients about risks and various possible scenarios so that the clients don't harbour unrealistic expectations.

Some advisors buy and sell financial products, such as mutual funds or insurance, or refer clients to other companies for products and services—for example, the preparation of taxes or wills. A number of advisors take on the responsibility of managing the clients' investments for them.

Finding clients and building a customer base is one of the most important of a financial advisor's job, because referrals from satisfied clients are an important source of new business. Many advisors also contact potential clients by giving seminars or lectures or meet clients through business and social contacts.

Working Conditions: Financial analysts and personal financial advisors usually work indoors in safe, comfortable offices or their own homes. Many of these workers enjoy the challenge of helping firms or people make financial decisions. However, financial analysts may face long hours, frequent travel to visit companies and talk to potential investors and the pressure of deadlines. Much of their research must be done after office hours, because their day is filled with telephone calls and meetings. Personal financial advisors usually work standard business hours, but they also schedule meetings with clients in the evenings or on weekends. Many teach evening classes or hold seminars in order to bring in more clients.

Training, Other Qualifications and Advancement: A college education is required for financial analysts and is strongly preferred for personal financial advisors. Most companies require financial analysts to have at least a bachelor's degree in business administration, accounting, statistics, or finance. Coursework in statistics, economics and business is required and knowledge of accounting policies and procedures, corporate budgeting and financial analysis methods is recommended. A master's degree in business administration is desirable. Advanced courses in options pricing or bond valuation and knowledge of risk management also are suggested.

Employers usually do not require a specific field of study for personal financial advisors, but a bachelor's degree in accounting, finance, economics, business, mathematics, or law provides good preparation for the occupation. Courses in investments, taxes, estate planning and risk management also are helpful. Programmes in financial planning are becoming more widely available in colleges and universities. Working for a broker-dealer is a good way to gain experience that can help individuals pass the security license exams needed to practice financial planning. Individuals who start out as independent financial planners may find it more difficult to build their client base and they often start by servicing their family members and friends. However, many financial planners enter the field after working in a related occupation, such as accountant; auditor; insurance sales agent; lawyer, or securities, commodities and financial services sales agent.

Mathematical, computer, analytical and problem-solving skills are essential qualifications for financial analysts and personal financial advisors. Good communication skills also are necessary, because these workers must present complex financial concepts and strategies in easy-to-understand language to clients and other professionals. Self-confidence, maturity and the ability to work independently are important as well. Financial analysts must be detail oriented, motivated to seek out obscure information and familiar with the workings of the economy, tax laws and money markets. Strong interpersonal skills and sales ability are crucial to the success of both financial analysts and personal financial advisors.

Although not required for financial analysts or personal financial advisors to practice, certification can enhance one's professional standing and is strongly recommended by many employers. Financial analysts may receive the Chartered Financial Analyst (CFA) designation, sponsored by the CFA Institute. To qualify for this designation, applicants need a bachelor's degree and 3 years of work experience in a related field and must pass a series of three examinations. These essay exams, administered once a year for 3 years, cover subjects such as accounting, economics, securities analysis, financial markets and instruments, corporate finance, asset valuation and portfolio management. Personal financial advisors may obtain the Certified Financial Planner credential, often referred to as CFP (R), demonstrating extensive training and competency in financial planning. This certification, issued by the Certified

Financial Planner Board of Standards, requires relevant experience, the completion of education requirements, passing a comprehensive examination and adherence to an enforceable code of ethics.

The CFP (R) exams test the candidate's knowledge of the financial planning process, insurance and risk management, employee benefits planning, taxes and retirement planning and investment and estate planning. The exam has been revised in recent years. Candidates are now required to have a working knowledge of debt management, planning liability, emergency fund reserves and statistical modelling. It may take from 2 to 3 years of study to complete these programmes.

Personal financial advisors also may obtain the Chartered Financial Consultant (ChFC) designation, issued by the American College in Bryn Mawr, Pennsylvania, which requires experience and the completion of an eight-course programme of study. The ChFC designation and other professional designations have continuing education requirements.

A license is not required to work as a personal financial advisor, but advisors who sell stocks, bonds, mutual funds, insurance, or real estate may need licenses to perform these additional services. Also, if legal advice is provided, a license to practice law may be required. Financial advisors who do not offer these additional services often refer clients to those who are qualified to provide them.

Financial analysts may advance by becoming portfolio managers or financial managers, directing the investment portfolios of their companies or of clients. Personal financial advisors who work in firms also may move into managerial positions, but most advisors advance by accumulating clients and managing more assets.

Employment: Financial analysts and personal financial advisors held 355,000 jobs in 2004, of which financial analysts held 197,000. Many financial analysts work at the headquarters of large financial companies, several of which are based in New York City. More than 4 out of 10 financial analysts work for finance and insurance industries, including securities and commodity brokers, banks and credit institutions and insurance carriers. Others worked throughout private industry and government.

Personal financial advisors held 158,000 jobs in 2004. Much like financial analysts, more than half work for finance and insurance industries, including securities and commodity brokers, banks, insurance carriers and financial investment firms. However, 4 out of 10 personal financial advisors are self-employed, operating small investment advisory firms, usually in urban areas.

Job Outlook: Overall employment of financial analysts and personal financial advisors is expected to increase faster than average for all occupations through 2014, resulting from increased investment by businesses and individuals. Personal financial advisors will benefit even more than financial analysts as baby boomers save for retirement and as a generally better educated and wealthier population requires investment advice. In addition, people are living longer and must plan to finance more years of retirement. The globalization of the securities markets also will increase the need for analysts and advisors to help investors make financial choices. Financial analysts and personal financial advisors who have earned a professional designation are expected to have the best opportunities.

Deregulation of the financial services industry is expected to spur demand for financial analysts and personal financial advisors. In recent years, banks, insurance companies and brokerage firms have been allowed to broaden their financial services. Many firms are adding investment advice to their list of services and are expected to increase their hiring of personal financial advisors. Many banks are entering the securities brokerage and investment banking fields and will increasingly need the skills of financial analysts.

Employment of personal financial advisors is projected to grow faster than the average for all occupations. The rapid expansion of self-directed retirement plans, such as 401(k) plans, is expected to continue. As the number and complexity of investments rises, more individuals will look to financial advisors to help manage their money.

Employment of financial analysts is expected to grow about as fast as the average for all occupations. As the number of mutual funds and the amount of assets invested in the funds increase, mutual fund companies will need increased numbers of financial analysts to recommend which financial products the funds should buy or sell.

Financial analysts also will be needed in the investment banking field, where they help companies raise money and work on corporate mergers and acquisitions. However, growth in demand for financial analysts to do company research has been and will continue to be, constrained by regulations that require investment firms to separate research from investment banking. As a result, firms have eliminated research jobs in an effort to contain the costs of implementing these regulations.

Demand for financial analysts in investment banking fluctuates because investment banking is sensitive to changes in the stock market. In addition, further consolidation in the finance industries may eliminate some financial analyst positions, dampening overall employment growth somewhat. Competition is expected to be keen for these highly lucrative positions, with many more applicants than jobs.

Earnings: Median annual earnings of financial analysts were \$61,910 in May 2004. The middle 50 percent earned between \$47,410 and \$82,730. The lowest 10 percent earned less than \$37,580 and the highest 10 percent earned more than \$113,490. Median annual earnings in the industries employing the largest numbers of financial analysts in 2004 were as follows:

Other financial investment activities	\$74,580
Securities and commodity contracts intermediation and brokerage	67,730
Management of companies and enterprises	62,890
Insurance carriers	58,120
Depository credit intermediation	56,860

Median annual earnings of personal financial advisors were \$62,700 in May 2004. The middle 50 percent earned between \$41,860 and \$108,280. Median annual earnings in the industries employing the largest number of personal financial advisors in 2004 were as follows:

Other financial investment activities	$78,350
Securities and commodity contracts intermediation and brokerage	63,310
Depository credit intermediation	57,180
Agencies, brokerages and other insurance related activities	56,950

Many financial analysts receive a bonus in addition to their salary and the bonus can add substantially to their earnings. Usually, the bonus is based on how well their predictions compare to the actual performance of a benchmark investment. Personal financial advisors who work for financial services firms are generally paid a salary plus bonus. Advisors who work for financial investment or planning firms or who are self-employed either charge hourly fees for their services or charge one set fee for a comprehensive plan, based on its complexity. Advisors who manage a client's assets may charge a percentage of those assets. Advisors generally receive commissions for financial products they sell, in addition to charging a fee.

Management Analysts

Significant Points: Despite fast employment growth, keen competition is expected for jobs; opportunities should be best for those with a graduate degree, specific industry expertise and a talent for salesmanship and public relations.

About 29 percent, more than 3 times the average for all occupations, are self-employed.

Most positions in private industry require a master's degree and additional years of specialized experience; a bachelor's degree is sufficient for entry-level government jobs.

Nature of the Work: As business becomes more complex, the Nation's firms are continually faced with new challenges. Firms increasingly rely on management analysts to help them remain competitive amidst these changes. Management analysts, often referred to as *management consultants* in private industry, analyze and propose ways to improve an organization's structure, efficiency, or profits. For example, a small but rapidly growing company that needs help improving the system of control over inventories and expenses may decide to employ a consultant who is an expert in just-in-time inventory management. In another case, a large company that has recently acquired a new division may hire management analysts to help reorganize the corporate structure and eliminate duplicate or nonessential jobs. In recent years, information technology and electronic commerce have provided new opportunities for management analysts. Companies hire consultants to develop strategies for entering and remaining competitive in the new electronic marketplace. (For information on computer specialists working in consulting, see the following statements elsewhere in the *Handbook*: computer software engineers; computer scientists and database administrators; and computer programmers.)

Firms providing management analysis range in size from a single practitioner to large international organizations employing thousands of consultants. Some analysts and consultants specialize in a specific industry, such as health care or telecommunications, while others specialize by type of business function, such as human resources, marketing, logistics, or information systems. In government, management analysts tend to specialize by type of agency. The work of management analysts and consultants varies with each client or employer and from project to project. Some projects require a team of consultants, each specializing in one area. In other projects, consultants work independently with the organization's managers. In all cases, analysts and consultants collect, review and analyze information in order to make recommendations to managers.

Both public and private organizations use consultants for a variety of reasons. Some lack the internal resources needed to handle a project, while others need a consultant's expertise to determine what resources will be required and what problems may be encountered if they pursue a particular opportunity. To retain a consultant, a company first solicits proposals from a number of consulting firms specializing in the area in which it needs assistance. These proposals include the estimated cost and scope of the project, staffing requirements, references from a number of previous clients and a completion deadline. The company then selects the proposal that best suits its needs.

After obtaining an assignment or contract, management analysts first define the nature and extent of the problem. During this phase, they analyze relevant data—which may include annual revenues, employment, or expenditures—and interview managers and employees while observing their operations. The analyst or consultant then develops solutions to the problem. While preparing their recommendations, they take into account the nature of the organization, the relationship it has with others in the industry and its internal organization and culture. Insight into the problem often is gained by building and solving mathematical models.

Once they have decided on a course of action, consultants report their findings and recommendations to the client. These suggestions usually are submitted in writing, but oral presentations regarding findings also are common. For some projects, management analysts are retained to help implement the suggestions they have made.

Like their private-sector colleagues, management analysts in government agencies try to increase efficiency and worker productivity and to control costs. For example, if an agency is planning to purchase personal computers, it must first determine which type to buy, given its budget and data-processing needs. In this case, management analysts would assess the prices and characteristics of various machines and determine which ones best meet the agency's needs. Analysts may manage contracts for a wide range of goods and services to ensure quality performance and to prevent cost over-runs.

Working Conditions: Management analysts usually divide their time between their offices and the client's site. In either situation, much of an analyst's time is spent indoors in clean, well-lit offices. Because they must spend a significant portion of their time with clients, analysts travel frequently.

Analysts and consultants generally work at least 40 hours a week. Uncompensated overtime is common, especially when project deadlines are approaching. Analysts may experience a great deal of stress as a result of trying to meet a client's demands, often on a tight schedule.

Self-employed consultants can set their workload and hours and work at home. On the other hand, their livelihood depends on their ability to maintain and expand their client base. Salaried consultants also must impress potential clients to get and keep clients for their company.

Training, Other Qualifications and Advancement: Educational requirements for entry-level jobs in this field vary widely between private industry and government. Most employers in private industry generally seek individuals with a master's degree in business administration or a related discipline.

Some employers also require additional years of experience in the field or industry in which the worker plans to consult, in addition to a master's degree. Some will hire workers with a bachelor's degree as a research analyst or associate. Research analysts usually need to pursue a master's degree in order to advance to a consulting position. Most government agencies hire people with a bachelor's degree and no pertinent work experience for entry-level management analyst positions.

Few universities or colleges offer formal programmes of study in management consulting; however, many fields of study provide a suitable educational background for this occupation because of the wide range of areas addressed by management analysts. Common educational backgrounds include most academic programmes in business and management, such as accounting and marketing, as well as economics, computer and information sciences and engineering. In addition to the appropriate formal education, most entrants to this occupation have years of experience in management, human resources, information technology, or other specialties. Analysts also routinely attend conferences to keep abreast of current developments in their field.

Management analysts often work with minimal supervision, so they need to be self-motivated and disciplined. Analytical skills, the ability to get along with a wide range of people, strong oral and written communication skills, good judgment, time management skills and creativity are other desirable qualities. The ability to work in teams also is an important attribute as consulting teams become more common.

As consultants gain experience, they often become solely responsible for a specific project, taking on more responsibility and managing their own hours. At the senior level, consultants may supervise teams working on more complex projects and become more involved in seeking out new business. Those with exceptional skills may eventually become a partner in the firm. Others with entrepreneurial ambition may open their own firm.

A high percentage of management consultants are self-employed, partly because business startup costs are low. Self-employed consultants also can share office space, administrative help and other resources with other self-employed consultants or small consulting firms, thus reducing overhead costs. Since many small consulting firms fail each year because of lack of managerial expertise and clients, persons interested in opening their own firm must have good organizational and marketing skills and several years of consulting experience.

The Institute of Management Consultants USA, Inc. (IMC USA) offers a wide range of professional development programmes and resources, such as meetings and workshops, which can be helpful for management consultants. The IMC USA also offers the Certified Management Consultant (CMC) designation to those who meet minimum levels of education and experience, submit client reviews and pass an interview and exam covering the IMC USA's Code of Ethics. Management consultants with a CMC designation must be re-certified every 3 years. Certification is not mandatory for management consultants, but it may give a jobseeker a competitive advantage.

Employment: Management analysts held about 605,000 jobs in 2004. About 29 percent of these workers, more than 3 times the average for all occupations, were self-employed. Management analysts are found throughout the country, but employ.ment is concentrated in large metropolitan areas. Management analyst jobs are found in a wide range of industries, including management, scientific and technical consulting firms; computer systems design and related services firms; and

Federal, State and local governments. The majority of those working for the Federal Government are in the US Department of Defense.

Job Outlook: Despite projected rapid employment growth, keen competition is expected for jobs as management analysts. The pool of applicants from which employers can draw is quite large since analysts can come from very diverse educational backgrounds. Furthermore, the independent and challenging nature of the work, combined with high earnings potential, makes this occupation attractive to many. Job opportunities are expected to be best for those with a graduate degree, specific industry expertise and a talent for salesmanship and public relations.

Employment of management analysts is expected to grow faster than the average for all occupations through 2014, as industry and government increasingly rely on outside expertise to improve the performance of their organizations. Job growth is projected in very large consulting firms with international expertise and in smaller consulting firms that specialize in specific areas, such as biotechnology, health care, information technology, human resources, engineering and marketing. Growth in the number of individual practitioners may be hindered by increasing use of consulting teams, that can expedite solutions to a variety of different issues and problems within an organization.

Employment growth of management analysts has been driven by a number of changes in the business environment that have forced firms to take a closer look at their operations. These changes include developments in information technology and the growth of electronic commerce. Traditional companies hire analysts to help design Intranets or company Web sites, or to establish online businesses. New Internet startup companies hire analysts not only to design Web sites but also to advise them in more traditional business practices, such as pricing strategies, marketing and inventory and human resource management. In order to offer clients better quality and a wider variety of services, consulting firms are partnering with traditional computer software and technology firms. Also, many computer firms are developing consulting practices of their own in order to take advantage of this expanding market. Although information technology consulting should remain one of the fastest growing consulting areas, the volatility of the computer services industry necessitates that the most successful management analysts have knowledge of traditional business practices in addition to computer applications, systems integration, Web design and management skills.

The growth of international business also has contributed to an increase in demand for management analysts. As US firms expand their business abroad, many will hire management analysts to help them form the right strategy for entering the market; to advise them on legal matters pertaining to specific countries; or to help them with organizational, administrative and other issues, especially if the US company is involved in a partnership or merger with a local firm. These trends provide management analysts with more opportunities to travel or work abroad but also require them to have a more comprehensive knowledge of international business and foreign cultures and languages.

Furthermore, as international and domestic markets have become more competitive, firms have needed to use resources more efficiently. Management analysts increasingly are sought to help reduce costs, streamline operations and develop marketing strategies. As this process continues and businesses downsize, even more opportunities will be created for analysts to perform duties that previously were handled internally. Finally, more management analysts also will be needed in the public sector, as Federal, State and local government agencies seek ways to become more efficient.

Though management consultants are continually expanding their services, employment growth could be hampered by increasing competition for clients from occupations that do not traditionally perform consulting work, such as accountants, financial analysts, lawyers and computer systems analysts. Furthermore, economic downturns also can have adverse effects on employment for some management consultants. In these times, businesses look to cut costs and consultants may be considered an excess expense. On the other hand, some consultants might experience an increase in work during recessions because they advise businesses on how to cut costs and remain profitable.

Earnings: Salaries for management analysts vary widely by years of experience and education, geographic location, sector of expertise and size of employer. Generally, management analysts employed in large firms or in metropolitan areas have the highest salaries. Median annual wage and salary earnings of management analysts in May 2004 were $63,450. The middle 50 percent earned between $48,340 and $86,650. The lowest 10 percent earned less than $37,680 and the highest 10 percent earned more than $120,220. Median annual earnings in the industries employing the largest numbers of management analysts in May 2004 were:

Management, scientific and technical consulting services	$72,480
Federal Government	72,440
Computer systems design and related services	69,800
Management of companies and enterprises	59,420
State government	48,070

According to a the Association of Management Consulting Firms, typical earnings in 2004—including bonuses and profit sharing—averaged $52,482 for research associates in member firms; $65,066 for entry-level consultants; $89,116 for management consultants; $123,305 for senior consultants; $191,664 for junior partners; and $317,339 for senior partners. Only the most experienced workers in highly successful management consulting firms earn these top salaries. Salaried management analysts usually receive common benefits, such as health and life insurance, a retirement plan, vacation and sick leave, as well as less common benefits, such as profit sharing and bonuses for outstanding work. In addition, all travel expenses usually are reimbursed by the employer. Self-employed consultants have to maintain their own office and provide their own benefits.

Market and Survey Researchers

Significant Points: Market and survey researchers need at least a bachelor's degree, but a master's degree may be required for employment; continuing education also is important.

Employment is expected to grow faster than average.

Job opportunities should be best for those with a master's or Ph.D. degree in marketing or a related field and strong quantitative skills.

Nature of the Work: *Market,* or *marketing, research analysts* are concerned with the potential sales of a product or service. Gathering statistical data on competitors and examining prices, sales and methods of marketing and distribution, they analyze data on past sales to predict future sales. Market research analysts devise methods and procedures for obtaining the data they need. Often, they design telephone, mail, or Internet surveys to assess consumer preferences. They conduct some surveys as personal interviews, going door-to-door, leading focus group discussions, or setting up booths in public places such as shopping malls. Trained interviewers usually conduct the surveys under the market research analyst's direction.

After compiling and evaluating the data, market research analysts make recommendations to their client or employer on the basis of their findings. They provide a company's management with information needed to make decisions on the promotion, distribution, design and pricing of products or services. The information also may be used to determine the advisability of adding new lines of merchandise, opening new branches, or otherwise diversifying the company's operations. Market research analysts also might develop advertising brochures and commercials, sales plans and product promotions such as rebates and giveaways.

Survey researchers design and conduct surveys for a variety of clients, such as corporations, government agencies, political candidates and providers of various services. The surveys collect information that is used for performing research, making fiscal or policy decisions, measuring the effectiveness of those decisions, or improving customer satisfaction. Analysts may conduct opinion research to determine public attitudes on various issues; the research results may help political or business leaders and others assess public support for their electoral prospects or social policies. Like market research analysts, survey researchers may use a variety of mediums to conduct surveys, such as the Internet, personal or telephone interviews, or questionnaires sent through the mail. They also may supervise interviewers who conduct surveys in person or over the telephone.

Survey researchers design surveys in many different formats, depending upon the scope of their research and the method of collection. Interview surveys, for example, are common because they can increase participation rates. Survey researchers may consult with economists, statisticians, market research analysts, or other data users in order to design surveys. They also may present survey results to clients.

Working Conditions: Market and survey researchers generally have structured work schedules. Some often work alone, writing reports, preparing statistical charts and using computers, but they also may be an integral part of a research team. Market researchers who conduct personal interviews have frequent contact with the public. Most work under pressure of deadlines and tight schedules, which may require overtime. Their routine may be interrupted by special requests for data, as well as by the need to attend meetings or conferences. Travel may be necessary.

Training, Other Qualifications and Advancement: A bachelor's degree is the minimum educational requirement for many market and survey research jobs. However, a master's degree may be required, especially for technical positions and increases opportunities for advancement to more responsible positions. Also, continuing education is important in order to keep current with the latest methods of developing, conducting and analyzing surveys and other data. Market and survey researchers may earn advanced degrees in business administration, marketing, statistics, communications, or some closely related discipline. Some schools help graduate students find internships or part-time employment in government agencies, consulting firms, financial institutions, or marketing research firms prior to graduation.

In addition to completing courses in business, marketing and consumer behaviour, prospective market and survey researchers should take other liberal arts and social science courses, including economics, psychology, English and sociology. Because of the importance of quantitative skills to market and survey researchers, courses in mathematics, statistics, sampling theory and survey design and computer science are extremely helpful. Many corporation and government executives have a strong background in marketing.

A master's degree is usually the minimum educational requirement for a job as a marketing or survey research instructor in junior and community colleges. In most colleges and universities, however, a Ph.D. is necessary for appointment as an instructor. A Ph.D. and extensive publications in academic journals are required for a professorship, tenure and promotion.

While in college, aspiring market and survey researchers should gain experience gathering and analyzing data, conducting interviews or surveys and writing reports on their findings. This experience can prove invaluable later in obtaining a full-time position in the field, because much of the initial work may centre on these duties. With experience, market and survey researchers eventually are assigned their own research projects.

Much of the market and survey researcher's time is spent on precise data analysis, so those considering careers in the occupation should be able to pay attention to detail. Patience and persistence are necessary qualities because these workers must spend long hours on independent study and problem solving. At the same time, they must work well with others: often, market and survey researchers oversee interviews of a wide variety of individuals. Communication skills are important, too, because researchers must be able to present their findings both orally and in writing, in a clear, concise manner.

While certification currently is not required for market and survey researchers, the Marketing Research Association (MRA) offers a certification programme for professional researchers. Certification is based on education and experience requirements, as well as on continuing education.

Employment: Market and survey researchers held about 212,000 jobs in 2004, most of which—190,000—were held by market research analysts. Because of the applicability of market research to many industries, market research analysts are employed throughout the economy. The industries that employ the largest number of market research analysts were management of companies and enterprises; management, scientific and technical consulting services; insurance carriers; credit intermediation and related activities; computer systems design and related services; marketing research and public opinion polling; software publishers; professional and commercial equipment and supplies merchant wholesalers; securities and commodity contracts intermediation and brokerage; and advertising and related services.

Survey researchers held about 22,000 jobs in 2004. Survey researchers were employed mainly by professional, scientific and technical services firms, especially in market research and public opinion polling; scientific research and development services; and management, scientific and technical consulting services. State government also provided many jobs for survey researchers.

A number of market and survey researchers combine a full-time job in government, academia, or business with part-time or consulting work in another setting. About nine percent of market and survey researchers are self-employed.

Besides holding the previously mentioned jobs, many market and survey researchers held faculty positions in colleges and universities. Marketing faculties have flexible work schedules and may divide their time among teaching, research, consulting and administration.

Job Outlook: Employment of market and survey researchers is expected to grow faster than average for all occupations through 2014. Many job openings are likely to result from the need to replace experienced workers who transfer to other occupations or who retire or leave the labour force for other reasons.

Job opportunities should be best for those with a master's or Ph.D. degree in marketing or a related field and strong quantitative skills. Bachelor's degree holders may face competition, as many positions, especially the more technical ones, require a master's or higher degree. Among bachelor's degree holders, those with good quantitative skills, including a strong background in mathematics, statistics, survey design and computer science, will have the best opportunities. Ph.D. degree holders in marketing and related fields should have a range of opportunities in industry and consulting firms. Like those in many other disciplines, however, Ph.D. holders probably will face keen competition for tenured teaching positions in colleges and universities.

Demand for market research analysts should be strong because of an increasingly competitive economy. Marketing research provides organizations valuable feedback from purchasers, allowing companies to evaluate consumer satisfaction and plan more effectively for the future. As companies seek to expand their market and as consumers become better informed, the need for marketing professionals will increase. In addition, as globalization of the marketplace continues, market researchers will increasingly be utilized to analyze foreign markets and competition for goods and services.

Market research analysts should have the best opportunities in consulting firms and marketing research firms as companies find it more profitable to contract for market research services rather than support their own marketing department. Increasingly, market research analysts not only are collecting and analyzing information, but also are helping clients implement the analysts' ideas and recommendations. Other organizations, including computer systems design companies, software publishers, financial services organizations, health care institutions, advertising firms and insurance companies, may offer job opportunities for market research analysts. Survey researchers will be needed to meet the growing demand for market and opinion research as an increasingly competitive economy requires businesses to allocate advertising funds more effectively and efficiently.

Earnings: Median annual earnings of market research analysts in May 2004 were $56,140. The middle 50 percent earned between $40,510 and $79,990. The lowest 10 percent earned less than $30,890 and the highest 10 percent earned more than $105,870. Median annual earnings in the industries employing the largest numbers of market research analysts in May 2004 were:

Management of companies and enterprises	$58,440
Computer systems design and related services	58,100
Insurance carriers	51,030
Other professional, scientific and technical services	50,950
Management, scientific and technical consulting services	49,080

Median annual earnings of survey researchers in May 2004 were $26,490. The middle 50 percent earned between $17,920 and $41,390. The lowest 10 percent earned less than $15,330 and the highest 10 percent earned more than $56,740. Median annual earnings of survey researchers in other professional, scientific and technical services were $22,880.

Mathematicians

Significant Points: A Ph.D. degree in mathematics usually is the minimum educational requirement, except in the Federal Government.

The number of jobs with the title "mathematician" is declining as the workforce becomes increasingly specialized; competition will be keen for the limited number of available jobs.

Master's and Ph.D. degree holders with a strong background in mathematics and a related field, such as computer science or engineering, should have better employment opportunities in related occupations.

Nature of the Work: Mathematics is one of the oldest and most fundamental sciences. Mathematicians use mathematical theory, computational techniques, algorithms and the latest computer technology to solve economic, scientific, engineering, physics and business problems. The work of mathematicians falls into two broad classes—theoretical (pure) mathematics and applied mathematics. These classes, however, are not sharply defined and often overlap.

Theoretical mathematicians advance mathematical knowledge by developing new principles and recognizing previously unknown relationships between existing principles of mathematics. Although these workers seek to increase basic knowledge without necessarily considering its practical use, such pure and abstract knowledge has been instrumental in producing or furthering many scientific and engineering achievements. Many theoretical mathematicians are employed as university faculty, dividing their time between teaching and conducting research.

Applied mathematicians, on the other hand, use theories and techniques, such as mathematical modelling and computational methods, to formulate and solve practical problems in business, government and engineering and in the physical, life and social sciences. For example, they may analyze the most efficient way to schedule airline routes between cities, the effects and safety of new drugs, the aerodynamic characteristics of an experimental automobile, or the cost-effectiveness of alternative manufacturing processes. Applied mathematicians working in industrial research and development may develop or enhance mathematical methods when solving a difficult problem. Some mathematicians, called cryptanalysts, analyze and decipher encryption systems designed to transmit military, political, financial, or law enforcement-related information in code.

Applied mathematicians start with a practical problem, envision the separate elements of the process under consideration and then reduce the elements to mathematical variables. They often use computers to analyze relationships among the variables and solve complex problems by developing models with alternative solutions.

Much of the work in applied mathematics is done by individuals with titles other than mathematician. In fact, because mathematics is the foundation on which so many other academic disciplines are built, the number of workers using mathematical techniques is much greater than the number formally designated as mathematicians. For example, engineers, computer scientists, physicists and economists are among those who use mathematics extensively. Some professionals, including statisticians, actuaries and operations research analysts, actually are specialists in a particular branch of mathematics. Frequently, applied mathematicians are required to collaborate with other workers in their organizations to achieve common solutions to problems.

Working Conditions: Mathematicians usually work in comfortable offices. They often are part of interdisciplinary teams that may include economists, engineers, computer scientists, physicists, technicians and others. Deadlines, overtime work, special requests for information or analysis and prolonged travel to attend seminars or conferences may be part of their jobs. Mathematicians who work in academia usually have a mix of teaching and research responsibilities. These mathematicians may conduct research alone or in close collaboration with other mathematicians. Collaborators may work together at the same institution or from different locations, using technology such as e-mail to communicate. Mathematicians in academia also may be aided by graduate students.

Training, Other Qualifications and Advancement: A Ph.D. degree in mathematics usually is the minimum educational requirement for prospective mathematicians, except in the Federal Government. In the Federal Government, entry-level job candidates usually must have a 4-year degree with a major in mathematics or a 4-year degree with the equivalent of a mathematics major—24 semester hours of mathematics courses.

In private industry, candidates for mathematician jobs typically need a Ph.D., although there may be opportunities for those with a master's degree. Most of the positions designated for mathematicians are in research and development laboratories, as part of technical teams. In such settings, mathematicians engage either in basic research on pure mathematical principles or in applied research on developing or improving specific products or processes. The majority of those with a bachelor's or master's degree in mathematics who work in private industry do so not as mathematicians but in related fields such as computer science, where they have titles such as computer programmer, systems analyst, or systems engineer.

A bachelor's degree in mathematics is offered by most colleges and universities. Mathematics courses usually required for this degree include calculus, differential equations and linear and abstract algebra. Additional courses might include probability theory and statistics, mathematical analysis, numerical analysis, topology, discrete mathematics and mathematical logic. Many colleges and universities urge or require students majoring in mathematics to take courses in a field that is closely related to mathematics, such as computer science, engineering, life science, physical science, or economics. A double major in mathematics and another related discipline is particularly desirable to many employers. High school students who are prospective college mathematics majors should take as many mathematics courses as possible while in high school.

In 2004, about 200 colleges and universities offered a master's degree as the highest degree in either pure or applied mathematics; about 200 offered a Ph.D. degree in pure or applied mathematics. In graduate school, students conduct research and take advanced courses, usually specializing in a subfield of mathematics.

For jobs in applied mathematics, training in the field in which the mathematics will be used is very important. Mathematics is used extensively in physics, actuarial science, statistics, engineering and operations research. Computer science, business and industrial management, economics, finance, chemistry, geology, life sciences and behavioural sciences are likewise dependent on applied mathematics. Mathematicians also should have substantial knowledge of computer programming, because most complex mathematical computation and much mathematical modelling are done on a computer.

Mathematicians need good reasoning ability and persistence to identify, analyze and apply basic principles to technical problems. Communication skills also are important, as mathematicians must be able to interact and discuss proposed solutions with people who may not have extensive knowledge of mathematics.

Employment: Mathematicians held about 2,500 jobs in 2004. Many people with mathematical backgrounds also worked in other occupations. For example, about 53,000 persons held positions as post-secondary mathematical science teachers in 2004.

Many mathematicians work for Federal or State governments. The US Department of Defense is the primary Federal employer, accounting for about three-fourths of the mathematicians employed by the Federal Government. Many of the other mathematicians employed by the Federal Government work for the National Aeronautics and Space Administration (NASA). In the private sector, major employers include scientific research and development services and management, scientific and technical consulting services. Some mathematicians also work for software publishers, insurance companies and in aerospace or pharmaceutical manufacturing.

Job Outlook: Employment of mathematicians is expected to decline through 2014, reflecting the reduction in the number of jobs with the title "mathematician." As a result, competition is expected to be keen for the limited number of jobs as mathematicians. Master's and Ph.D. degree holders with a strong background in mathematics and a related discipline, such as engineering or computer science, should have the best opportunities. Many of these workers have job titles that reflect their occupation, such as systems analyst, rather than the title mathematician, reflecting their primary educational background.

Advancements in technology usually lead to expanding applications of mathematics and more workers with knowledge of mathematics will be required in the future. However, jobs in industry and government often require advanced knowledge of related scientific disciplines in addition to mathematics. The most common fields in which mathematicians study and find work are computer science and software development, physics, engineering and operations research. More mathematicians also are becoming involved in financial analysis. Mathematicians must compete for jobs, however, with people who have degrees in these other disciplines. The most successful jobseekers will be able to apply mathematical theory to real-world problems and will possess good communication, teamwork and computer skills.

Private industry jobs require at least a master's degree in mathematics or in a related field. Bachelor's degree holders in mathematics usually are not qualified for most jobs and many seek advanced degrees in mathematics or a related discipline. However, bachelor's degree holders who meet State certification requirements may become primary or secondary school mathematics teachers. (For additional information, see the statement on teachers—preschool, kindergarten, elementary, middle and secondary elsewhere in the *Handbook*.)

Holders of a master's degree in mathematics will face very strong competition for jobs in theoretical research. Because the number of Ph.D. degrees awarded in mathematics continues to exceed the number of university positions available, many of these graduates will need to find employment in industry and government.

Earnings: Median annual earnings of mathematicians were $81,240 in May 2004. The middle 50 percent earned between $60,050 and $101,360. The lowest 10 percent had earnings of less than $43,160, while the highest 10 percent earned over $120,900.

In early 2005, the average annual salary for mathematicians employed by the Federal Government in supervisory, nonsupervisory and managerial positions was $88,194; that for mathematical statisticians was $91,446; and for cryptanalysts the average was $70,774.

Actuaries

Significant Points: A strong background in mathematics is essential; actuaries must pass a series of examinations to gain full professional status.

About 6 out of 10 actuaries are employed in the insurance industry.

Employment opportunities should remain good for those who qualify, because the stringent qualifying examination system restricts the number of candidates.

Nature of the Work: One of the main functions of actuaries is to help businesses assess the risk of certain events occurring and to formulate policies that minimize the cost of that risk. For this reason, actuaries are essential to the insurance industry. Actuaries assemble and analyze data to estimate the probability and likely cost of the occurrence of an event such as death, sickness, injury, disability, or loss of property.

Actuaries also address financial questions, including those involving the level of pension contributions required to produce a certain retirement income and the way in which a company should invest resources to maximize its return on investments in light of potential risk. Using their broad knowledge of statistics, finance and business, actuaries help design insurance policies, pension plans and other financial strategies in a manner which will help ensure that the plans are maintained on a sound financial basis.

Most actuaries are employed in the insurance industry, specializing in life and health insurance or property and casualty insurance. They produce probability tables which determine the likelihood that a potential future event will generate a claim. From these tables, they estimate the amount a company can expect to pay in claims. For example, property and casualty actuaries calculate the expected amount payable in claims resulting from automobile accidents, an amount that varies with the insured person's age, sex, driving history, type of car and other factors.

Actuaries ensure that the price, or premium, charged for such insurance will enable the company to cover claims and other expenses. The premium must be profitable, yet competitive with other insurance companies. Within the life and health insurance fields, actuaries are helping to develop long-term-care insurance and annuity policies, the latter a growing investment tool for many individuals.

Actuaries in other financial services industries manage credit and price corporate security offerings. They also devise new investment tools to help their firms compete with other financial services companies. Pension actuaries working under the provisions of the Employee Retirement Income Security Act (ERISA) of 1974 evaluate pension plans covered by that Act and report on the plans' financial soundness to participants, sponsors and Federal regulators. Actuaries working in government help manage social programmes such as Social Security and Medicare.

Actuaries may play a role in determining company policy and may need to explain complex technical matters to company executives, government officials, shareholders, policyholders, or the public in general. They may testify before public agencies on proposed legislation affecting their businesses or explain changes in contract provisions to customers. They also may help companies develop plans to enter new lines of business or new geographic markets with existing lines of business by forecasting demand in competitive settings.

Both staff actuaries employed by businesses and consulting actuaries provide advice to clients on a contract basis. The duties of most consulting actuaries are similar to those of other actuaries. For example, some may evaluate company pension plans by calculating the future value of employee and employer contributions and determining whether the amounts are sufficient to meet the future needs of retirees. Others help companies reduce their insurance costs by lowering the level of risk the companies assume. For instance, they may provide advice on how to lessen the risk of injury on the job, which will lower worker's compensation costs. Consulting actuaries sometimes testify in court regarding the value of the potential lifetime earnings of a person who is disabled or killed in an accident, the current value of future pension benefits (in divorce cases), or other values arrived at by complex calculations. Many consulting actuaries work in reinsurance, a field in which one insurance company arranges to share a large prospective liability policy with another insurance company in exchange for a percentage of the premium.

Working Conditions: Actuaries have desk jobs and their offices usually are comfortable and pleasant. They often work at least 40 hours a week. Some actuaries—particularly consulting actuaries—may travel to meet with clients. Consulting actuaries also may experience more erratic employment and be expected to work more than 40 hours per week.

Training, Other Qualifications and Advancement: Actuaries need a strong background in mathematics. Applicants for beginning actuarial jobs usually have a bachelor's degree in mathematics, actuarial science, statistics, or a business-related discipline such as economics, finance, or accounting. About 100 colleges and universities offer an actuarial science programme and most offer a degree in mathematics, statistics, economics, or finance.

Some companies hire applicants without specifying a major, provided that the applicant has a working knowledge of mathematics, including calculus, probability and statistics and has demonstrated this knowledge by passing one or two actuarial exams required for professional designation. Courses in economics, accounting, finance and insurance also are useful. Companies increasingly prefer well-rounded individuals who, in addition to having acquired a strong technical background, have some training in liberal arts and business and possess strong communication skills.

In addition to knowledge of mathematics, computer skills are becoming increasingly important. Actuaries should be able to develop and use spreadsheets and databases, as well as standard statistical analysis software. Knowledge of computer programming languages, such as Visual Basic, also is useful.

Two professional societies sponsor programmes leading to full professional status in their specialty. The Society of Actuaries (SOA) administers a series of actuarial examinations in the life insurance, health benefits systems, retirement systems and finance and investment fields. The Casualty Actuarial Society (CAS) gives a series of examinations in the property and casualty field, which includes fire, accident, medical malpractice, worker's compensation and personal injury liability.

The first four exams in the SOA and CAS examination series are jointly sponsored by the two societies and cover the same material. For this reason, students do not need to commit themselves to a specialty until they have taken the initial examinations, which test an individual's competence in probability, calculus, statistics and other branches of mathematics. The first few examinations help students evaluate their potential as actuaries. Many prospective actuaries begin taking the exams in college with the help of self-study guides and courses. Those who pass one or more examinations have better opportunities for employment at higher starting salaries than those who do not.

After graduating from college, most prospective actuaries gain on-the job experience at an insurance company or consulting firm, while at the same time working to complete the examination process. Actuaries are encouraged to finish the entire series of examinations as soon as possible, advancing first to the Associate level (with an ASA or ACAS designation) and then to the Fellowship level (FSA or FCAS designation). Advanced topics in the casualty field include investment and assets, dynamic financial analysis and valuation of insurance.

Candidates in the SOA examination series must choose a specialty—group and health benefits, individual life and annuities, pensions, investments, or finance. Examinations are given twice a year, in the spring and the fall. Although many companies allot time to their employees for study, home study is required to pass the examinations and many actuaries study for months to prepare for each examination. It is likewise common for employers to pay the hundreds of dollars for examination fees and study materials. Most actuaries reach the Associate level within 4 to 6 years and the Fellowship level a few years later.

Specific requirements apply to pension actuaries, who verify the financial status of defined benefit pension plans for the Federal Government. These actuaries must be enrolled by the Joint Board of the US Treasury Department and the US Department of Labour for the Enrolment of Actuaries. To qualify for enrolment, applicants must meet certain experience and examination requirements, as stipulated by the Board.

To perform their duties effectively, actuaries must keep up with current economic and social trends and legislation, as well as with health, business, finance and economic developments that could affect insurance or investment practices. Good communication and interpersonal skills also are important, particularly for prospective consulting actuaries.

Beginning actuaries often rotate among different jobs in an organization to learn various actuarial operations and phases of insurance work, such as marketing, underwriting and product development. At first, they prepare data for actuarial projects or perform other simple tasks. As they gain experience, actuaries may supervise clerks, prepare correspondence, draft reports and conduct research. They may move from one company to another early in their careers as they advance to higher positions.

Advancement depends largely on job performance and the number of actuarial examinations passed. Actuaries with a broad knowledge of the insurance, pension, investment, or employee benefits fields can rise to administrative and executive positions in their companies. Actuaries with supervisory ability may advance to management positions in other areas, such as underwriting, accounting, data processing, marketing and advertising. Some actuaries assume college and university faculty positions.

Employment: Actuaries held about 18,000 jobs in 2004, with 6 out of 10 employed in the insurance industry. A growing number of actuaries work for firms providing a variety of corporate services, especially management and public relations, or for firms offering consulting services. A relatively small number of actuaries are employed by security and commodity brokers or by government agencies.

Job Outlook: Employment of actuaries is expected to grow faster than average for all occupations through 2014. Employment opportunities should remain good for those who qualify, because the stringent qualifying examination system restricts the number of candidates. Employment growth in the insurance industry is expected to continue at a stable pace, while more significant job growth is likely in some other industries. In addition, a small number of jobs will open up each year to replace actuaries who leave the occupation to retire or who find new jobs.

Steady demand by the insurance industry—the largest employer of actuaries—should ensure the creation of new actuary jobs in this key industry over the projection period.

Actuaries will continue to be needed to develop, price and evaluate a variety of insurance products and calculate the costs of new risks. Although employment of actuaries in life insurance had begun to decline recently, the growing popularity of annuities, a financial product offered primarily by life insurance companies, has resulted in some job growth in this specialty. Also, new actuarial positions have been created in property-casualty insurance to analyze evolving risks, such as terrorism.

Some new employment opportunities for actuaries should also become available in the health care field as health care issues and Medicare reform continue to receive growing attention. Increased regulation of managed health care companies and the desire to contain health care costs will continue to provide job opportunities for actuaries, who will also be needed to evaluate the risks associated with new medical issues, such as genetic testing and the impact of new diseases. Others in this field are involved in drafting health care legislation.

A significant proportion of new actuaries will find employment with consulting firms. Companies that may not find it cost effective to hire their own actuaries are increasingly hiring consulting actuaries to analyze various risks. Other areas with notable growth prospects are information services and accounting services. Also, because actuarial skills are increasingly seen as useful to other industries that deal with risk, such as the airline and the banking industries, additional job openings may be created in these industries.

The best job prospects for entry-level positions will be for those candidates who have passed at least one or two of the initial actuarial exams. Candidates with additional knowledge or experience, such as those who possess computer programming skills, will be particularly attractive to employers. Most jobs in this occupation are located in urban areas, but opportunities vary by geographic location. States in which actuary jobs are concentrated include Illinois, New Jersey, New York and Connecticut.

Earnings: Median annual earnings of actuaries were \$76,340 in May 2004. The middle 50 percent earned between

$54,770 and $107,650. According to the National Association of Colleges and Employers, annual starting salaries for graduates with a bachelor's degree in actuarial science averaged $52,741 in 2005. Insurance companies and consulting firms give merit increases to actuaries as they gain experience and pass examinations. Some companies also offer cash bonuses for each professional designation achieved.

Accountants and Auditors

Significant Points: Most jobs require at least a bachelor's degree in accounting or a related field.

Overall job opportunities should be favourable; jobseekers who obtain professional recognition through certification or licensure, a master's degree, proficiency in accounting and auditing computer software, or specialized expertise will have the best opportunities.

An increase in the number of businesses, changing financial laws and regulations and greater scrutiny of company finances will drive faster-than-average growth of accountants and auditors.

Nature of the Work: Accountants and auditors help to ensure that the Nation's firms are run efficiently, its public records kept accurately and its taxes paid properly and on time. They perform these vital functions by offering an increasingly wide array of business and accounting services, including public, management and government accounting, as well as internal auditing, to their clients.

Beyond carrying out the fundamental tasks of the occupation—preparing, analyzing and verifying financial documents in order to provide information to clients—many accountants now are required to possess a wide range of knowledge and skills. Accountants and auditors are broadening the services they offer to include budget analysis, financial and investment planning, information technology consulting and limited legal services.

Specific job duties vary widely among the four major fields of accounting: *public*, *management* and *government accounting* and *internal auditing*.

Public accountants perform a broad range of accounting, auditing, tax and consulting activities for their clients, which may be corporations, governments, non-profit organizations, or individuals. For example, some public accountants concentrate on tax matters, such as advising companies about the tax advantages and disadvantages of certain business decisions and preparing individual income tax returns. Others offer advice in areas such as compensation or employee health care benefits, the design of accounting and data-processing systems and the selection of controls to safeguard assets. Still others audit clients' financial statements and inform investors and authorities that the statements have been correctly prepared and reported. Public accountants, many of whom are Certified Public Accountants (CPAs), generally have their own businesses or work for public accounting firms.

Some public accountants specialize in forensic accounting—investigating and interpreting white-collar crimes such as securities fraud and embezzlement, bankruptcies and contract disputes and other complex and possibly criminal financial transactions, including money laundering by organized criminals. Forensic accountants combine their knowledge of accounting and finance with law and investigative techniques in order to determine whether an activity is illegal. Many forensic accountants work closely with law enforcement personnel and lawyers during investigations and often appear as expert witnesses during trials.

In response to recent accounting scandals, new Federal legislation restricts the non-auditing services that public accountants can provide to clients. If an accounting firm audits a client's financial statements, that same firm cannot provide advice on human resources, technology, investment banking, or legal matters, although accountants may still advise on tax issues, such as establishing a tax shelter. Accountants may still advise other clients in these areas or may provide advice within their own firm.

Management accountants—also called cost, managerial, industrial, corporate, or private accountants—record and analyze the financial information of the companies for which they work. Among their other responsibilities are budgeting, performance evaluation, cost management and asset management. Usually, management accountants are part of executive teams involved in strategic planning or the development of new products. They analyze and interpret the financial information that corporate executives need in order to make sound business decisions. They also prepare financial reports for other groups, including stockholders, creditors, regulatory agencies and tax authorities. Within accounting departments, management accountants may work in various areas, including financial analysis, planning and budgeting and cost accounting.

Government accountants and auditors work in the public sector, maintaining and examining the records of government agencies and auditing private businesses and individuals whose activities are subject to government regulations or taxation. Accountants employed by Federal, State and local governments guarantee that revenues are received and expenditures are made in accordance with laws and regulations. Those employed by the Federal Government may work as Internal Revenue Service agents or in financial management, financial institution examination, or budget analysis and administration.

Internal auditors verify the accuracy of their organization's internal records and check for mismanagement, waste, or fraud. Internal auditing is an increasingly important area of accounting and auditing. Internal auditors examine and evaluate their firms' financial and information systems, management procedures and internal controls to ensure that records are accurate and controls are adequate to protect against fraud and waste.

They also review company operations, evaluating their efficiency, effectiveness and compliance with corporate policies and procedures, laws and government regulations. There are many types of highly specialized auditors, such as electronic data-processing, environmental, engineering, legal, insurance premium, bank and health care auditors. As computer systems make information timelier, internal auditors help managers to base their decisions on actual data, rather than personal observation. Internal auditors also may recommend controls for their organization's computer system, to ensure the reliability of the system and the integrity of the data.

Computers are rapidly changing the nature of the work of most accountants and auditors. With the aid of special software packages, accountants summarize transactions in standard formats used by financial records and organize data in special formats employed in financial analysis. These accounting packages greatly reduce the amount of tedious manual work associated with data management and record-keeping. Computers enable accountants and auditors to be more mobile and to use their clients' computer systems to extract information from databases and the Internet.

As a result, a growing number of accountants and auditors with extensive computer skills are specializing in correcting problems with software or in developing software to meet unique data management and analytical needs. Accountants also are beginning to perform more technical duties, such as implementing, controlling and auditing systems and networks, developing technology plans and analyzing and devising budgets.

Increasingly, accountants also are assuming the role of a personal financial advisor. They not only provide clients with accounting and tax help, but also help them develop personal budgets, manage assets and investments, plan for retirement and recognize and reduce their exposure to risks. This role is a response to clients' demands for a single trustworthy individual or firm to meet all of their financial needs. However, accountants are restricted from providing these services to clients whose financial statements they also prepare.

Working Conditions: Most accountants and auditors work in a typical office setting. Self-employed accountants may be able to do part of their work at home. Accountants and auditors employed by public accounting firms and government agencies may travel frequently to perform audits at branches of their firm, clients' places of business, or government facilities.

Most accountants and auditors generally work a standard 40-hour week, but many work longer hours, particularly if they are self-employed and have numerous clients. Tax specialists often work long hours during the tax season.

Training, Other Qualifications and Advancement: Most accountant and auditor positions require at least a bachelor's degree in accounting or a related field. Beginning accounting and auditing positions in the Federal Government, for example, usually require 4 years of college (including 24 semester hours in accounting or auditing) or an equivalent combination of education and experience. Some employers prefer applicants with a master's degree in accounting, or with a master's degree in business administration with a concentration in accounting.

Previous experience in accounting or auditing can help an applicant get a job. Many colleges offer students an opportunity to gain experience through summer or part-time internship programmes conducted by public accounting or business firms. In addition, practical knowledge of computers and their applications in accounting and internal auditing is a great asset for jobseekers in the accounting field.

Professional recognition through certification or licensure provides a distinct advantage in the job market. CPAs are licensed by a State Board of Accountancy. The vast majority of States require CPA candidates to be college graduates, but a few States substitute a number of years of public accounting experience for a college degree.

As of early 2005, on the basis of recommendations made by the American Institute of Certified Public Accountants (AICPA), 42 States and the District of Columbia required CPA candidates to complete 150 semester hours of college coursework—an additional 30 hours beyond the usual 4-year bachelor's degree. Another five States have adopted similar legislation that will become effective between 2006 and 2009. Colorado, Delaware, New Hampshire and Vermont are the only States that do not require 150 semester hours. In response to this trend, many schools have altered their curricula accordingly, with most programmes offering master's degrees as part of the 150 hours, so prospective accounting majors should carefully research accounting curricula and the requirements of any States in which they hope to become licensed.

All States use the four-part Uniform CPA Examinaticn prepared by the AICPA. The 2-day CPA examination is rigorous and only about one-quarter of those who take it each year pass every part they attempt. Candidates are not required to pass all four parts at once, but most States require candidates to pass at least two parts for partial credit and to complete all four sections within a certain period. The CPA exam is now computerized and is offered quarterly at various testing centres throughout the United States. Most States also require applicants for a CPA certificate to have some accounting experience.

The AICPA also offers members with valid CPA certificates the option to receive any or all of the Accredited in Business Valuation (ABV), Certified Information Technology Professional (CITP), or Personal Financial Specialist (PFS) designations. CPA's with these designations may claim a certain level of expertise in the non-traditional areas in which accountants are practicing ever more frequently. The ABV designation requires a written exam, as well as the completion of a minimum of 10 business valuation projects that demonstrate a candidate's experience and competence. The CITP requires payment of a fee, a written statement of intent and the achievement of a set number of points awarded for business experience and education. Those who do not meet the required number of points may substitute a written exam. Candidates for the PFS designation also must achieve a certain level of points, based on experience and education and must pass a written exam and submit references.

Nearly all States require CPAs and other public accountants to complete a certain number of hours of continuing professional education before their licenses can be renewed. The professional associations representing accountants sponsor numerous courses, seminars, group study programmes and other forms of continuing education.

Accountants and auditors also can seek to obtain other forms of credentials from professional societies on a voluntary basis. Voluntary certification can attest to professional competence in a specialized field of accounting and auditing. It also can certify that a recognized level of professional competence has been achieved by accountants and auditors who have acquired some skills on the job, without the formal education or public accounting work experience needed to meet the rigorous standards required to take the CPA examination.

The Institute of Management Accountants (IMA) confers the Certified Management Accountant (CMA) designation upon applicants who complete a bachelor's degree or who attain a minimum score or higher on specified graduate school entrance exams. Applicants, who must have worked at least 2 years in management accounting, also must pass a four-part examination, agree to meet continuing education requirements and comply with standards of professional conduct. The CMA exam provides an in-depth measure of competence in areas such as financial statement analysis, working-capital policy, capital structure, valuation issues and risk management. The CMA programme is administered by the Institute of Certified Management Accountants, an affiliate of the IMA.

Graduates from accredited colleges and universities who have worked for 2 years as internal auditors and have passed a four-part examination may earn the Certified Internal Auditor (CIA) designation from the Institute of Internal Auditors (IIA). The IIA recently implemented three new specialty designations: Certification in Control Self-Assessment (CCSA), Certified Government Auditing Professional (CGAP) and Certified Financial Services Auditor (CFSA). Requirements are similar to those of the CIA.

The Information Systems Audit and Control Association confers the Certified Information Systems Auditor (CISA) designation upon candidates who pass an examination and have 5 years of experience auditing information systems. Auditing or data-processing experience and a college education may be substituted for up to 2 years of work experience in this programme. Accountants and auditors may hold multiple designations. For instance, an internal auditor might be a CPA, CIA and CISA.

The Accreditation Council for Accountancy and Taxation, a satellite organization of the National Society of Public Accountants, confers four designations—Accredited Business Accountant (ABA), Accredited Tax Advisor (ATA), Accredited Tax Preparer (ATP) and Elder Care Specialist (ECS)—on accountants specializing in tax preparation for small and medium-sized businesses. Candidates for the ABA must pass an exam; candidates for the ATA, ATP and ECS must complete the required coursework and pass an exam. Often, a practitioner will hold multiple licenses and designations.

The Association of Government Accountants grants the Certified Government Financial Manager (CGFM) designation for accountants, auditors and other government financial personnel at the Federal, State and local levels. Candidates must have a minimum of a bachelor's degree, 24 hours of study in financial management and 2 years' experience in government and must pass a series of three exams. The exams cover topics in governmental environment; governmental accounting, financial reporting and budgeting; and financial management and control.

Persons planning a career in accounting should have an aptitude for mathematics and be able to analyze, compare and interpret facts and figures quickly. They must be able to clearly communicate the results of their work to clients and managers both verbally and in writing. Accountants and auditors must be good at working with people, as well as with business systems and computers. At a minimum, accountants should be familiar with basic accounting software packages. Because financial decisions are made on the basis of their statements and services, accountants and auditors should have high standards of integrity.

Capable accountants and auditors may advance rapidly; those having inadequate academic preparation may be assigned routine jobs and find promotion difficult. Many graduates of junior colleges or business or correspondence schools, as well as bookkeepers and accounting clerks who meet the education and experience requirements set by their employers, can obtain junior accounting positions and advance to positions with more responsibilities by demonstrating their accounting skills on the job.

Beginning public accountants usually start by assisting with work for several clients. They may advance to positions with more responsibility in 1 or 2 years and to senior positions within another few years. Those who excel may become supervisors, managers, or partners; open their own public accounting firm; or transfer to executive positions in management accounting or internal auditing in private firms.

Management accountants often start as cost accountants, junior internal auditors, or trainees for other accounting positions. As they rise through the organization, they may advance to accounting manager, chief cost accountant, budget director, or manager of internal auditing. Some become controllers, treasurers, financial vice presidents, chief financial officers, or corporation presidents. Many senior corporation executives have a background in accounting, internal auditing, or finance.

In general, public accountants, management accountants and internal auditors have much occupational mobility. Practitioners often shift into management accounting or internal auditing from public accounting, or between internal auditing and management accounting. It is less common for accountants and auditors to move from either management accounting or internal auditing into public accounting.

Employment: Accountants and auditors held about 1.2 million jobs in 2004. They worked throughout private industry and government, but 1 out of 4 wage and salary accountants worked for accounting, tax preparation, bookkeeping and payroll services firms. Approximately 1 out of 10 accountants or auditors was self-employed.

Many accountants and auditors are unlicensed management accountants, internal auditors, or government accountants and auditors; however, a large number are licensed CPAs. Most accountants and auditors work in urban areas, where public accounting firms and central or regional offices of businesses are concentrated.

Some individuals with backgrounds in accounting and auditing are full-time college and university faculty; others teach part time while working as self-employed accountants or as accountants for private industry or government.

Job Outlook: Employment of accountants and auditors is expected to grow faster than average for all occupations through the year 2014. An increase in the number of businesses, changing financial laws and regulations and increased scrutiny of company finances will drive growth. In addition to openings resulting from growth, the need to replace accountants and auditors who retire or transfer to other occupations will produce numerous job openings in this large occupation.

As the economy grows, the number of business establishments will increase, requiring more accountants and auditors to set up books, prepare taxes and provide management advice. As these businesses grow, the volume and complexity of information developed by accountants and auditors regarding costs, expenditures and taxes will increase as well. An increased need for accountants and auditors will arise from changes in legislation related to taxes, financial reporting standards, business investments, mergers and other financial events. The growth of international business also has led to more demand for accounting expertise and services related to international trade and accounting rules, as well as to international mergers and acquisitions. These trends should create more jobs for accountants and auditors.

As a result of accounting scandals at several large corporate companies, Congress passed legislation in an effort to curb corporate accounting fraud. This legislation requires public companies to maintain well-functioning internal controls to ensure the accuracy and reliability of their financial reporting. It also holds the company's chief executive personally responsible for falsely reporting financial information.

These changes should lead to increased scrutiny of company finances and accounting procedures and should create opportunities for accountants and auditors, particularly CPAs, to audit financial records more thoroughly. In order to ensure that finances comply with the law before public accountants conduct audits, management accountants and internal auditors increasingly will be needed to discover and eliminate fraud. Also, in an effort to make government agencies more efficient and accountable, demand for government accountants should increase.

Increased awareness of financial crimes such as embezzlement, bribery and securities fraud will increase the demand for forensic accountants, to detect illegal financial activity by individuals, companies and organized crime rings. Computer technology has made these crimes easier to commit and they are on the rise. At the same time, the development of new computer software and electronic surveillance technology has made tracking down financial criminals easier, thus increasing the ease with which and likelihood that, forensic accountants will discover their crimes. As success rates of investigations grow, demand also will grow for forensic accountants.

The changing role of accountants and auditors also will spur job growth, although this growth will be limited as a result of financial scandals. In response to demand, some accountants were offering more financial management and consulting services as they assumed a greater advisory role and developed more sophisticated accounting systems. Because Federal legislation now prohibits accountants from providing non-traditional services to clients whose books they audit, opportunities for accountants to offer such services could be limited. However, accountants will still be able to advise on other financial matters for clients that are not publicly traded companies and for non-audit clients, but growth in these areas will be slower than in the past. Also, due to the increasing popularity of tax preparation firms and computer software, accountants will shift away from tax preparation. As computer programmes continue to simplify some accounting-related tasks, clerical staff will increasingly handle many routine calculations.

Overall, job opportunities for accountants and auditors should be favourable. After most States instituted the 150-hour rule for CPAs, enrolment in accounting programmes declined; however, enrolment is slowly beginning to grow again as more students become attracted to the profession because of the attention from the accounting scandals. Those who earn a CPA should have excellent job prospects. However, many accounting graduates are instead pursuing other certifications, such as the CMA and CIA, so job prospects may not be as favourable in management accounting and internal auditing as in public accounting. Regardless of specialty, accountants and auditors who have earned professional recognition through certification or licensure should have the best job prospects. Applicants with a master's degree in accounting, or a master's degree in business administration with a concentration in accounting, also will have an advantage. In the aftermath of the accounting scandals, professional certification is even more important in order to ensure that accountants' credentials and ethics are sound.

Proficiency in accounting and auditing computer software, or expertise in specialized areas such as international business, specific industries, or current legislation, may be helpful in landing certain accounting and auditing jobs. In addition, employers increasingly are seeking applicants with strong interpersonal and communication skills. Because many accountants work on teams with others from different backgrounds, they must be able to communicate accounting and financial information clearly and concisely. Regardless of one's qualifications, however, competition will remain keen for the most prestigious jobs in major accounting and business firms.

Earnings: Median annual wage and salary earnings of accountants and auditors were $50,770 in May 2004. The middle half of the occupation earned between $39,890 and $66,900. The top 10 percent of accountants and auditors earned more than $88,610 and the bottom 10 percent earned less than $32,320. In May 2004, median annual earnings in the industries employing the largest numbers of accountants and auditors were as follows:

Federal executive branch and United St®ates Postal Service	$56,900
Accounting, tax preparation, bookkeeping and payroll services	53,870
Management of companies and enterprises	52,260
Local government	47,440
State government	43,400

According to a salary survey conducted by the National Association of Colleges and Employers, bachelor's degree candidates in accounting received starting offers averaging $43,269 a year in 2005; master's degree candidates in accounting were offered $46,251 initially.

According to a 2005 salary survey conducted by Robert Half International, a staffing services firm specializing in accounting and finance, accountants and auditors with up to 1 year of experience earned between $28,250 and $45,000 a year. Those with 1 to 3 years of experience earned between $33,000 and $52,000. Senior accountants and auditors earned between $40,750 and $69,750, managers between $48,000 and $90,000 and directors of accounting and auditing between $64,750 and $200,750. The variation in salaries reflects differences in size of firm, location, level of education and professional credentials.

In the Federal Government, the starting annual salary for junior accountants and auditors was $24,677 in 2005. Candidates who had a superior academic record might start at $30,567, while applicants with a master's degree or 2 years of professional experience usually began at $37,390. Beginning salaries were slightly higher in selected areas where the prevailing local pay level was higher. Accountants employed by the Federal Government in nonsupervisory, supervisory and managerial positions averaged $74,907 a year in 2005; auditors averaged $78,890.

Budget Analysts

Significant Points: Competition for jobs is expected.

Although a bachelor's degree generally is the minimum educational requirement, many employers prefer or require a master's degree.

About 52 percent of all budget analysts work in Federal, State and local governments.

Nature of the Work: Deciding how to efficiently distribute limited financial resources is an important challenge in all organizations. In most large and complex organizations, this task would be nearly impossible without budget analysts. These workers play the primary role in the development, analysis and execution of budgets, which are used to allocate current resources and estimate future financial requirements. Without effective budget analysis and feedback about budgetary problems, many private and public organizations could become bankrupt.

Budget analysts can be found in private industry, non-profit organizations and the public sector. In private sector firms, a budget analyst examines budgets and seeks new ways to improve efficiency and increase profits. Although analysts working in non-profit and governmental organizations usually are not concerned with profits, they still try to find the most efficient distribution of funds and other resources among various departments and programmes.

Budget analysts have many responsibilities in these organizations, but their primary task is providing advice and technical assistance in the preparation of annual budgets. At the beginning of each budget cycle, managers and department heads submit proposed operational and financial plans to budget analysts for review. These plans outline prospective programmes, including proposed funding increases and new initiatives, estimated costs and expenses and capital expenditures needed to finance these programmes.

Analysts examine the budget estimates or proposals for completeness; accuracy; and conformance with established procedures, regulations and organizational objectives. Sometimes, they employ cost-benefit analysis to review financial requests, assess programme tradeoffs and explore alternative funding methods. They also examine past and current budgets and research economic and financial developments that affect the organization's spending. This process enables analysts to evaluate proposals in terms of the organization's priorities and financial resources.

After the initial review process, budget analysts consolidate individual departmental budgets into operating and capital budget summaries. These summaries contain comments and statements that support or argue against funding requests. Budget summaries then are submitted to senior management, or, as is often the case in local and State governments, to appointed or elected officials. Budget analysts then help the chief operating officer, agency head, or other top managers analyze the proposed plan and devise possible alternatives if the projected results are unsatisfactory. The final decision to approve the budget, however, usually is made by the organization head in a private firm or by elected officials in government, such as the State legislature.

Throughout the remainder of the year, analysts periodically monitor the budget by reviewing reports and accounting records to determine if allocated funds have been spent as specified. If deviations appear between the approved budget and actual performance, budget analysts may write a report providing reasons for the variations, along with recommendations for new or revised budget procedures. To avoid or alleviate deficits, budget analysts may recommend programme cuts or reallocation of excess funds. They also inform programme managers and others within their organization of the status and availability of funds in different budget accounts. Before any changes are made to an existing programme, or before a new one is implemented, a budget analyst must assess the programme's efficiency and effectiveness. Analysts also may be involved in long-range planning activities such as projecting future budget needs.

The amount of data and information that budget analysts are able to analyze has greatly increased through the use of computerized financial software programmes. The analysts also make extensive use of spreadsheet, database and word-processing software.

Budget analysts have seen their role broadened as limited funding has led to downsizing and restructuring throughout private industry and government. Not only do they develop guidelines and policies governing the formulation and maintenance of the budget, but they also measure organizational performance, assess the effects of various programmes and policies on the budget and help draft budget-related legislation. In addition, budget analysts sometimes conduct training sessions for company or government agency personnel regarding new budget procedures.

Working Conditions: Budget analysts usually work in a comfortable office setting. Long hours are common among these workers, especially during the initial development and midyear and final reviews of budgets. The pressures of deadlines and tight work schedules during these periods can be stressful and analysts usually are required to work more than the routine 40 hours a week.

Budget analysts spend the majority of their time working independently, compiling and analyzing data and preparing budget proposals. Nevertheless, their schedules sometimes are interrupted by special budget requests, meetings and training sessions. Some budget analysts travel to obtain budget details and explanations of various programmes from coworkers, or to personally verify funding allocation.

Training, Other Qualifications and Advancement: Private firms and government agencies generally require candidates for budget analyst positions to have at least a bachelor's degree, but many prefer or require a master's degree. Within the Federal Government, a bachelor's degree in any field is sufficient for an entry-level budget analyst position, but, again, master's degrees are preferred. State and local governments have varying requirements, but a bachelor's degree in one of many areas—accounting, finance, business, public administration, economics, statistics, political science, or sociology—may qualify one for employment. Many States, especially larger, more urban States, require a master's degree. Sometimes a degree in a field closely related to that of the employing industry or organization, such as engineering, may be preferred. Some firms prefer candidates with a degree in business because business courses emphasize quantitative and analytical skills. Many government employers prefer candidates with strong analytic and policy analysis backgrounds that may be obtained through such majors as political science, economics, public administration, or public finance. Occasionally, budget-related or finance-related work experience can be substituted for formal education.

Because developing a budget involves manipulating numbers and requires strong analytical skills, courses in statistics or accounting are helpful, regardless of the prospective budget analyst's major field of study. Financial analysis is automated in almost every organization and, therefore, familiarity with word-processing programmes and with financial software packages used in budget analysis often is required. Software packages commonly used by budget analysts include electronic spreadsheet, database and graphics programmes. Employers usually prefer candidates who already possess these computer skills.

Those seeking a career as a budget analyst also must be able to work under strict time constraints. Strong oral and written communication skills are essential for analysts because they must prepare, present and defend budget proposals to decision makers.

In addition, budget analysts, along with all other financial officers, must abide by strict ethical standards. Integrity, objectivity and confidentiality are all important to budget analysis and budget analysts must avoid any personal conflicts of interest.

Entry-level budget analysts may receive some formal training when they begin their jobs, but most employers feel that the best training is obtained by working through one complete budget cycle. During the cycle, which typically is 1 year, analysts become familiar with the various steps involved in the budgeting process. The Federal Government, on the other hand, offers extensive on-the-job and classroom training for entry-level trainees. In addition to on-the-job training, budget analysts are encouraged to participate in various professional development classes throughout their careers.

Some government budget analysts employed at the Federal, State, or local level may earn the Certified Government Financial Manager (CGFM) designation granted by the Association of Government Accountants. Other government financial officers also may earn this designation. To do so, candidates must have a minimum of a bachelor's degree, 24 hours of study in financial management and 2 years of government work experience in financial management. They also must pass a series of three exams that cover topics on the organization and structure of government; governmental accounting, financial reporting and budgeting; and financial management and control. To maintain the CGFM designation, individuals must complete 80 hours of continuing professional education every 2 years.

Budget analysts start their careers with limited responsibilities. In the Federal Government, for example, beginning budget analysts compare projected costs with prior expenditures, consolidate and enter data prepared by others and assist higher grade analysts by doing research. As analysts progress in their careers, they begin to develop and formulate budget estimates and justification statements, perform detailed analyses of budget requests, write statements supporting funding requests, advise programme managers and others on the status and availability of funds for various budget activities and present and defend budget proposals to senior managers.

Beginning analysts usually work under close supervision. Capable entry-level analysts can be promoted to intermediate-level positions within 1 to 2 years and then to senior positions within a few more years. Progressing to higher levels means added budgetary responsibility and can lead to a supervisory role. Because of the importance and high visibility of their jobs, senior budget analysts are prime candidates for promotion to management positions in various parts of their organizations, or with other organizations with which they have worked.

Employment: Budget analysts held 58,000 jobs throughout private industry and government in 2004. Federal, State and local governments are major employers, accounting for 52 percent of budget analyst jobs. About 23 percent worked for the Federal Government. Many other budget analysts worked in manufacturing, financial services, or management services. Other employers include schools and hospitals.

Job Outlook: Competition for budget analyst jobs is expected over the 2004-14 projection period. Candidates with a master's degree should have the best job opportunities. Familiarity with computer financial software packages also should enhance a jobseeker's employment prospects.

Employment of budget analysts is expected to grow about as fast as the average for all occupations through 2014.

Employment growth will be driven by the continuing demand for sound financial analysis in both the public and the private sectors. In addition to employment growth, many job openings will result from the need to replace experienced budget analysts who transfer to other occupations or leave the labour force.

The increasing efficiency of computer applications used in budget analysis has increased worker productivity by enabling analysts to process more data in less time. However, because budget analysts now have much more data available to them, their jobs are becoming more complicated. In addition, as businesses and other organizations become more complex and specialized, budget planning and financial control will demand greater attention. These factors should offset any adverse effects of computer applications on employment of budget analysts.

In coming years, all types of organizations will continue to rely heavily on budget analysts to develop and analyze budgets. Because of the importance of financial analysis performed by budget analysts, employment of these workers should remain relatively unaffected by any downsizing in the Nation's workplaces. In addition, budget analysts usually are less subject to layoffs than are many other workers during economic downturns because financial and budget reports must be completed during periods of both economic growth and slowdowns.

Earnings: Salaries of budget analysts vary widely by experience, education and employer. Median annual earnings of budget analysts in May 2004 were $56,040. The middle 50 percent earned between $45,170 and $70,530. The lowest 10 percent earned less than $36,850 and the highest 10 percent earned more than $87,380. Median annual earnings in the industries employing the largest numbers of budget analysts in May 2004 were:

Federal Government	$61,640
Local government	52,520
State government	51,870

According to a 2005 survey conducted by Robert Half International—a staffing services firm specializing in accounting and finance—starting salaries of financial, budget, treasury and cost analysts in small companies ranged from $29,750 to $36,250. In large companies, starting salaries ranged from $33,500 to $40,000.

In the Federal Government, budget analysts usually started as trainees earning $24,677 or $30,567 year in 2005. Candidates with a master's degree began at $37,390. Beginning salaries were slightly higher in areas where the prevailing local pay level was higher. The average annual salary in 2005 for budget analysts employed by the Federal Government in nonsupervisory, supervisory and managerial positions was $67,767.

Cost Estimators

Significant Points: More than half of all cost estimators work in the construction industry and another 17 percent are employed in manufacturing industries.

Growth of the construction industry will account for most new jobs.

In construction and manufacturing, job prospects should be best for those with industry work experience and a bachelor's degree in a related field.

Nature of the Work: Accurately forecasting the cost of future projects is vital to the survival of any business. Cost estimators develop the cost information that business owners or managers need to make a bid for a contract or to decide whether a proposed new product will be profitable. They also determine which endeavours are making a profit.

Regardless of the industry in which they work, estimators compile and analyze data on all of the factors that can influence costs—such as materials, labour, location and special machinery requirements, including computer hardware and software. Job duties vary widely depending on the type and size of the project.

The methods and motivations for estimating costs can differ greatly by industry. On a construction project, for example, the estimating process begins with the decision to submit a bid. After reviewing various preliminary drawings and specifications, the estimator visits the site of the proposed project. The estimator needs to gather information on access to the site and the availability of electricity, water and other services, as well as on surface topography and drainage. The information developed during the site visit usually is recorded in a signed report that is included in the final project estimate.

After the site visit, the estimator determines the quantity of materials and labour the firm will need to furnish. This process, called the quantity survey or "takeoff," involves completing standard estimating forms, filling in dimensions, numbers of units and other information. A cost estimator working for a general contractor, for example, estimates the costs of all of the items that the contractor must provide.

Although subcontractors estimate their costs as part of their own bidding process, the general contractor's cost estimator often analyzes bids made by subcontractors as well. Also during the takeoff process, the estimator must make decisions concerning equipment needs, the sequence of operations, the size of the crew required and physical constraints at the site. Allowances for wasted materials, inclement weather, shipping delays and other factors that may increase costs also must be incorporated in the estimate.

On completion of the quantity surveys, the estimator prepares a cost summary for the entire project, including the costs of labour, equipment, materials, subcontracts, overhead, taxes, insurance, markup and any other costs that may affect the project. The chief estimator then prepares the bid proposal for submission to the owner.

Construction cost estimators also may be employed by the project's architect or owner to estimate costs or to track actual costs relative to bid specifications as the project develops. In large construction companies employing more than one estimator, it is common practice for estimators to specialize. For example, one may estimate only electrical work and another may concentrate on excavation, concrete and forms.

In manufacturing and other firms, cost estimators usually are assigned to the engineering, cost, or pricing department. The estimator's goal in manufacturing is to accurately estimate the costs associated with making products. The job may begin when management requests an estimate of the costs associated with a major redesign of an existing product or the development of a new product or production process. When estimating the cost of developing a new product, for example, the estimator works with engineers, first reviewing blueprints or conceptual drawings to determine the machining operations, tools, gauges and materials that would be required for the job.

The estimator then prepares a parts list and determines whether it is more efficient to produce or to purchase the parts. To do this, the estimator must initiate inquiries for price information from potential suppliers. The next step is to determine the cost of manufacturing each component of the product. Some high-technology products require a considerable amount of computer programming during the design phase. The cost of software development is one of the fastest growing and most difficult activities to estimate. As a result, some cost estimators now specialize in estimating only computer software development and related costs.

The cost estimator then prepares time-phase charts and learning curves. Time-phase charts indicate the time required for tool design and fabrication, tool "debugging"—finding and correcting all problems—manufacturing of parts, assembly and testing. Learning curves graphically represent the rate at which the performance of workers producing parts for the new product improves with practice. These curves are commonly called "cost reduction" curves, because many problems—such as engineering changes, rework, shortages of parts and lack of operator skills—diminish as the number of units produced increases, resulting in lower unit costs.

Using all of this information, the estimator then calculates the standard labour hours necessary to produce a specified number of units. Standard labour hours are then converted to dollar values, to which are added factors for waste, overhead and profit to yield the unit cost in dollars. The estimator then compares the cost of purchasing parts with the firm's cost of manufacturing them to determine which is cheaper.

Computers play an integral role in cost estimation, because estimating often involves complex mathematical calculations and requires advanced mathematical techniques. For example, to undertake a parametric analysis (a process used to estimate project costs on a per unit basis, subject to the specific requirements of a project), cost estimators use a computer database containing information on the costs and conditions of many other similar projects. Although computers cannot be used for the entire estimating process, they can relieve estimators of much of the drudgery associated with routine, repetitive and time-consuming calculations. Computer word-processing and spreadsheet software is used to produce all of the necessary documentation for cost-estimation results, leaving estimators more time to study and analyze projects.

Operations research, production control, cost and price analysts who work for government agencies may do significant amounts of cost estimating in the course of their regular duties. In addition, the duties of construction managers may include estimating costs.

Working Conditions: Although estimators spend most of their time in an office, construction estimators must make visits to project worksites that can be dusty, dirty and occasionally hazardous. Likewise, estimators in manufacturing must spend time on the factory floor, where it also can be noisy and dirty. In some industries, frequent travel between a firm's headquarters and its subsidiaries or subcontractors may be required.

Although estimators normally work a 40-hour week, overtime is common. Cost estimators often work under pressure and stress, especially when facing bid deadlines. Inaccurate estimating can cause a firm to lose a bid or to lose money on a job that was not accurately estimated.

Training, Other Qualifications and Advancement: Job entry requirements for cost estimators vary by industry. In the construction industry, employers increasingly prefer individuals with a degree in building construction, construction management, construction science, engineering, or architecture. However, most construction estimators also have considerable construction experience, gained through work in the industry, internships, or cooperative education programmes. Applicants with a thorough knowledge of construction materials, costs and procedures in areas ranging from heavy construction to electrical work, plumbing systems, or masonry work have a competitive edge.

In manufacturing industries, employers prefer to hire individuals with a degree in engineering, physical science, operations research, mathematics, or statistics; or in accounting, finance, business, economics, or a related subject. In most industries, great emphasis is placed on experience involving quantitative techniques.

Cost estimators should have an aptitude for mathematics; be able to quickly analyze, compare and interpret detailed but sometimes poorly defined information; and be able to make sound and accurate judgments based on this information. Assertiveness and self-confidence in presenting and supporting one's conclusions are important, as are strong communications and interpersonal skills, because estimators may work as part of a project team alongside managers, owners, engineers and design professionals. Cost estimators also need knowledge of computers, including word-processing and spreadsheet packages. In some instances, familiarity with special estimation software or programming skills also may be required.

Regardless of their background, estimators receive much training on the job, because every company has its own way of handling estimates. Working with an experienced estimator, newcomers become familiar with each step in the process. Those with no experience reading construction specifications or blueprints first learn that aspect of the work. Then they may accompany an experienced estimator to the construction site or shop floor, where they observe the work being done, take measurements, or perform other routine tasks. As they become more knowledgeable, estimators learn how to tabulate quantities and dimensions from drawings and how to select the appropriate prices for materials.

For most estimators, advancement takes the form of higher pay and prestige. Some move into management positions, such as project manager for a construction firm or manager of the industrial engineering department for a manufacturer. Others may go into business for themselves as consultants, providing estimating services for a fee to government or to construction or manufacturing firms.

Many colleges and universities include cost estimating as part of bachelor's and associate's degree curriculums in civil engineering, industrial engineering and construction management or construction engineering technology. In addition, cost estimating is a significant part of many master's degree programmes in construction science or construction management. Organizations representing cost estimators, such as the Association for the Advancement of Cost Engineering (AACE International) and the Society of Cost Estimating and Analysis (SCEA), also sponsor educational and professional development programmes. These programmes help students, estimators-in-training and experienced estimators stay abreast of changes affecting the profession. Specialized courses and programmes in cost-estimating techniques and procedures also are offered by many technical schools, community colleges and universities.

Voluntary certification can be valuable to cost estimators because it provides professional recognition of the estimator's competence and experience. In some instances, individual employers may even require professional certification for employment. Both AACE International and SCEA administer certification programmes. To become certified, estimators usually must have between 2 and 8 years of estimating experience and must pass an examination. In addition, certification requirements may include the publication of at least one article or paper in the field.

Employment: Cost estimators held about 198,000 jobs in 2004. About 58 percent of estimators were in the construction industry and another 17 percent were employed in manufacturing. The remainder worked in a wide range of other industries.

Cost estimators work throughout the country, usually in or near major industrial, commercial and government centres and in cities and suburban areas undergoing rapid change or development.

Job Outlook: Overall employment of cost estimators is expected to grow faster than average for all occupations through the year 2014. In addition to openings created by growth, some job openings will arise from the need to replace workers who transfer to other occupations or leave the labour force. In construction and manufacturing—the primary employers of cost estimators—job prospects should be best for those with industry work experience and a bachelor's degree in a related field.

Employment growth in the construction industry, in which most cost estimators are employed, will account for most new jobs in this occupation. Construction and repair of highways, streets and bridges, as well as construction of more subway systems, airports, water and sewage systems and electric power plants and transmission lines, will stimulate demand for many more cost estimators. Similarly, increasing population and changing demographics will boost demand for residential construction and remodelling and school construction and repair, spurring demand for more cost estimators. As the population ages, the demand for nursing and extended-care facilities will increase. Job prospects in construction should be best for cost estimators who have a degree in construction management or in construction science, engineering, or architecture and who have practical experience in various phases of construction or in a specialty craft area.

Employment of cost estimators also will grow in manufacturing, but not as fast as in construction, as firms continue to use cost estimators to identify and control operating costs. Experienced estimators with degrees in engineering, science, mathematics, business administration, or economics should have the best job prospects in manufacturing.

Earnings: Salaries of cost estimators vary widely by experience, education, size of firm and industry. Median annual earnings of cost estimators in May 2004 were $49,940. The middle 50 percent earned between $38,420 and $65,620. The lowest 10 percent earned less than $30,240 and the highest 10 percent earned more than $84,870. Median annual earnings in the industries employing the largest numbers of cost estimators in May 2004 were:

Nonresidential building construction	$56,570
Building equipment contractors	53,310
Residential building construction	49,830
Foundation, structure and building exterior contractors	49,500
Building finishing contractors	47,980

College graduates with degrees in fields that provide a strong background in cost estimating, such as engineering or construction management, could start at a higher level. According to a July 2005 salary survey by the National Association of Colleges and Employers, those with bachelor's degrees in construction science/management received job offers averaging $42,923 a year.

Bill and Account Collectors

Significant Points: About 1 in 5 collectors works for a collection agency; others work in banks, retail stores, government, physicians' offices, hospitals and other institutions that lend money and extend credit.

Most jobs in this occupation require only a high school diploma, though many employers prefer workers with some post-secondary training.

Faster-than-average employment growth is expected as companies focus more efforts on collecting unpaid debts.

Nature of the Work: Bill and account collectors, called simply *collectors*, keep track of accounts that are overdue and attempt to collect payment on them. Some are employed by third-party collection agencies, while others—known as "in-house collectors"—work directly for the original creditors, such as department stores, hospitals, or banks.

The duties of bill and account collectors are similar in the many different organizations in which they are employed. First, collectors are called upon to locate and notify customers of delinquent accounts, usually over the telephone, but sometimes by letter. When customers move without leaving a forwarding address, collectors may check with the post office, telephone companies, credit bureaus, or former neighbours to obtain the new address. The attempt to find the new address is called "skip tracing." New computer systems assist in tracing by automatically tracking when customers change their address or contact information on any of their open accounts.

Once collectors find the debtor, they inform him or her of the overdue account and solicit payment. If necessary, they review the terms of the sale, service, or credit contract with the customer. Collectors also may attempt to learn the cause of the delay in payment. Where feasible, they offer the customer advice on how to pay off the debts, such as by taking out a bill consolidation loan. However, the collector's prime objective is always to ensure that the customer pays the debt in question.

If a customer agrees to pay, collectors record this commitment and check later to verify that the payment was indeed made. Collectors may have authority to grant an extension of time if customers ask for one. If a customer fails to respond, collectors prepare a statement indicating the customer's action for the credit department of the establishment. In more extreme cases, collectors may initiate repossession proceedings, disconnect the customer's service, or hand the account over to an attorney for legal action. Most collectors handle other administrative functions for the accounts assigned to them, including recording changes of addresses and purging the records of the deceased.

Collectors use computers and a variety of automated systems to keep track of overdue accounts. Typically, collectors work at video display terminals that are linked to computers. In sophisticated predictive dialer systems, a computer dials the telephone automatically and the collector speaks only when a connection has been made. Such systems eliminate time spent calling busy or non-answering numbers. Many collectors use regular telephones, but others wear headsets like those used by telephone operators.

Working Conditions: In-house bill and account collectors typically are employed in an office environment, while those who work for third-party collection agencies may work in a call-centre environment. Workers spend most of their time on the phone tracking down and contacting people with debts. The work can be stressful as some customers can be confrontational when pressed about their debts, although some appreciate assistance in resolving their outstanding debt. Collectors may also feel pressured to meet targets for the amount of debt they are expected recover in a certain period.

Bill and account collectors often have to work evenings and weekends, when it usually is easier to reach people. As a result, it is not uncommon for workers to work part time or on flexible work schedules, though the majority work 40 hours per week.

Training, Other Qualifications and Advancement: Most bill and account collectors are required to have at least a high school diploma. However, employers prefer workers who have completed some college or who have experience in other occupations that involve contact with the public. Workers should have good communication skills and be computer literate; experience with advanced telecommunications equipment is also useful.

Once hired, workers usually receive on-the-job training. Under the guidance of a supervisor or some other senior worker, new employees learn company procedures. Some formal classroom training also may be necessary, such as training in specific computer software. Additional training topics usually include telephone techniques and negotiation skills. Workers are also instructed in the laws governing the collection of debt as mandated by the Fair Debt Collection Practices Act (FDCPA), which applies to all third party and some in-house collectors.

Workers usually advance by taking on more duties in the same occupation for higher pay or by transferring to a closely related occupation. Many companies fill supervisory positions by promoting individuals from within the organization and workers who acquire additional skills, experience and training improve their advancement opportunities.

Employment: Bill and account collectors held about 456,000 jobs in 2004. About 1 in 5 collectors works for a collection agency. Many others work in banks, retail stores, government, physician's offices, hospitals and other institutions that lend money and extend credit.

Job Outlook: Employment of bill and account collectors is expected to grow faster than the average for all occupations through 2014. Cash flow is becoming increasingly important to companies, which are now placing greater emphasis on collecting unpaid debts sooner. Thus, the workload for collectors is expected to continue to increase as they seek to collect not only debts that are relatively old, but ones that are more recent. Also, as more companies in a wide range of industries get involved in lending money and issuing their own credit cards, they will need to hire collectors, because debt levels will likely continue to rise. In addition to job openings from employment growth, a significant number of openings will result from the high level of turnover in the occupation. As a result, job opportunities should be favourable.

Hospitals and physicians' offices are two of the fastest growing industries requiring collectors. With insurance reimbursements not keeping up with cost increases, the health care industry is seeking to recover more money from patients. Government agencies also are making more use of collectors to collect on everything from parking tickets to child-support payments and past-due taxes. Finally, the Internal Revenue Service (IRS) is looking into outsourcing the collection of overdue Federal taxes to third-party collection agencies. If the IRS does outsource, more collectors will be required for this large job.

Despite the increasing demand for bill collectors, employment growth may be limited due to an increased use of third party debt collectors, who are generally more efficient than in-house collectors. Also, some firms are beginning to use offshore collection agencies, whose lower cost structures allow them to collect debts that are too small for domestic collection agencies. Contrary to the pattern in most occupations, employment of bill and account collectors tends to rise during recessions, reflecting the difficulty that many people have in meeting their financial obligations. However, collectors usually have more success at getting people to repay their debts when the economy is good.

Earnings: Median hourly earnings of bill and account collectors were $13.20 in May 2004. The middle 50 percent earned between $10.87 and $16.28. The lowest 10 percent earned less than $9.22 and the highest 10 percent earned more than $20.10. In addition to a basic rate of pay, many bill and account collectors earn commissions based on the amount of debt they recover.

Credit Authorizers, Checkers and Clerks

Significant Points: Most jobs require only a high school diploma.

Employment is expected to decline.

Nature of the Work: Credit authorizers, checkers and clerks review credit history and obtain the information needed to determine the creditworthiness of individuals or businesses applying for credit. They spend much of their day on the telephone or on the Internet obtaining information from credit bureaus, employers, banks, credit institutions and other sources to determine applicants' credit history and ability to repay what they borrow or charge.

Credit authorizers, checkers and clerks process and authorize applications for credit, including applications for credit cards. Although the distinctions among the three job titles are disappearing, some general differences remain. *Credit clerks* typically handle the processing of credit applications by verifying the information on the application, calling applicants if additional data are needed, contacting credit bureaus for a credit rating and obtaining any other information necessary to determine applicants' creditworthiness. If clerks work in a department store or other establishment that offers instant credit, they enter the applicant's information into a computer at the point of sale. A credit rating is then transmitted from a central office within seconds to indicate whether the application should be rejected or approved.

Credit checkers investigate the credit history and current credit standing of a person or business prior to the issuance of a loan or line of credit. Credit checkers also may contact credit departments of businesses and service companies to obtain information about an applicant's credit standing. Credit reporting agencies and bureaus hire checkers to secure, update and verify information for credit reports. These workers often are called *credit investigators* or *credit reporters*.

Credit authorizers approve charges against customers' existing accounts. Most charges are approved automatically by computer. However, when accounts are past due, overextended, or invalid, or when they show a change of address, salespersons refer the associated transactions to credit authorizers located in a central office. These authorizers evaluate the customers' computerized credit records and payment histories and quickly decide whether to approve new charges.

Working Conditions: Credit authorizers, checkers and clerks usually work a standard 40-hour week. However, they may work overtime during particularly busy periods, such as holiday shopping seasons and store sales. Most credit authorizers, checkers and clerks work in areas that are clean, well lit and relatively quiet. These workers sit for long periods of time in front of computer screens, which may cause eyestrain and headaches. Part-time work is available and temporary workers are often hired during peak workloads.

Training, Other Qualifications and Advancement: A high school diploma or its equivalent is usually the minimum requirement for these workers. Other requirements of the job include good telephone and organizational skills and the ability to pay close attention to details and meet tight deadlines. Computer skills also are important in order to enter and retrieve data quickly.

Most new employees are trained on the job, working under close supervision of more experienced employees. Some firms offer formal training that may include courses in telephone etiquette, computer use and customer service skills. Some credit authorizers, checkers and clerks also take courses in credit offered by banking and credit associations, public and private vocational schools and colleges and universities. These workers typically can advance to loan or credit department supervisor or team leader of a small group of clerks.

Employment: Credit authorizers, checkers and clerks held about 67,000 jobs in 2004. Nearly half of these workers were employed by finance and insurance industries, mainly firms in credit intermediation and related activities, such as commercial and savings banks; credit unions; and mortgage, finance and loan companies. Credit bureaus, collection agencies and wholesale and retail trade establishments also employ these clerks.

Job Outlook: Employment of credit authorizers, checkers and clerks is expected to decline through 2014. Despite a projected increase in the number of credit applications, technology will allow these applications to be processed, checked and authorized by fewer workers than were required in the past. Credit scoring is a major development that has improved the productivity of credit authorizers, checkers and clerks, thus limiting employment growth in the occupation. Companies and credit bureaus now can purchase software that quickly analyzes an applicant's creditworthiness and summarizes it with a "score." Credit issuers then can easily decide whether to accept or reject an application on the basis of its score, speeding up the authorization of loans or credit. Obtaining credit ratings also has become much easier for credit checkers and authorizers because businesses now have computer systems directly linked to credit bureaus that provide immediate access to a person's credit history.

The job outlook for credit authorizers, checkers and clerks is sensitive to overall economic activity. A downturn in the economy or a rise in interest rates usually leads to a decline in demand for credit. Even in slow economic times, however, job openings will arise from the need to replace workers who leave the occupation for various reasons.

Earnings: Median hourly earnings of credit authorizers, checkers and clerks in May 2004 were $13.97. The middle 50 percent earned between $11.27 and $17.56. The lowest 10 percent earned less than $9.19 and the highest 10 percent earned more than $21.90. Median hourly earnings in Non-depository credit intermediation were $13.74 in 2004, while median earnings in depository credit intermediation were $13.62.

Securities, Commodities and Financial Services Sales Agents

Significant Points: A college degree, sales ability, good interpersonal and communication skills and a strong desire to succeed are important qualifications. Securities and commodities sales agents must pass licensing exams.

Competition for entry-level jobs usually is keen, especially in larger firms; opportunities should be better in smaller firms.

Turnover is high for beginning agents, who often are unable to establish a sizable clientele; once established, securities and commodities sales agents have a very strong attachment to their occupation because of their high earnings and considerable investment in training.

Nature of the Work: Most investors, whether they are individuals with a few hundred dollars to invest or large institutions with millions, use *securities, commodities and financial services sales agents* when buying or selling stocks, bonds, shares in mutual funds, insurance annuities, or other financial products. In addition, many clients seek out these agents for advice on investments, insurance, tax planning, estate planning and other financial matters.

Securities and commodities sales agents, also called brokers, stockbrokers, registered representatives, account executives, or financial consultants, perform a variety of tasks, depending on their specific job duties. When an investor wishes to buy or sell a security, for example, sales agents may relay the order through their firm's computers to the floor of a securities exchange, such as the New York Stock Exchange.

There, securities and commodities sales agents known as *floor brokers* negotiate the price with other floor brokers, make the sale and forward the purchase price to the sales agents. If a security is not traded on an exchange, as in the case of bonds and over-the-counter stocks, the broker sends the order to the firm's trading department. Here, using their own funds or those of the firm, other securities sales agents, known as *dealers*, buy and sell securities directly from other dealers, with the intention of reselling the security to customers at a profit. After the transaction has been completed, the broker notifies the customer of the final price.

Securities and commodities sales agents also provide many related services for their customers. They may explain stock market terms and trading practices, offer financial counselling or advice on the purchase or sale of particular securities and design an individual client's financial portfolio, which could include securities, life insurance, corporate and municipal bonds, mutual funds, certificates of deposit, annuities and other investments.

Not all customers have the same investment goals. Some individuals prefer long-term investments, for capital growth or to provide income over a number of years; others might want to invest in speculative securities, which they hope will quickly rise in price. On the basis of each customer's objectives, securities and commodities sales agents furnish information about the advantages and disadvantages of an investment. They also supply the latest price quotes on any securities, as well as information on the activities and financial positions of the corporations issuing the securities.

Most securities and commodities sales agents serve individual investors; others specialize in institutional investors, such as banks and pension funds. In institutional investing, sales agents usually concentrate on a specific financial product, such as stocks, bonds, options, annuities, or commodity futures. At other times, they may also handle the sale of new issues, such as corporate securities issued to finance the expansion of a plant.

The most important part of a sales representative's job is finding clients and building a customer base. Thus, beginning securities and commodities sales agents spend much of their time searching for customers—relying heavily on telephone solicitation. They also may meet clients through business and social contacts. Agents often join civic organizations and other social organizations to expand their networks. Many sales agents find it useful to contact potential clients by teaching adult education investment courses or by giving lectures at libraries or social clubs. Brokerage firms may give sales agents lists of people with whom the firm has done business in the past. Some agents inherit the clients of agents who have retired. After an agent is established, referrals from satisfied clients are an important source of new business.

Financial services sales agents sell a wide variety of banking and related services. They contact potential customers to explain their services and to ascertain customers' banking and other financial needs. In doing so, they discuss services such as loans, deposit accounts, lines of credit, sales or inventory financing, certificates of deposit, cash management, mutual funds, or investment services. They also may solicit businesses to participate in consumer credit card programmes. Financial services sales agents who serve all the financial needs of a single affluent individual or a business often are called private bankers or relationship managers.

With deregulation of the financial services industry, the distinctions among sales agents are becoming less clear as securities firms, banks and insurance companies venture further into each other's products and services. The agents' jobs also are becoming more important as competition between the firms intensifies.

Working Conditions: Most securities and commodities sales agents work in offices under fairly stressful conditions. They have access to "quote boards" or computer terminals that continually provide information on the prices of securities. When sales activity increases, due perhaps to unanticipated changes in the economy, the pace can become very hectic.

Established securities and commodities sales agents usually work a standard 40-hour week. Beginners who are seeking customers usually work longer hours. New brokers spend a great deal of time learning the firm's products and services and studying for exams in order to qualify to sell other products, such as insurance and commodities. Most securities and commodities sales agents accommodate customers by meeting with them in the evenings or on weekends.

A growing number of securities sales agents, employed mostly by discount or online brokerage firms, work in call-centre environments. In these centres, hundreds of agents spend much of the day on the telephone taking orders from clients or offering advice and information on different securities. Often, such call centres operate 24 hours a day, requiring agents to work in shifts.

Financial services sales agents normally work 40 hours a week in a comfortable, less stressful office environment. They may spend considerable time outside the office, meeting with current and prospective clients, attending civic functions and participating in trade association meetings. Some financial services sales agents work exclusively inside banks, providing service to walk-in customers.

Training, Other Qualifications and Advancement: Because securities and commodities sales agents must be knowledgeable about economic conditions and trends, a college education is important, especially in larger securities firms. In fact, the overwhelming majority of workers in this occupation are college graduates. Although employers seldom require specialized academic training, courses in business administration, economics and finance are helpful.

Many employers consider personal qualities and skills more important than academic training. Employers seek applicants who have considerable sales ability, good interpersonal and communication skills and a strong desire to succeed. Some employers also make sure that applicants have a good credit history and a clean record. Self-confidence and an ability to handle frequent rejections are important ingredients for success.

Because maturity and the ability to work independently are important, many employers prefer to hire those who have achieved success in other jobs. Most firms prefer candidates with sales experience, particularly those who have worked on commission in areas such as real estate or insurance. Therefore, most entrants to this occupation transfer from other jobs. Some begin working as securities and commodities sales agents following retirement from other fields.

Securities and commodities sales agents must meet State licensing requirements, which usually include passing an examination and, in some cases, furnishing a personal bond. In addition, sales agents must register as representatives of their firm with the National Association of Securities Dealers, Inc. (NASD). Before beginners can qualify as registered representatives, they must pass the General Securities Registered Representative Examination (Series 7 exam), administered by the NASD and be an employee of a registered firm for at least 4 months.

Most States require a second examination—the Uniform Securities Agents State Law Examination. This test measures the prospective representative's knowledge of the securities business in general, customer protection requirements and record-keeping procedures. Many take correspondence courses in preparation for the securities examinations. Within 2 years, brokers are encouraged to take additional licensing exams in order to sell mutual funds, insurance and commodities.

Most employers provide on-the-job training to help securities and commodities sales agents meet the registration requirements for certification. In most firms, the training period takes about 4 months. Trainees in large firms may receive classroom instruction in securities analysis, effective speaking and the finer points of selling; may take courses offered by business schools and associations; and may undergo a period of on-the-job training lasting up to 2 years. Many firms like to rotate their trainees among various departments, to give them a broad perspective of the securities business. In small firms, sales agents often receive training in outside institutions and on the job.

Securities and commodities sales agents must understand the basic characteristics of the wide variety of financial products offered by brokerage firms. Brokers periodically take training through their firms or outside institutions in order to keep abreast of new financial products and to improve their sales techniques. Computer training also is important, because the securities sales business is highly automated. It is mandatory for all registered securities and commodities sales agents to attend periodic continuing education classes to maintain their licenses. Courses consist of computer-based training in regulatory matters and company training on new products and services. In addition, more sales agents are taking courses to become certified financial planners. The Certified Financial Planner credential issued by the Certified Financial Planner Board of Standards, requires relevant experience, completion of education requirements, passing a comprehensive examination and adherence to an enforceable code of ethics. The CFP exams test the candidate's knowledge of the financial planning process, insurance and risk management, employee benefits planning, taxes and retirement planning and investment and estate planning.

The principal form of advancement for securities and commodities sales agents is an increase in the number and size of the accounts they handle. Although beginners usually service the accounts of individual investors, they may eventually handle very large institutional accounts, such as those of banks and pension funds. After taking a series of tests, some brokers become portfolio managers and have greater authority to make investment decisions regarding an account. Some experienced sales agents become branch office managers and supervise other sales agents while continuing to provide services for their own customers. A few agents advance to top management positions or become partners in their firms.

Banks and other credit institutions prefer to hire college graduates for financial services sales jobs. A business administration degree with a specialization in finance or a liberal arts degree that includes courses in accounting, economics and marketing serves as excellent preparation for this job. Often, financial services sales agents learn their jobs through on-the-job training under the supervision of bank officers. However, those who wish to sell mutual funds and insurance products may need to undergo formal training and pass some of the same exams required of securities sales agents.

Employment: Securities, commodities and financial services sales agents held about 281,000 jobs in 2004. More than half of jobs were found in securities, commodity contracts and other financial investments and related activities. One in 5 worked in depository and Non-depository credit intermediation, including commercial banks, savings institutions and credit unions. Although securities and commodities sales agents are employed by firms in all parts of the country, many work for a small number of large securities and investment banking firms headquartered in New York City. About 1 out of 8 securities, commodities and financial services sales agents were self-employed.

Job Outlook: Employment of securities, commodities and financial services sales agents is expected to grow about as fast as average for all occupations through 2014. As people's incomes continue to climb, they will increasingly seek the advice and services of securities, commodities and financial services sales agents to realize their financial goals. Growth in the volume of stocks traded over the Internet will limit job growth. Nevertheless, the overall increase in investment is expected to spur employment growth among these workers, with a majority of transactions still requiring the advice and services of securities, commodities and financial services sales agents.

Baby boomers in their peak savings years will fuel much of this increase in investment. Saving for retirement has been made much easier by the government, which continues to offer a number of tax-favourable pension plans, such as the 401(k) and the Roth IRA. The participation of more women in the workforce also means higher household incomes and more women qualifying for pensions. Many of these pensions are self-directed, meaning that the recipient has the responsibility for investing the money. With such large amounts of money to invest, sales agents, in their role as financial advisors, will be in great demand.

Other factors that will affect the demand for brokers are the increasing number and complexity of investment products, as well as the effects of globalization. As the public and businesses become more sophisticated about investing, they are venturing into the options and futures markets. Brokers are needed to buy or sell these products, which are not traded online. Also, markets for investment are expanding with the increase in global trading of stocks and bonds. Furthermore, the New York Stock Exchange has extended its trading hours to accommodate trading in foreign stocks and compete with foreign exchanges.

Employment of sales agents is adversely affected by downturns in the stock market or the economy. Turnover is high for beginning agents, who often are unable to establish a sizable clientele even in good times. Once established, securities and commodities sales agents have a very strong attachment to their occupation because of their high earnings and considerable investment in training. Competition usually is keen, especially in larger companies with more applicants than jobs. Opportunities for beginning sales agents should be better in smaller firms.

Employment of financial services sales agents in banks will increase as banks expand their product offerings in order to compete directly with other investment firms.

Earnings: Median annual earnings of securities, commodities and financial services sales agents were $69,200 in May 2004. The middle half earned between $40,750 and $131,290.

Median annual earnings in the industries employing the largest numbers of securities, commodities and financial services sales agents in 2004 were:

Other financial investment activities	$94,670
Securities and commodity contracts intermediation and brokerage	85,350
Management of companies and enterprises	67,690
Non-depository credit intermediation	51,820
Depository credit intermediation	44,670

Stockbrokers, who provide personalized service and more guidance with respect to a client's investments, usually are paid a commission based on the amount of stocks, bonds, mutual funds, insurance and other products they sell. Earnings from commissions are likely to be high when there is much buying and selling and low when there is a slump in market activity. Most firms provide sales agents with a steady income by paying a "draw against commission"—a minimum salary based on commissions they can be expected to earn. Securities and commodities sales agents who can provide their clients with the most thorough financial services should enjoy the greatest income stability. Trainee brokers usually are paid a salary until they develop a client base. The salary gradually decreases in favour of commissions as the broker gains clients. A small, but increasing, number of full-service brokers are paid a percentage of the assets they oversee. This fee often covers a certain number of trades done for free.

Brokers who work for discount brokerage firms that promote the use of telephone and online trading services usually are paid a salary, sometimes boosted by bonuses that reflect the profitability of the office. Financial services sales agents usually are paid a salary also; however, bonuses or commissions from sales are starting to account for a larger share of their income.

Bookkeeping, Accounting and Auditing Clerks

Significant Points: Bookkeeping, accounting and auditing clerks held more than 2 million jobs in 2004 and are employed in every industry.

Employment is projected to grow more slowly than average as the spread of office automation lifts worker productivity.

The large size of this occupation ensures plentiful job openings, including many opportunities for temporary and part-time work; those who can carry out a wider range of bookkeeping and accounting activities will be in greater demand than specialized clerks.

Nature of the Work: Bookkeeping, accounting and auditing clerks are an organization's financial record-keepers. They update and maintain one or more accounting records, including those which tabulate expenditures, receipts, accounts payable and receivable and profit and loss. They represent a wide range of skills and knowledge from full-charge bookkeepers who can maintain an entire company's books to accounting clerks who handle specific accounts. All of these clerks make numerous computations each day and increasingly must be comfortable using computers to calculate and record data.

In small establishments, *bookkeeping clerks* handle all financial transactions and record-keeping. They record all transactions, post debits and credits, produce financial statements and prepare reports and summaries for supervisors and managers. Bookkeepers also prepare bank deposits by compiling data from cashiers, verifying and balancing receipts and sending cash, checks, or other forms of payment to the bank. They also may handle payroll, make purchases, prepare invoices and keep track of overdue accounts.

In large offices and accounting departments, *accounting clerks* have more specialized tasks. Their titles, such as accounts payable clerk or accounts receivable clerk, often reflect the type of accounting they do. In addition, their responsibilities vary by level of experience. Entry-level accounting clerks post details of transactions, total accounts and compute interest charges. They also may monitor loans and accounts to ensure that payments are up to date.

More advanced accounting clerks may total, balance and reconcile billing vouchers; ensure the completeness and accuracy of data on accounts; and code documents according to company procedures. These workers post transactions in journals and on computer files and update the files when needed. Senior clerks also review computer printouts against manually maintained journals and make necessary corrections. They may review invoices and statements to ensure that all the information appearing on them is accurate and complete and they may reconcile computer reports with operating reports.

Auditing clerks verify records of transactions posted by other workers. They check figures, postings and documents to ensure that they are correct, mathematically accurate and properly coded. They also correct or note errors for accountants or other workers to adjust.

As organizations continue to computerize their financial records, many bookkeeping, accounting and auditing clerks are using specialized accounting software on personal computers. With manual posting to general ledgers becoming obsolete, these clerks increasingly are posting charges to accounts on computer spreadsheets and databases. They now enter information from receipts or bills into computers and the information is then stored either electronically or as computer printouts (or both). The widespread use of computers also has enabled bookkeeping, accounting and auditing clerks to take on additional responsibilities, such as payroll, procurement and billing. Many of these functions require these clerks to write letters, make phone calls to customers or clients and interact with colleagues. Therefore, good communication skills are becoming increasingly important in the occupation.

Working Conditions: Bookkeeping, accounting and auditing clerks work in an office environment. They may experience eye and muscle strain, backaches, headaches and repetitive motion injuries as a result of using computers on a daily basis. Clerks may have to sit for extended periods while reviewing detailed data.

Many bookkeeping, accounting and auditing clerks work regular business hours and a standard 40-hour week. A substantial number work just part time. Full-time and part-time clerks may work some evenings and weekends. Bookkeeping, accounting and auditing clerks may work longer hours to meet deadlines at the end of the fiscal year, during tax time, or when monthly or yearly accounting audits are performed. Those who work in hotels, restaurants and stores may put in overtime during peak holiday and vacation seasons.

Training, Other Qualifications and Advancement: Most bookkeeping, accounting and auditing clerks are required to have a high school degree at a minimum. However, having some college is increasingly important and an associate degree in business or accounting is required for some positions. Although a college degree is rarely required, graduates may accept bookkeeping, accounting and auditing clerk positions to get into a particular company or to enter the accounting or finance field with the hope of eventually being promoted to professional or managerial positions.

Experience in a related job and working in an office environment also is recommended. Employers prefer workers who are computer-literate; knowledge of word processing and spreadsheet software is especially valuable.

Once hired, bookkeeping, accounting and auditing clerks usually receive on-the-job training. Under the guidance of a supervisor or other senior worker, new employees learn company procedures. Some formal classroom training also may be necessary, such as training in specific computer software. Bookkeeping, accounting and auditing clerks must be careful, orderly and detail-oriented in order to avoid making errors and to recognize errors made by others. These workers also should be discreet and trustworthy, because they frequently come in contact with confidential material. In addition, all bookkeeping, accounting and auditing clerks should have a strong aptitude for numbers.

Bookkeepers, particularly those who handle all the record-keeping for companies, may find it beneficial to become certified. The Certified Bookkeeper designation, awarded by the American Institute of Professional Bookkeepers, assures employers that individuals have the skills and knowledge required to carry out all the bookkeeping and accounting functions up through the adjusted trial balance, including payroll functions. For certification, candidates must have at least 2 years of bookkeeping experience, pass three tests and adhere to a code of ethics. More than 100 colleges and universities offer a preparatory course for certification and another 150 offer a course online.

The Universal Accounting Centre offers the Professional Bookkeeper designation. Bookkeeping, accounting and auditing clerks usually advance by taking on more duties in the same occupation for higher pay or by transferring to a closely related occupation. Most companies fill office and administrative support supervisory and managerial positions by promoting individuals from within their organizations, so clerks who acquire additional skills, experience and training improve their advancement opportunities. With appropriate experience and education, some bookkeeping, accounting and auditing clerks may become accountants or auditors.

Employment: Bookkeeping, accounting and auditing clerks held more than 2 million jobs in 2004. They are found in all industries and at all levels of government. Local government and the accounting, tax preparation, bookkeeping and payroll services industry are among the individual industries employing the largest numbers of these clerks. A growing number work for employment services firms, the result of an increase in outsourcing of this occupation. About 1 out of 4 bookkeeping, accounting and auditing clerks worked part time in 2004.

Job Outlook: Employment of bookkeeping, accounting and auditing clerks is projected to grow more slowly than average for all occupations through 2014. More job openings will stem from replacement needs than from job growth. Each year, numerous jobs will become available as these clerks transfer to other occupations or leave the labour force. The large size of this occupation ensures plentiful job openings, including many opportunities for temporary and part-time work.

Although a growing economy will result in more financial transactions and other activities that require these clerical workers, the continuing spread of office automation will lift worker productivity and contribute to the slower-than-average increase in employment.

In addition, organizations of all sizes will continue to downsize and consolidate various record-keeping functions, thus reducing the demand for bookkeeping, accounting and auditing clerks. Furthermore, some work performed by these workers will be outsourced to lower-wage foreign countries. Those who can carry out a wider range of bookkeeping and accounting activities will be in greater demand than specialized clerks. Demand for full-charge bookkeepers is expected to increase, because they are called upon to do much of the work of accountants, as well as perform a wider variety of financial transactions, from payroll to billing. Certified bookkeepers and those with several years of accounting or bookkeeper experience will have the best job prospects.

Earnings: In May 2004, the median wage and salary annual earnings of bookkeeping, accounting and auditing clerks were $28,570. The middle half of the occupation earned between $22,960 and $35,450. The top 10 percent of bookkeeping, accounting and auditing clerks more than $43,570 and the bottom 10 percent earned less than $18,580.

Payroll and Timekeeping Clerks

Significant Points: Payroll and timekeeping clerks are found in every industry.

Most employers prefer applicants with a high school diploma; computer skills are very desirable.

Those who have completed a certification programme, indicating that they can handle more complex payroll issues, will have an advantage in the job market.

Nature of the Work: Payroll and timekeeping clerks perform a vital function: ensuring that employees are paid on time and that their paychecks are accurate. If inaccuracies occur, such as monetary errors or incorrect amounts of vacation time, these workers research and correct the records. In addition, they may perform various other clerical tasks.

Automated timekeeping systems that allow employees to enter the number of hours they have worked directly into a computer have eliminated much of the data entry and review by timekeepers and have elevated the job of payroll clerk. In offices that have not automated this function, however, payroll and timekeeping clerks still perform many of the traditional job functions.

The fundamental task of *timekeeping clerks* is distributing and collecting timecards each pay period. These workers review employee work charts, timesheets and timecards to ensure that information is properly recorded and that records have the signatures of authorizing officials. In companies that bill for the time spent by staff, such as law or accounting firms, timekeeping clerks make sure that the hours recorded are charged to the correct job so that clients can be properly billed. These clerks also review computer reports listing timecards that cannot be processed because of errors and they contact the employee or the employee's supervisor to resolve the problem. In addition, timekeeping clerks are responsible for informing managers and other employees about procedural changes in payroll policies.

Payroll clerks, also called payroll technicians, screen timecards for calculating, coding, or other errors. They compute pay by subtracting allotments, including Federal and State taxes and contributions to retirement, insurance and savings plans, from gross earnings. Increasingly, computers are performing these calculations and alerting payroll clerks to problems or errors in the data. In small organizations or for new employees whose records are not yet entered into a computer system, clerks may perform the necessary calculations manually. In some small offices, clerks or other employees in the accounting department process payroll.

Payroll clerks record changes in employees' addresses; close out files when workers retire, resign, or transfer; and advise employees on income tax withholding and other mandatory deductions. They also issue and record adjustments to workers' pay because of previous errors or retroactive increases. Payroll clerks need to follow changes in tax and deduction laws, so they are aware of the most recent revisions. Finally, they prepare and mail earnings and tax-withholding statements for employees' use in preparing income tax returns.

In small offices, payroll and timekeeping duties are likely to be included in the duties of a general office clerk, a secretary, or an accounting clerk. However, large organizations employ specialized payroll and timekeeping clerks to perform these functions. In offices that have automated timekeeping systems, payroll clerks perform more analysis of the data, examine trends and work with computer systems. They also spend more time answering employees' questions and processing unique data.

Working Conditions: Payroll and timekeeping clerks usually work in clean, pleasant and comfortable office settings. Clerks usually work a standard 35- to 40-hour week; however, longer hours might be necessary during busy periods. Payroll and timekeeping clerks also may face stress at times, particularly from the pressure to meet deadlines.

Training, Other Qualifications and Advancement: Most employers prefer applicants with a high school diploma or GED. Computer skills are very desirable. Payroll and timekeeping clerks learn their skills through a combination of on-the-job experience and informal training. Training also can be attained through programmes in high schools, business schools and community colleges. New workers receive training in payroll, timekeeping, personnel issues, workplace practices and company policies.

Payroll and timekeeping clerks must be able to interact and communicate with individuals at all levels of the organization. In addition, clerks should demonstrate poise, tactfulness and diplomacy and have a high level of interpersonal skills in order to handle sensitive and confidential situations.

Most organizations specializing in payroll and timekeeping offer classes intended to enhance the marketable skills of their members. Some organizations offer certification programmes; completion of a certification programme indicates competence and can enhance one's advancement opportunities. For example, the American Payroll Association offers two levels of certification, the Fundamental Payroll Certification (FPC) and the Certified Payroll Professional (CPP). The FPC is open to all individuals who wish to demonstrate basic payroll competency. The more advanced CPP is available those who have been employed in the practice of payroll for at least 3 years and who have obtained the FPC within the last 18 months. Both require experience and a passing score on a comprehensive exam.

Employment: Payroll and timekeeping clerks held about 214,000 jobs in 2004. They can be found in every industry, but a growing number work for employment services companies as temporary employees, or for accounting, tax preparation, bookkeeping and payroll services firms, which increasingly are taking on the payroll function as a service to other companies. Approximately 18 percent of all payroll and timekeeping clerks worked part time in 2004.

Job Outlook: Employment of payroll and timekeeping clerks is expected to grow about as fast as average for all occupations through 2014. In addition to job growth, numerous job openings will arise each year as payroll and timekeeping clerks leave the labour force or transfer to other occupations. Those who have completed a certification programme, indicating that they can handle more complex payroll issues, will have an advantage in the job market.

As entering and recording payroll and timekeeping information becomes more simplified, the job itself is becoming more complex, with companies now offering a greater variety of pension, 401(k) and other investment plans to their employees. Also, the growing use of transhipment of wages for child support is adding to the complexity. These developments will fuel the demand for payroll and timekeeping clerks, who will be needed to record and monitor such information.

Firms increasingly are outsourcing the payroll function. As a result, the best employment opportunities are expected to be in companies that specialize in payroll, including companies in the employment services industry and the accounting, tax preparation, bookkeeping and payroll services industry. Many of these companies are data processing facilities, but accounting firms also are taking on the payroll function to supplement their accounting work.

The increasing use of computers will limit employment growth of payroll and timekeeping clerks. For example, automated time clocks, which calculate employee hours, allow large organizations to centralize their timekeeping duties in one location. At individual sites, employee hours increasingly are tracked by computer and verified by managers. This information is compiled and sent to a central office to be processed by payroll clerks. In addition, the growing use of direct deposit will reduce the need to draft paychecks, because these funds are transferred automatically each pay period. Also, more organizations are allowing employees to update their payroll records electronically. In smaller organizations, payroll and timekeeping duties are being assigned to secretaries, general office clerks, or accounting clerks. Furthermore, the greater complexity of the job, coupled with the automation of records that is simplifying data entry, is resulting in payroll professionals, not payroll and timekeeping clerks, doing more of the work.

Earnings: Salaries of payroll and timekeeping clerks may vary considerably. The region of the country, size of city and type and size of establishment all influence salary levels. Also, the level of expertise required and the complexity and uniqueness of a clerk's responsibilities may affect earnings.

Median annual earnings of payroll and timekeeping clerks in May 2004 were $30,350. The middle 50 percent earned between $24,430 and $36,930. The lowest 10 percent earned less than $19,680 and the highest 10 percent earned more than $44,270. Median annual earnings in the industries employing the largest numbers of payroll and timekeeping clerks in May 2004 were:

Management of companies and enterprises	$32,600
Elementary and secondary schools	32,390
Local government	31,620
Accounting, tax preparation, bookkeeping and payroll services	29,040
Employment services	28,010

Some employers offer educational assistance to payroll and timekeeping clerks.

Real Estate Brokers and Sales Agents

Significant Points: Real estate brokers and sales agents often work evenings and weekends and usually are on call to suit the needs of clients.

A license is required in every State and the District of Columbia.

Although gaining a job may be relatively easy, beginning workers may face competition from well-established, more experienced agents and brokers in obtaining listings and in closing an adequate number of sales.

Employment is sensitive to swings in the economy, especially interest rates; during periods of declining economic activity and increasing interest rates, the volume of sales and the resulting demand for sales workers fall.

Nature of the Work: One of the most complex and significant financial events in peoples' lives is the purchase or sale of a home or investment property. Because of this complexity and significance, people typically seek the help of real estate brokers and sales agents when buying or selling real estate.

Real estate brokers and sales agents have a thorough knowledge of the real estate market in their communities. They know which neighbourhoods will best fit clients' needs and budgets. They are familiar with local zoning and tax laws and know where to obtain financing. Agents and brokers also act as intermediaries in price negotiations between buyers and sellers.

Real estate agents usually are independent sales workers who provide their services to a licensed real estate broker on a contract basis. In return, the broker pays the agent a portion of the commission earned from the agent's sale of the property. Brokers are independent business people who sell real estate owned by others; they also may rent or manage properties for a fee. When selling real estate, brokers arrange for title searches and for meetings between buyers and sellers during which the details of the transactions are agreed upon and the new owners take possession of the property. A broker may help to arrange favourable financing from a lender for the prospective buyer; often, this makes the difference between success and failure in closing a sale. In some cases, brokers and agents assume primary responsibility for closing sales; in others, lawyers or lenders do. Brokers supervise agents who may have many of the same job duties. Brokers also supervise their own offices, advertise properties and handle other business matters. Some combine other types of work, such as selling insurance or practicing law, with their real estate business.

Besides making sales, agents and brokers must have properties to sell. Consequently, they spend a significant amount of time obtaining listings—agreements by owners to place properties for sale with the firm. When listing a property for sale, agents and brokers compare the listed property with similar properties that recently sold, in order to determine a competitive market price for the property. Once the property is sold, both the agent who sold it and the agent who obtained the listing receive a portion of the commission. Thus, agents who sell a property that they themselves have listed can increase their commission.

Most real estate brokers and sales agents sell residential property. A small number—usually employed in large or specialized firms—sell commercial, industrial, agricultural, or other types of real estate. Every specialty requires knowledge of that particular type of property and clientele. Selling or leasing business property requires an understanding of leasing practices, business trends and the location of the property. Agents who sell or lease industrial properties must know about the region's transportation, utilities and labour supply. Whatever the type of property, the agent or broker must know how to meet the client's particular requirements.

Before showing residential properties to potential buyers, agents meet with them to get a feeling for the type of home the buyers would like. In this prequalifying phase, the agent determines how much the buyers can afford to spend.

In addition, the agent and the buyer usually sign a loyalty contract which states that the agent will be the only one to show houses to buyers. An agent or broker then generates lists of properties for sale, their location and description and available sources of financing. In some cases, agents and brokers use computers to give buyers a virtual tour of properties in which they are interested. With a computer, buyers can view interior and exterior images or floor plans without leaving the real estate office.

Agents may meet several times with prospective buyers to discuss and visit available properties. Agents identify and emphasize the most pertinent selling points. To a young family looking for a house, they may emphasize the convenient floor plan, the area's low crime rate and the proximity to schools and shopping centres. To a potential investor, they may point out the tax advantages of owning a rental property and the ease of finding a renter. If bargaining over price becomes necessary, agents must follow their client's instructions carefully and may have to present counteroffers in order to get the best possible price.

Once both parties have signed the contract, the real estate broker or agent must make sure that all special terms of the contract are met before the closing date. For example, the agent must make sure that the mandated and agreed-upon inspections, including that of the home and termite and radon inspections, take place.

Also, if the seller agrees to any repairs, the broker or agent must see that they are made. Increasingly, brokers and agents are handling environmental problems as well, by making sure that the properties they sell meet environmental regulations. For example, they may be responsible for dealing with lead paint on the walls. While loan officers, attorneys, or other persons handle many details, the agent must ensure that they are carried out.

Working Conditions: Advances in telecommunications and the ability to retrieve data about properties over the Internet allow many real estate brokers and sales agents to work out of their homes instead of real estate offices. Even with this convenience, much of the time of these workers is spent away from their desks—showing properties to customers, analyzing properties for sale, meeting with prospective clients, or researching the state of the market.

Agents and brokers often work more than a standard 40-hour week. They usually work evenings and weekends and are always on call to suit the needs of clients. Although the hours are long and frequently irregular, most agents and brokers have the freedom to determine their own schedule. Consequently, they can arrange their work so that they can have time off when they want it. Business usually is slower during the winter season.

Training, Other Qualifications and Advancement: In every State and the District of Columbia, real estate brokers and sales agents must be licensed. Prospective agents must be high school graduates, be at least 18 years old and pass a written test. The examination—more comprehensive for brokers than for agents—includes questions on basic real estate transactions and laws affecting the sale of property. Most States require candidates for the general sales license to complete between 30 and 90 hours of classroom instruction. Those seeking a broker's license need between 60 and 90 hours of formal training and a specific amount of experience selling real estate, usually 1 to 3 years. Some States waive the experience requirements for the broker's license for applicants who have a bachelor's degree in real estate.

State licenses typically must be renewed every 1 or 2 years; usually, no examination needs to be taken. However, many States require continuing education for license renewals. Prospective agents and brokers should contact the real estate licensing commission of the State in which they wish to work in order to verify the exact licensing requirements.

As real estate transactions have become more legally complex, many firms have turned to college graduates to fill positions. A large number of agents and brokers have some college training. College courses in real estate, finance, business administration, statistics, economics, law and English are helpful. For those who intend to start their own company, business courses such as marketing and accounting are as significant as courses in real estate or finance.

Personality traits are equally as important as one's academic background. Brokers look for applicants who possess a pleasant personality, are honest and present a neat appearance. Maturity, good judgment, trustworthiness and enthusiasm for the job are required in order to encourage prospective customers in this highly competitive field. Agents should be well organized, be detail oriented and have a good memory for names, faces and business particulars.

Those interested in jobs as real estate agents often begin in their own communities. Their knowledge of local neighbourhoods is a clear advantage. Under the direction of an experienced agent, beginners learn the practical aspects of the job, including the use of computers to locate or list available properties and identify sources of financing.

Many firms offer formal training programmes for both beginners and experienced agents. Larger firms usually offer more extensive programmes than smaller firms. More than a thousand universities, colleges and junior colleges offer courses in real estate. At some, a student can earn an associate's or bachelor's degree with a major in real estate; several offer advanced degrees. Many local real estate associations that are members of the National Association of Realtors sponsor courses covering the fundamentals and legal aspects of the field. Advanced courses in mortgage financing, property development and management and other subjects also are available.

Advancement opportunities for agents may take the form of higher rates of commission. As agents gain knowledge and expertise, they become more efficient in closing a greater number of transactions and increase their earnings. In many large firms, experienced agents can advance to sales manager or general manager. Persons who have received their broker's license may open their own offices. Others with experience and training in estimating property value may become real estate appraisers and people familiar with operating and maintaining rental properties may become property managers. Experienced agents and brokers with a thorough knowledge of business conditions and property values in their localities may enter mortgage financing or real estate investment counselling.

Employment: In 2004, real estate brokers and sales agents held about 460,000 jobs; real estate sales agents held approximately 24 percent of these jobs. Many worked part time, combining their real estate activities with other careers. About 6 out of 10 real estate agents and brokers were self-employed. Real estate is sold in all areas, but employment is concentrated in large urban areas and in rapidly growing communities.

Most real estate firms are relatively small; indeed, some are one-person businesses. By contrast, some large real estate firms have several hundred agents operating out of numerous branch offices. Many brokers have franchise agreements with national or regional real estate organizations. Under this type of arrangement, the broker pays a fee in exchange for the privilege of using the more widely known name of the parent organization. Although franchised brokers often receive help in training sales staff and running their offices, they bear the ultimate responsibility for the success or failure of their firms.

Real estate brokers and sales agents are older, on average, than most other workers. Historically, many homemakers and retired persons were attracted to real estate sales by the flexible and part-time work schedules characteristic of the field. These individuals could enter, leave and later return to the occupation, depending on the strength of the real estate market, their family responsibilities, or other personal circumstances. Recently, however, the attractiveness of part-time real estate work has declined, as increasingly complex legal and technological requirements are raising startup costs associated with becoming an agent.

Job Outlook: Employment of real estate brokers and sales agents is expected to grow about as fast as average for all occupations through the year 2014, because of the increasing housing needs of a growing population, as well as the perception that real estate is a good investment. Relatively low interest rates should continue to stimulate sales of real estate, resulting in the need for more agents and brokers. In addition, a large number of job openings will arise each year from the need to replace workers who transfer to other occupations or leave the labour force.

However, job growth will be somewhat limited by the increasing use of technology, which is improving the productivity of agents and brokers. For example, prospective customers often can perform their own searches for properties that meet their criteria by accessing real estate information on the Internet. The increasing use of technology is likely to be more detrimental to part-time or temporary real estate agents than to full-time agents, because part-time agents generally are not able to compete with full-time agents who have invested in new technology. Changing legal requirements, such as disclosure laws, also may dissuade some who are not serious about practicing full time from continuing to work part time.

This occupation is relatively easy to enter and is attractive because of its flexible working conditions; the high interest in and familiarity with, local real estate markets that entrants often have; and the potential for high earnings. Therefore, although gaining a job as a real estate agent or broker may be relatively easy, beginning agents and brokers may face competition from their well-established, more experienced counterparts in obtaining listings and in closing an adequate number of sales. Well-trained, ambitious people who enjoy selling—particularly those with extensive social and business connections in their communities—should have the best chance for success.

Employment of real estate brokers and sales agents often is sensitive to swings in the economy, especially interest rates. During periods of declining economic activity and increasing interest rates, the volume of sales and the resulting demand for sales workers falls. As a result, the earnings of agents and brokers decline and many work fewer hours or leave the occupation altogether.

Earnings: The median annual earnings of salaried real estate sales agents, including commissions, were $35,670 in May 2004. The middle 50 percent earned between $23,500 and $58,110 a year. The lowest 10 percent earned less than $17,600 and the highest 10 percent earned more than $92,770. Median hourly earnings in the industries employing the largest number of real estate sales agents in May 2004 were as follows:

Residential building construction	$54,770
Offices of real estate agents and brokers	37,970
Activities related to real estate	32,460
Lessors of real estate	25,840

Median annual earnings of salaried real estate brokers, including commission, were $58,720 in May 2004. The middle 50 percent earned between $33,480 and $99,820 a year. Median annual earning of real estate brokers were $61,550 in offices of real estate agents and brokers and $44,920 in activities related to real estate.

Commissions on sales are the main source of earnings of real estate agents and brokers. The rate of commission varies according to whatever the agent and broker agree on, the type of property and its value. The percentage paid on the sale of farm and commercial properties or unimproved land is typically higher than the percentage paid for selling a home.

Commissions may be divided among several agents and brokers. When the property is sold, the broker or agent who obtained the listing usually shares the commission with the broker or agent who made the sale and with the firm that employs each of them. Although an agent's share varies greatly from one firm to another, often it is about half of the total amount received by the firm. Agents who both list and sell a property maximize their commission.

Income usually increases as an agent gains experience, but individual motivation, economic conditions and the type and location of the property also affect earnings. Sales workers who are active in community organizations and in local real estate associations can broaden their contacts and increase their earnings. A beginner's earnings often are irregular, because a few weeks or even months may go by without a sale. Although some brokers allow an agent to draw against future earnings from a special account, the practice is not common with new employees. The beginner, therefore, should have enough money to live for about 6 months or until commissions increase.

Brokerage Clerks

Significant Points: More than 9 out of 10 worked for securities and commodities, banks and other finance industries.

Brokerage clerks be may high school or college graduates, but positions dealing with the public, such as broker's or sales assistant and those dealing with more complicated financial records are increasingly being held by college graduates.

Although a growing economy will result in more financial transactions that require these workers, the continuing spread of office automation and the emergence of online trading will result in slower-than-average growth in employment.

Nature of the Work: Brokerage clerks handle much of the day-to-day operations of brokerages, performing a number of different jobs with a wide range of responsibilities; all involve computing and recording data pertaining to securities transactions. Brokerage clerks also may contact customers, take orders and inform clients of changes to their accounts. Some of these jobs are more clerical and require only a high school diploma, while others are considered entry-level positions for which a bachelor's degree is needed. Brokerage clerks, who work in the operations departments of securities firms, on trading floors and in branch offices, also are called margin clerks, dividend clerks, transfer clerks and broker's assistants.

The broker's assistant, also called sales assistant, is the most common type of brokerage clerk. These workers typically assist two brokers, for whom they take calls from clients, write up order tickets, process the paperwork for opening and closing accounts, record a client's purchases and sales and inform clients of changes to their accounts. All broker's assistants must be knowledgeable about investment products so that they can communicate clearly with clients. Those with a "Series 7" license can make recommendations to clients at the instruction of the broker. This license, issued to securities and commodities sales representatives by the National Association of Securities Dealers (NASD), allows them to provide advice on securities to the public.

Brokerage clerks in the operations areas of securities firms perform many duties to facilitate the sale and purchase of stocks, bonds, commodities and other kinds of investments. These clerks produce the necessary records of all transactions that occur in their area of the business. Job titles for many of them depend upon the type of work that they perform. Purchase-and-sale clerks, for example, match orders to buy with orders to sell.

They balance and verify trades of stock by comparing the records of the selling firm with those of the buying firm. Dividend clerks ensure timely payments of stock or cash dividends to clients of a particular brokerage firm. Transfer clerks execute customer requests for changes to security registration and examine stock certificates to make sure that they adhere to banking regulations.

Receive-and-deliver clerks facilitate the receipt and delivery of securities among firms and institutions. Margin clerks record and monitor activity in customers' accounts to ensure that clients make payments and stay within legal boundaries concerning their purchases of stock.

Technology is changing the nature of many of these jobs. A significant and growing number of brokerage clerks use custom-designed software programmes to process transactions more quickly. Only a few customized accounts are still handled manually. Furthermore, the rapid expansion of online trading reduces the amount of paperwork because brokerage clerks are able to make trades electronically.

Working Conditions: Brokerage clerks work in offices. Usually the work flow is fairly regular; however, when sales activity increases, the pace can become hectic.

Brokerage clerks generally work a standard 40-hour week, but, they may work overtime during particularly busy periods. Most brokerage clerks work in areas that are clean and well lit, but may be noisy at times.

Training, Other Qualifications and Advancement: Depending on the job description, brokerage clerks can be high school or college graduates. Positions dealing with the public, such as broker's or sales assistant and those dealing with more complicated financial records are increasingly being held by college graduates.

Brokerage clerk jobs require good organizational and communication skills, as well as attention to detail. Computer skills also are important in order to enter and retrieve data quickly. A Series 7 brokerage license can make a clerk more valuable to the broker because it gives the assistant the ability to answer more of a client's questions and to pass along securities recommendations from the broker. Before clerks can obtain a license, however, they must pass the General Securities Registered Representative Examination (Series 7 exam), administered by the NASD and be an employee of a registered firm for at least 4 months.

Most new employees are trained on the job, working under the close supervision of more experienced employees. Some firms offer formal training that may include courses in telephone etiquette, computer use and customer service skills.

Clerks may be promoted to sales representative positions or other professional positions within the securities industry. Some of the larger firms have training programmes, especially for their college graduates, that provide clerks with the skills they need for advancement.

Employment: Brokerage clerks held about 75,000 jobs in 2004. More than 9 out of 10 worked for securities and commodities, banks and other finance industries.

Job Outlook: Employment of brokerage clerks is expected to grow more slowly than average for all occupations through the year 2014. Although a growing economy will result in more financial transactions and other activities that require these workers, the continuing spread of office automation will lift worker productivity and restrict job growth.

With people increasingly investing in securities, brokerage clerks will be required to process larger volumes of transactions.

Moreover, some brokerage clerks will still be needed to update records, enter changes into customers' accounts and verify transfers of securities. However, the emergence of online trading and widespread automation in the securities and commodities industry will limit demand for brokerage clerks in the coming decade. Some job openings will stem from the need to replace clerks who transfer to other occupations or stop working.

Earnings: Median hourly earnings of brokerage clerks were $16.94 in May 2004. The middle 50 percent earned between $13.52 and $21.60. The lowest 10 percent earned less than $11.22 and the highest 10 percent earned more than $27.11.

Order Clerks

Significant Points: Employment is expected to decline because of growth in online retailing and in business-to-business electronic commerce and the use of automated systems that make placing orders easy and convenient.

A high school diploma or its equivalent is the most common educational requirement.

Nature of the Work: Order clerks receive and process orders for a variety of goods or services, such as spare parts for machines, consumer appliances, gas and electric power connections, film rentals and articles of clothing. They sometimes are called order-entry clerks, sales representatives, order processors, or order takers.

Orders for materials, merchandise, or services can come from inside or from outside of an organization. In large companies with many worksites, such as automobile manufacturers, clerks order parts and equipment from the company's warehouses. Inside order clerks receive orders from other workers employed by the same company or from salespersons in the field.

Many other order clerks, however, receive orders from outside companies or individuals. Order clerks in wholesale businesses, for instance, receive orders from retail establishments for merchandise that the retailer, in turn, sells to the public. An increasing number of order clerks are working for catalogue companies and online retailers, receiving orders from individual customers by telephone, fax, regular mail, or e-mail. Order clerks dealing primarily with the public sometimes are referred to as outside order clerks.

Computers provide order clerks with ready access to information such as stock numbers, prices and inventory. The successful filling of an order frequently depends on having the right products in stock and being able to determine which products are most appropriate for the customer's needs. Some order clerks—especially those in industrial settings—must be able to give price estimates for entire jobs, not just single parts. Others must be able to take special orders, give expected arrival dates, prepare contracts and handle complaints.

Many order clerks receive orders directly by telephone, entering the required information as the customer places the order. However, a rapidly increasing number of orders now are received through computer systems, the Internet, faxes and e-mail. In some cases, these orders are sent directly from the customer's terminal to the order clerk's terminal. Orders received by regular mail are sometimes scanned into a database that is instantly accessible to clerks.

Clerks review orders for completeness and clarity. They may fill in missing information or contact the customer for the information. Clerks also contact customers if the customers need additional information, such as prices or shipping dates, or if delays in filling the order are anticipated. For orders received by regular mail, clerks extract checks or money orders, sort them and send them for processing.

After an order has been verified and entered, the customer's final cost is calculated. The clerk then routes the order to the proper department—such as the warehouse—which actually sends out or delivers the item in question.

In organizations with sophisticated computer systems, inventory records are adjusted automatically, as sales are made. In less automated organizations, order clerks may adjust inventory records. Clerks also may notify other departments when inventories are low or when filling certain orders would deplete supplies.

Some order clerks must establish priorities in filling orders. For example, an order clerk in a blood bank may receive a request from a hospital for a certain type of blood. The clerk must first find out whether the request is routine or an emergency and then take appropriate action.

Working Conditions: Order clerks usually work a standard 40-hour workweek. Most order clerks work in areas that are clean, well lit and relatively quiet. These workers sit for long periods of time in front of computer terminals, which may cause eyestrain and headaches. Order clerks in retail establishments typically work overtime during peak holiday seasons, when sales volume is high.

Training, Other Qualifications and Advancement: Employers prefer applicants with a high school diploma or its equivalent or a mix of education and related experience. Most employers prefer workers who are computer literate and have a working knowledge of word-processing and spreadsheet software.

Most order clerks are trained on the job under the close supervision of more experienced employees. Proficiency with computer software is becoming increasingly important because most orders are being filed electronically. By taking on more duties, ambitious order clerks can receive higher pay or become eligible for advancement opportunities. Some use their experience as an order clerk to move into sales positions.

Employment: Order clerks held about 293,000 jobs in 2004. Over 50 percent of order clerks were employed in wholesale and retail trade establishments and another 16 percent were employed in manufacturing firms. Other jobs for order clerks were in industries such as information, warehousing and storage, couriers and business support services.

Job Outlook: Job openings for order clerks likely will be limited, as improvements in technology and office automation continue to increase worker productivity. While overall employment of order clerks is expected to decline through the year 2014, numerous openings will occur each year to replace order clerks who transfer to other occupations or leave the labour force completely. Many of these openings will be for seasonal work, especially in catalogue companies or online retailers catering to holiday gift buyers.

The growth in online retailing and in business-to-business electronic commerce and the use of automated systems that make placing orders easy and convenient, will decrease demand for order clerks. The spread of electronic data interchange, which enables computers to communicate directly with each other, allows orders within establishments to be placed with little human intervention. In addition, internal systems allowing a firm's employees to place orders directly are becoming increasingly common. Outside orders placed over the Internet often are entered directly into the computer by the customer; thus, the order clerk is not involved at all in placing the order. Some companies also use automated phone menus that are accessible with a touch-tone phone to receive orders and others use answering machines. Developments in voice recognition technology may further reduce the demand for order clerks.

Furthermore, increased automation will allow current order clerks to be more productive, with each clerk able to handle an increasingly higher volume of orders. Sophisticated inventory control and automatic billing systems permit companies to track inventory and accounts with much less help from order clerks than in the past.

Earnings: Median hourly earnings of order clerks in May 2004 were $12.07. The middle 50 percent earned between $9.45 and $15.53. The lowest 10 percent earned less than $7.75 and the highest 10 percent earned more than $19.34. Median hourly earnings in electronic shopping and mail-order houses was $9.83 while median earnings in machinery, equipment and supplies merchant wholesalers was $14.05 in May 2004. In business support services, median hourly earning was $9.71 in May 2004.

Accountant

Professionally qualified accountants (sometimes known as chartered or certified accountants) work with financial and management information, using their specialist knowledge to advise a range of clients, from individuals to large organisations. There are several different professional bodies in accountancy and the first years of employment could be linked to the specialist activities of a particular body. In practice, however, there is considerable overlap between the various professional qualifications and accountants regularly move between sectors later in their career. In fact, many of the major bodies are currently in the midst of merger negotiations.

Areas of work include private practice (also known, confusingly, as public practice), the public sector and industry/ commerce. In the first of these, accountants work in a specialist firm of accountants offering services ranging from basic bookkeeping to audit (independent assessment of a client's current financial position), taxation advice, management consultancy and corporate financial planning. Accountants working in the public sector handle very large budgets in local or central government, the National Health Service, colleges or universities. In industry/commerce, they might be involved in keeping financial records for a company, overseeing credit control systems and possibly participating in strategic planning for the organisation's future development.

Entry Level: To gain recognition as a qualified accountant, you would need to spend several years pursuing the professional training route of one of the six main bodies. While most of the bodies would accept you with at least two A level/Advanced Higher/three Higher or equivalent qualifications, together with three GCSE/S Grade passes A-C/1-3, including English and maths, in practice, the most common entry route to professional accountancy training is with a degree in any academic subject. If you choose an accountancy-related degree subject, you should gain exemption from some of the exams set by the professional bodies.

Making the Grade: With so many different bodies, there are many routes to professional qualification. Most take three to five years and usually involve work experience in an approved organisation, part-time study and lots of exams.

Alongside the exam training, employers provide in-house training on technical and general skills to help you perform well in your job. Professional accountants must remain up to date on technical and business issues, so there is a strong emphasis on continuing professional development after qualification.

You may also opt to start as an accounting technician and then work your way towards professional status.

Personal Qualities: You would need to be very methodical, with good IT skills. You would not have to be brilliant at maths but you should enjoy working with figures and problem solving, as well as being extremely accurate. Employers look for skills such as leadership, communication, numeracy, interest in finance and business, self-motivation and commitment.

Looking Ahead: An accountancy qualification is a very useful tool and demand for accountants is currently growing in all sectors. As your career develops, you could choose to work for a very large organisation, you could become self-employed and work as a freelance consultant or you could take advantage of the worldwide recognition of UK accountancy qualifications and travel extensively.

Alternative Suggestions: Other possibilities might include accountancy as a profession, actuary, banking executive, chartered secretary, civil servant, economist, financial adviser, insurance underwriter, investment banking, management consultant or tax inspector.

Take-home Pay: Starting salaries for graduate trainees vary according to location and the size of the organisation employing you. You could start on around £18,000 to £25,000 in a large company but on around £14,000 to £19,000 in a smaller company. Starting salaries for school leaver trainees are rather lower. On achieving full qualification, you could expect to earn between £36,000 and £42,000 and, if you rise to become a partner in private practice or a senior manager in industry or the public sector, you could easily command a six-figure salary.

Effects: Normal working hours are Monday to Friday, nine to five, but your lifestyle as an accountant would depend very much on the sort of organisation you join and the area of specialisation you choose. Audits can take you all over the country and a large international partnership would expect you to travel. High salaries are possible but are usually associated with increased stress and longer working hours. You may have to move a few times to develop your career.

Accountancy as a Profession

So you arc not sure what you what to do after you graduate? At this juncture of your life, it is time to make sure that you make the right decision. This article will hopefully help you to decide whether a career in finance is suitable for you.

Accountacy boring? Humbug! Today's accountancy market offers more than ever. Firms can no longer afford to be prehistoric and long gone are the days of "Bob Crathoic" and large manual ledgers. Firms are having to adapt to ensure they meet the needs of the clients. The company audit is now a mature product in the market place and the accountant of today must fulfil the role of business advisor and must provide an added value service. As a result of increasing market expectations the industry is thus demanding high quality graduates that are looking for a challenging and rewarding career.

The experience gained from working with clients is just one side of the coin as training to be an accountant with an authorised training firms leads to obtaining a premier business qualification. It thus remains essential that applicants still have a strong desire to continue studying after university. Trainees will spend most of their time away from the office and visit a wide variety of work places where they will be expected to deal personally with the clients. Combining this with a demanding exam structure means accountancy is not for people that are not willing to travel and work hard!

Graduates begin their careers as trainee chartered accountants with a three year training contract. Initially trainees will be fully supervises on every assignment but encourages and expected to take on responsibility as quickly as possible. As the student progresses they in turn will be expected to supervise the work of the latest juniors. Learning to be a part of a team is essential. Rapid progression and early responsibility are the hallmarks of a firm that offers opportunities to its trainees. Emphasis is placed on the ability to communicate effectively, to learn quickly and apply that knowledge, to analyse and resolve problems and have an outgoing personality.

Most firms enrol their students with leading specialist tutorial firms for their professional examinations. In house training is designed to be responsive to the trainees speed of development and promote key competencies, both technical and interpersonal required at each stage. When the training contract has been completed and the student has celebrated exam success the training and experience still continues. Accountants need to keep up to date with developments within the profession and to broaden managerial and interpersonal skills throughout their career.

Apart from auditing the trainee should gain experience in accounts preparation, taxation and information technology. This great variety of experience helps the trainee to develop different talents and the broadest possible commercial awareness and understanding of all aspects of business matters relating to clients from very small concerns to publicly quoted groups. Not only does this stretch the trainee but it also gives the an opportunity to decide where their interests lie. It is important to train staff to think like entrepreneurs so that they can give all round management and not see the problems through the "eyes of an auditor".

Firms today are not "Scrooge-like" when it comes to salary and career prospects. A combination of exams and practical experience on a wide Variety of clients gives the right environment for swift advancement.

Many firms offer the opportunity for secondments to departments outside audit. A few graduates take the change to specialise in tax or corporate finance towards the end of their training contract. Other opportunities exists for those who decide not to stay in the profession in the longer term, as the professional qualification holds worldwide recognition and continues to open many doors in the job market.

In conclusion—Do you have the potential to be a good accountant?

You will need to pass exams, interact as a team member, be adaptable, tactful, organised, honest and presentable. Training to be a chartered accountant is not easy and requires a firm commitment from the individual. Accountancy is primarily a "social business" where it is essential to have an outgoing personality and good communication skills with both clients and colleagues. The team spirit that is built up with colleges often continues outside office hours.

Making the right choice of professional firm after university is important as this is where your core training will be undertaken. Choosing a firm with a strong commitment to staff development and where training is taken very seriously is of paramount importance.

Don't be left behind in the Dicken's era, consider accountancy as a career for the future.

Accounting Technician

Accounting technicians work at all levels of finance and in all industries, from accounts staff to financial controllers. In a small company, they may be the only trained and qualified employee looking after the financial records, invoices and wages. In a larger company, they may be working as part of a team alongside chartered accountants and administrative staff and they would report to an accounting manager. The work can be similar to that of an accountant. For many, working as an accounting technician is a practical introduction to accounting. It can provide a stepping stone while studying towards a qualification as a chartered accountant.

As a broad rule, accounting technicians are more likely to be involved with the detailed, practical applications of day-to-day accounting issues than with the wider areas of financial management dealt with by professionally qualified accountants.

Entry Level: Accountancy technicians do not need formal academic qualifications, but employers often ask for a good standard of English and maths. You can improve your earning potential and career development by taking professional accountancy qualifications.

Many employers accept older recruits. The Association of Accounting Technicians (AAT) and the Association of Chartered Certified Accountants (ACCA) training schemes welcome applications from adult entrants and no previous qualifications are required. In fact, 20% of students enrolled with AAT are aged over 40. They train in exactly the same way as people who start straight from school or college.

The AAT offers an accounting qualification based on an occupational training scheme, recognising work abilities as well as exam results. Many universities recognise the AAT qualification and it may exempt you from parts of an accountancy degree course. The Institute of Chartered Accountants in Scotland (ICAS) and AAT have teamed up to run a joint venture which promotes the role of accounting technicians in Scotland. AAT also offers NVQ/SVQ Levels 2 and 3 in Payroll Administration, a diploma in government finance and an ABC book-keeping certificate.

The ACCA Certified Accounting Technician (CAT) qualification is internationally recognised and takes approximately one year to complete.

A number of awarding bodies offer NVQ training in Accountancy at Levels 2, 3 and 4.

Making the Grade: There are many opportunities for career progression. In many small to medium-sized companies, accounting technicians are the only trained financial staff and they have major responsibilities. They may have to work with senior managers, reporting on how the business is performing and suggesting ways to improve profitability and performance. Some accounting technicians also become self-employed, providing book-keeping and advisory support to smaller organisations.

Personal Qualities: As an accounting technician, you should be confident about working with numbers, have good IT skills and be able to communicate and convey information clearly.

You must inspire trust and be discreet and tactful when handling confidential information. You would have to be extremely accurate in your work, while keeping to tight deadlines.

Looking Ahead: There is a growing demand for accounting technicians in all areas, including accounting practice, commerce and industry and the public sector. There are good career opportunities, in all parts of the UK, in commercial companies, accountancy practices, local and central government, the NHS, shops, hotels, charities and voluntary organisations.

Financial Adviser

Financial advisers work with clients to find financial products that suit their needs. A client could be one person, an organisation or a group of individuals. The sorts of products they give advice on may include investments, life insurance and critical illness cover, pensions and savings plans, mortgages and other borrowings, secured and unsecured.

There are two quite distinct types of financial adviser:

- They may be tied to an individual bank, building society or insurance company, advising solely on the financial products of that organisation.
- They may have a broader role as an independent adviser, recommending suitable investments, mortgages, pensions and insurance policies on an impartial basis.

When they have identified a product that is appropriate, financial advisers need to explain all the details clearly, with the minimum of jargon. They need to point out the potential benefits and any limitations so that the client can make an informed decision.

Entry Level: While there are no formal academic entry requirements, the most prestigious employers would require a high standard of education. Many financial advisers are graduates. A degree in finance and accountancy, business studies or related subjects may be an advantage, but a confident, professional character is just as important. Clients look for maturity in their adviser, so school leavers are rarely employed directly into this role.

Entry to a degree is with at least two A levels/three H grades and five GCSEs/S grades (A-C/1-3), or equivalent qualifications.

Making the Grade: You would have to undertake recognised industry training, regulated by the Financial Services Authority (FSA).

Training for an FSA-recognised qualification normally takes between two and three years. Employers tend to be fully supportive of all professional qualifications and most would provide training and pay for exams, but you would be expected to put in a lot of study time outside your normal working hours. To pass, you would need to show a good understanding of the financial services sector and to be able to share this knowledge with clients.

Younger financial advisers tend to start as tied consultants. As they gain experience, they may join a firm of independent financial advisers, or go into business by themselves. If you are enthusiastic, can make clients feel comfortable and have good product knowledge, you can progress quickly.

Personal Qualities: As a financial adviser, you would need to be capable of understanding financial products, which may be complex, yet able to communicate the benefits of these products simply.

You must be a clear and concise communicator, with good listening and questioning skills, you must be numerate and comfortable using computers and you must be able to inspire trust.

Looking Ahead: Financial advisers can work anywhere in the UK, although the opportunities are mostly centred on the major cities and the suburbs. Although tied advisers may be on the payroll of a bank or insurance company, a significant proportion of financial advisers are self-employed.

As you gain more experience, you may move on to advising on other financial products, which will require you to obtain further qualifications. The Financial Services Authority (FSA) is currently reviewing the large number of qualifications issued by the approved institutes.

IT Careers in Financial Services

Inna Rozel might be obsessed with money, but don't get the idea that she is a greedy or narrow-minded person. She isn't. It's just that Rozel is one of a growing number of IT grads who are launching their careers in the financial services industry.

The financial services market encompasses an array of companies spread across many different types of businesses, including banks, brokerages, credit card issuers and mortgage providers. This diverse industry requires experts who are skilled in the complete gamut of IT specialties, including programming, operations, databases, systems design and analysis, networks and telecommunications.

Rozel, for instance, is a business analyst for Chase Home Mortgage in Edison, N. J. "My responsibilities include gathering requirements, translating user needs into functional and technical specifications and managing small projects and initiatives," she says. Rozel also creates various types of in-house tests and represents users' interests on various IT projects and initiatives.

Hiring the Best Money can Buy

Since financial services companies must handle great quantities of numbers and documents in a variety of different ways, they have historically been among the earliest and eagerest IT adopters. "We use technology to minimize costs," says Gary Simms, operational risk management director for Freddie Mac, the US government chartered company, located in McLean, Va. The company helps keep money flowing to mortgage lenders that support the home and rental housing markets. "If a technology can help make us more efficient and lower costs, we'll adopt it," says Simms.

Like most major financial services companies, Freddie Mac employs an army of IT specialists. "We have over 2,700 technology employees spread across the country," says Simms. That's out of total workforce of about 5,200 people. Simms notes that Freddie Mac's IT workforce focuses on four basic areas: software development, infrastructure management, database management and technical project management.

When hiring new IT workers, Freddie Mac seeks grads with various types of skills, but nothing too specialized. "We mostly look for development capabilities," says Simms. "We look for C++, Java, WebLogic, COBOL, HTML, SQL, UML and various other development skills." Additionally, Freddie Mac gives preferences to candidates with what Simms describes as "soft skills."

"We also look for the ability to comprehend technical platforms, operating systems, basic system security principles and network architectures," he says. Simms adds that job candidates should also possess a set of basic business skills, including the ability to coordinate and monitor work, interact with a diverse workforce, communicate effectively and work in their own area with minimal supervision. "Rather than one specific talent, we look for an entire range of skills in the people we consider for employment," says Simms.

Rozel was hired by Chase directly out of college, where she earned a B.S. in computer science. "Doing IT at a financial services company seemed to be a great opportunity to apply the basics of technology that I had learned in college," she says.

Over her 10-year career at Chase, Rozel has steadily worked her way up the ladder, progressing from entry-level programmer to project manager and business analyst. Like many financial services IT workers, Rozel recently decided to advance her career by adding a graduate degree to her resume. She now has a master's degree in management of technology in financial services from New York's Polytechnic University. "I would like to use the knowledge I acquired in the master's programme to look at and assess the bigger picture in my future assignments and endeavours," she says.

Growing Trend Towards Combined Education

A growing number of colleges and universities are beginning to offer courses and programmes that are focused on financial IT. Polytechnic University, for example, offers a master's degree in financial engineering, as well as the management of technology in financial services. The University of California at Berkeley, Kent State College, Claremont Graduate University and Princeton University are among the many other schools offering similar graduate-level programmes.

Given the fact that IT plays such an important role at financial services, it's only natural that there's a growing trend toward combined technology and finance education, says Bob Biolsi, a Polytechnic University adjunct professor and vice president of quantitative analysis at the New York Mercantile Exchange.

"Traditionally, finance was taught in the abstract and certainly not in combination with technology management," he explains. "The current demand is for IT people with some knowledge of finance theory and practice and for finance people who have the skills to manage the technology process."

Biolsi believes that a new generation of trained financial technology specialists will help the industry correct some of its past IT mistakes. "Finance people had difficulty communicating their technology needs while IT departments built systems that really didn't understand what was expected of them," he says. The two sides, working in near isolation, wasted both time and money. "Tens of millions of dollars were spent without accomplishing what was truly needed by the industry," says Biolsi.

Ron Thompson, an associate professor of information technology at Wake Forest University's Babcock Graduate School of Management, located in Winston-Salem, N.C., sees a growing overlap of financial and IT interests at the graduate level. He believes finance students are taking IT courses and more IT students are studying finance. "It's becoming quite common for finance students to learn some Visual Basic programming so they can build decision support systems using Microsoft Excel as the platform and Visual Basic for the logic," he says. "On the flip side, for IT students who want to work in the financial services industry, it's helpful to have a basic understanding of financial accounting and basic financial industry regulations and practices."

Rozel asserts that financial IT can be a fascinating and fulfilling career. "Starting as a programmer, I was able to observe how the whole development cycle works and, from that, I was able to move up to the tasks that would build on my existing skills and help me develop new abilities," she says. "Financial services IT is for those who are looking for a fast paced environment filled with challenges and overcoming obstacles in the most efficient manner."

Auditor

Auditors carry out checks on the accounts of companies and public bodies. They ensure that organisations meet all the legal and financial reporting standards required of them.

Work Activities: Auditors are professionally qualified specialist accountants. They examine a client's accounts to check they have been accurately prepared in accordance with the Companies Act. This covers accounts and financial reporting standards.

Limited companies are required by law to have their accounts audited by a certified or chartered accountant. Government departments are also audited, normally by public finance accountants.

Auditors often conduct their work on the client's premises. They start by gaining a thorough knowledge of a client's business and continue gathering evidence until they are certain that there are no significant errors in the accounts.

Auditors carry out audit tests and examine samples of documents and records to check that all transactions, assets and liabilities have been properly recorded. Techniques include inspecting assets and seeking further details from both within and outside a company. They may also compare current accounts with the previous year, or with a comparable company's accounts.

Auditors complete their work by preparing a report for presentation to the company's shareholders and management.

Personal Qualities and Skills: To be an auditor you need to be highly numerate and capable of interpreting complicated accounts. You should have an enquiring mind, a good eye for detail and be accurate and methodical in your work. An ability to communicate effectively and explain results clearly and concisely is essential. Good report writing skills are also necessary.

Pay and Opportunities: The pay rates given below are approximate.

Starting salaries for trainees are from around £11,000 a year (AAT trainee), graduate trainees from £15,000. Qualified accountants earn in the range of £24,500 - £30,000 a year and senior accountants earn £38,000 - £47,000. Higher earners can make around £50,000 - £80,000 a year.

Auditors usually work 35 - 40 hours Monday to Friday. However, they may need to work late/weekends at peak times, for example, at the end of the financial year.

Jobs exist throughout the UK, particularly in cities and larger towns. Employers in the private sector are accountancy practices (known as private practice). Auditors in the public sector in Scotland work for Audit Scotland which supports the Auditor General and the Accounts Commission. There are similar structures in England, Northern Ireland and Wales.

The following information is sourced from government statistics. The government's definition of types of job is slightly different to that used in this programme. For this type of job, the most relevant Government-defined occupation is 'Chartered and certified accountants'.

In 2001 there were 10,200 people working as 'Chartered and certified accountants' in Scotland. 47 in every 10,000 employees working in Scotland were employed as 'Chartered and certified accountants'.

Entry Routes and Training

To become an auditor you must register as a student with the Institute of Chartered Accountants of Scotland (ICAS), the Association of Chartered Certified Accountants (ACCA), the Chartered Institute of Public Finance and Accountancy (CIPFA) or the Association of International Accountants (AIA). The majority of students who register with ICAS, CIPFA and ACCA are graduates.

To qualify you must pass professional examinations. Study is possible through day-release, block-release, full-time study or distance learning, depending on the professional body and your employer.

Qualifications: For entry to a relevant degree course the minimum requirements is 3/4 Highers (A-C) plus Standard Grades (1-3) in 2 other subjects. Some popular courses ask for higher entry qualifications.

Entry requirements vary between courses and alternative qualifications may be accepted - check prospectuses for details.

Adult Opportunities: The Institute of Internal Auditors (IIA) will consider applications from those who do not have the minimum qualifications, provided their employer confirms their ability to cope with the demands of the programme.

IIA offer distance learning with some face-to-face induction/ revision attended sessions.

Suitable applicants aged 21 or over may do a college or university Access course. No formal qualifications are required to enter an Access course, but you should check individual course details. They lead to relevant degree/HND courses.

Auditing qualifications may also be studied as a fully experienced accounting technician.

Sponsorships from some of the larger accounting or professional services firms and from public sector organisations such as the National Audit Office (NAO) can be available for those on degree-level study.

- 10% of people who work in occupations such as auditor work part-time.
- 15% have flexible hours.
- 2% of employees work on a temporary basis.

Stock Broking

Indian stock exchanges, today, are dealing with big numbers and big buyers.

The capital markets are undergoing transformation. Today's progressive brokers deal in billions rather than in millions.

Brokers now have all their operations computerized and employ qualified industry specialists to advise on buying and selling of stocks.

Brokers or stock market professionals are now either playing host to foreign investment bankers, who are looking for opportunities on the Indian stock market, or visiting fund managers abroad seeking investment here. Stock market houses are redefining themselves and the business of stock broking is highly visible today. Communication links between the dealing room and the trading ring are being improved. The National Stock Exchange or NSE (inaugurated on 23 July 1994) provides nationwide facilities with access to investors all over the country. The automated, screen-based trading system using state-of-the-art technology makes market operations transparent.

The Securities and Exchange Board of India (SEBI) has been empowered by an Act of Parliament to protect the rights of investors and ensure the promotion and regulation of the capital markets. It is the regulatory body in charge of the country's capital markets.

Eligibility: Stock broking business requires the services of specialists (in varied fields) - economists, accountants, finance managers, financial analysts, capital market specialists and investments and financial planners.

Postgraduate courses in economics and commerce are available in most universities in the country. Finance managers may be MBAs with specialization in finance from the reputed institutes of management or from the departments of business administration of the major universities.

The Institute of Chartered Accountants of India (ICAI), New Delhi, conducts the chartered accountancy course for the plus two level through the foundation course and directly for graduates.

Job Prospects: Prospects for the stock broking business are bright and for those who are qualified to handle this business and have the necessary personality traits to cope with it, the openings are many. Foreign firms are waiting in the wings to secure government clearance for participating in the stock exchanges. Indian brokers will, therefore, have to come to terms with real competition and ensure international standards of services to the investor.

Where to Apply?: Institute of Company Secretaries of India, New Delhi

Postgraduate membership course in capital market and financial services.

Institute of Capital Market Development, 1965, Arya Samaj Road, Karol Bagh, New Delhi-110005

One year postgraduate programme in fundamentals of capital market development.

All India Centre for Capital Market Studies, J. D. C. Byte Institute of Management Studies and Research, Nashik-422 005

One year post graduate programme in capital market studies, in collaboration with the Mumbai Stock Exchange Training Institute, leading to a diploma from the University of Pune. The course is open to graduates through an all-India selection process.

Mumbai Stock Exchange Training Institute, Stock Exchange Building, Fort, Mumbai

Certificate courses are run periodically throughout the year.

Institute of Financial and Investment Planning, B/303, Ventex Vikas, M. V. Road andheri East, Mumbai

One year correspondence cum lecture course leading to a diploma in financial and investment planning.

Institute of Chartered Financial Analysts of India, Road No. 3, Banjara Hills, Hyderabad

Courses on Chartered Financial Analyst Equity Research. The institute is also planning a number of other related programmes.

Debt and Structured Finance Jobs and Advice

The Debt and Structured Finance business at Michael Page Financial Services works at all levels across a broad range of sectors between which there is ever-increasing cross-over. The teams draw upon significant banking experience and an excellent reputation to ensure that they are able to recruit into the following sectors:

Credit Analysis/Counterparty Credit

We deal with everything from Financial Institutions to Sovereigns and Corporates; from Credit Analysis to Counterparty Credit and Credit Research. With the growth in the Structured Finance businesses, the team is well positioned to work in the Project Finance, Property Finance, Leveraged Portfolio Management and Securitisation Credit areas.

Relationship Management/Corporate Banking

Corporate banking provides the foundations for the debt markets, there continues to be a shift in this space towards more sector-focused cross-product coverage rather than traditional large-cap corporate banking. As margins are being squeezed, deals are becoming increasingly structured. Our expertise covering both vanilla and more structured debt means that we are well placed to help you with this market shift.

Trade Finance/Structured Trade Finance

The team has a unique perspective on this niche market and a successful record of working with the major players from top tier Investment Banks to Commodity Traders.

Project Finance

This has always been a key market to Michael Page Financial Services as it possesses a proven capability to weather the downturns in the Debt market. There has been a pronounced switch away from the UK to the European market and therefore candidates combining good languages and strong technical skills are highly sought after.

Leveraged Finance

This is currently a booming market - the team have successfully filled roles at all levels from Analyst to Head of team, in all areas of the market. With 2 ex-Leveraged Finance bankers in the team, this team will continue to be one of our most active areas of focus.

Distressed Debt/Workouts

This is an area that we are expecting an imminent increase in activity as the result of the boom in the Leveraged business.

Securitisation

The team has worked with clients focused on Origination/ Structuring and Securitisation Credit and Credit Research at all levels. The MBS and CDO markets have been particularly active in the last 18 months.

Property Finance/Structured Property Finance

The team have recently successfully completed a number of national campaigns for all levels for Banks, Funds and Specialist Property companies including advisory clients.

Tax Structured Finance/Asset Finance

This is a very specialised business and an area Michael Page Financial Services have had a presence in for a number of years. The team have worked with the top teams in the industry sourcing candidates from Legal and Accounting practice as well as more experienced market players.

3

Career in Insurance Sector

Insurance

Insurance is the equitable transfer of the risk of a potential loss, from one entity to another, in exchange for a premium. Insurer is the company that sells the insurance policy and schemes. Insurance rate is a factor used to determine the amount, called the premium, to be charged for a certain amount of insurance coverage. Risk management or insurance as the practice of appraising and controlling risk, has evolved as a hot career option in the post-liberalization era in India. As a result, not only insurance agents but also marketers and actuaries are in great demand in the insurance sector.

Insurance Companies deal in two main areas - Life insurance and General insurance. With the liberalization and opening up of this field several companies have come up in the field of Life insurance and general insurance.

Insurance Agents: Agents are not on the payrolls of the insurance company. The insurance agents get a fixed commission on each policy they (insurance-agent) manage to sell

Eligibility and Process: People who wish to become insurance agents are required to undergo 100 hours of training by the respective insurance company. Once the training is complete, the candidate is eligible to appear for an online examination conducted by the Insurance Regulatory Development Authority (IRDA) with at least 50 per cent marks set for qualifying.

Composite Agent—is the one who sells both life and general insurance policies. One has to put in 100 hours promoting life insurance products assuming that you are a general insurance agent. A life insurance agent, before appearing for another exam, has to dedicate 50 hours towards promoting general insurance products. A composite agent has to appear for another test also (conducted by the IRDA).

The agent is supposed to renew his license after three years, by putting in another 25 hours (and 50 hours for composite insurance agent) of training. An agent can register under a development officer in any insurance company. The training institutes are accredited by the IRDA and the insurance Company merely sponsors its agents. An agent works with the Development Officer in the insurance Company and the credit for the policy of the insurance agents goes to the Development Officers within the organization. Nevertheless, this job is as good as freelancing. Secondly, the insurance companies also provide incentive schemes for the insurance agents from time to time.

Surveyors, Loss Adjusters and Assessors are technically qualified professionals who perform the job of assessing the losses, according to their qualifications and experience. They work as 'consultants' for the company. A surveyor with a background in mechanical engineering assesses industrial accidents. Here the surveyor would investigate, evaluate, assess, adjust and determine the liability, negotiate and then finally submit a report.

A surveyor must hold either a fellowship or associateship from one of the following

- The Institute of Insurance surveyors and Adjusters (IISA), Mumbai
- A degree or diploma in architecture from a recognized university or institute
- Fellowship or Associateship from the Institute of Chartered Accountants or Costs and Works Accountants
- A degree or diploma from a recognized institute of engineering or a degree or diploma in naval architecture.

- They have to apply to the IRDA for a license that further categorizes them as Class A, B, C, or D. A surveyor, loss adjuster or assessor is the only specialized link between the insurers and the insured.

Qualifications

Qualifications for Insurance Surveyor: For membership of the Institute the candidate should fulfil the parameters listed below besides the satisfaction of the Managing Committee:

a. The candidate should be in the business or profession of Insurance Surveyor or Adjuster:
b. Should have attained the age of twenty one years
c. Should be been in professional practice either as a Principal or Head or responsible surveyor of any firm company or corporation connected with the profession or business of Insurance Surveyors or Adjusters for at least two years consecutively immediately preceding the date of his application for admission and membership but the Managing Committee may in its absolute discretion waive or relax this restriction in a special case or cases and admit a person to membership;
d. Should be able to furnish proofs of his professional ability as the Managing Committee may in their absolute discretion require;
e. Is not directly or indirectly connected or otherwise works as broker or agent or solicits or canvasses or procures insurance business;
f. Is not an owner, partner or otherwise directly or indirectly connected with a workshop or motor garage undertaking repairs of accident job and;
g. Is not an employee of an Insurer or a Principal or Chief Agent of an Insurer:

Norms for Membership

Fellow	Ten Years after empanelment
Associate	Five Years after empanelment
Licentiate	Ten Years after empanelment
Student	Undergoing Apprenticeship

Fellow, Associate, Licentiate and Student are four categories in which IISA grants membership

Student: Any individual undergoing apprenticeship with a licensed practicing surveyor is eligible to apply for student membership of IISA. Student Membership can be upgraded to Licentiate Membership on obtaining a Surveyors' License from Insurance Regulatory and Development Authority of India

Licentiate: Two years after empanelment and duly licensed by the Insurance Regulatory And Development Authority Of India, any individual is eligible to apply for Licentiate Membership of IISA

Associate: Any individual duly licensed by the Insurance Regulatory and Development Authority of India, is eligible to apply for Licentiate Membership of IISA.

Actuaries: An actuary is a business professional who analyses the financial consequences of risk. Actuaries use mathematics, statistics and financial theory to study uncertain future events, especially those of concern to insurance and pension programmes.

Eligibility: Graduate with 55 per cent marks and should have either completed a course in maths/ stats/ econometrics/ computer science, or are engineers in any discipline, or have done an MBA in finance. People who have also completed their CA/ CWA/ MCA are eligible to join

Training as an actuary can be pursued from the Actuarial Society of India (ASI), Mumbai or The Institute And Faculty of Actuaries, London, UK. Actuaries are paid very well and the consolidated salary figure can go up to Rs 8 lakhs per year in India.

Job Prospects: Agents get about 25 to 32 percent of the premium amount in the first year of the policy. In the second and third year they get about 7.5 percent and in fourth and fifth year they get about 5 percent of the premium. After about four years of good performance, an agent may also be entitled to office facilities, car, computer, telephone, maintenance, housing loan etc.

Insurance & Actuarials

The opening up of the Insurance sector to private enterprises will usher in a new phase in this century old sector.

In 1950, with the enactment of the Insurance Act, the entire business of life insurance was nationalised. The central office of LIC was set up in Mumbai with seven zonal offices. The head office was responsible for formulation of policies and the zonal offices for coordinating with and supervising divisional offices. The LIC operates through almost a hundred divisional offices and nearly 2000 branch offices located across the country and in some locations abroad.

Insurance companies deal in 3 main areas, life insurance, health insurance, property and accident insurance. Companies may specialise in one or all the three types of insurance coverage. While LIC deals with insurance of life, the General Insurance Company (GIC) is another insurance firm concerned with motor, marine, personal accident and fire insurance.

Both LIC and GIC have branches all over the country. GIC has four subsidiaries - Oriental Insurance, United India Insurance, New India Assurance and National Insurance, netting business in India and in over thirty locations abroad.

Insurance Underwriters

Significant Points: Most large insurance companies prefer college graduates who have a degree in business administration or finance with courses in accounting; however, a bachelor's degree in any field—plus courses in business law and accounting—may be sufficient to qualify.

Continuing education is necessary for advancement.

Employment is expected to grow more slowly than average as the continuing spread of underwriting software increases worker productivity.

Job opportunities should be best for those with a background in finance and strong computer and communication skills.

Nature of the Work: Insurance companies protect individuals and organizations from financial loss by assuming billions of dollars in risk each year. Underwriters are needed to identify and calculate the risk of loss from policyholders, establish appropriate premium rates and write policies that cover this risk. An insurance company may lose business to competitors if the underwriter appraises risks too conservatively, or it may have to pay excessive claims if the underwriting actions are too liberal.

With the aid of computers, underwriters analyze information in insurance applications to determine whether a risk is acceptable and will not result in a loss. Applications often are supplemented with reports from loss-control consultants, medical reports, reports from data vendors and actuarial studies. Underwriters then must decide whether to issue the policy and, if so, the appropriate premium to charge. In making this determination, underwriters serve as the main link between the insurance carrier and the insurance agent. On occasion, they accompany sales agents to make presentations to prospective clients.

Technology plays an important role in an underwriter's job. Underwriters use computer applications called "smart systems" to manage risks more efficiently and accurately. These systems automatically analyze and rate insurance applications, recommend acceptance or denial of the risk and adjust the premium rate in accordance with the risk. With these systems, underwriters are better equipped to make sound decisions and avoid excessive losses.

The Internet also has affected the work of underwriters. Many insurance carriers' computer systems are now linked to different databases on the Internet that allow immediate access to information—such as driving records—necessary in determining a potential client's risk. This kind of access reduces the amount of time and paperwork necessary for an underwriter to complete a risk assessment.

Most underwriters specialize in one of three major categories of insurance: life, health and property and casualty. Life and health insurance underwriters may further specialize in group or individual policies.

Property and casualty underwriters usually specialize in either commercial or personal insurance and then by type of risk insured, as in fire, homeowners', automobile, marine, or liability insurance, or workers' compensation. In cases where casualty companies provide insurance through a single "package" policy covering various types of risks, the underwriter must be familiar with different lines of insurance. For business insurance, the underwriter often must be able to evaluate the firm's entire operation in appraising its application for insurance.

An increasing proportion of insurance sales, particularly in life and health insurance, is being made through group contracts. A standard group policy insures everyone in a specified group through a single contract at a standard premium rate. The group underwriter analyzes the overall composition of the group to ensure that the total risk is not excessive. Another type of group policy provides members of a group—a labour union, for example—with individual policies reflecting their needs. These usually are casualty policies, such as those covering automobiles. The casualty underwriter analyzes the application of each group member and makes individual appraisals. Some group underwriters meet with union or employer representatives to discuss the types of policies available to their group.

Working Conditions: Underwriters have desk jobs that require no unusual physical activity. Their offices usually are comfortable and pleasant. Although underwriters typically work a standard 40-hour week, more are working longer hours due to the downsizing of many insurance companies. Most underwriters are based in a home or regional branch office, but they occasionally attend meetings away from home for several days. Construction and marine underwriters frequently travel to inspect worksites and assess risks.

Training, Other Qualifications and Advancement: For entry-level underwriting jobs, most large insurance companies prefer college graduates who have a degree in business administration or finance with courses or experience in accounting. However, a bachelor's degree in almost any field—plus courses in business law and accounting—provides a good general background and may be sufficient to qualify an individual. Because computers are an integral part of most underwriters' jobs, computer skills are essential.

New employees usually start as underwriter trainees or assistant underwriters. They may help collect information on applicants and evaluate routine applications under the supervision of an experienced risk analyst. Property and casualty trainees study claims files to become familiar with factors associated with certain types of losses. Many larger insurers offer work-study training programmes, lasting from a few months to a year. As trainees gain experience, they are assigned policy applications that are more complex and cover greater risks. Analyzing and processing these applications efficiently requires the use of computers.

Underwriting can be a satisfying career for people who enjoy analyzing information and paying attention to detail. In addition, underwriters must possess good judgment in order to make sound decisions. Excellent communication and interpersonal skills also are essential, as much of the underwriter's work involves dealing with agents and other insurance professionals.

Continuing education is necessary for advancement. Insurance companies usually pay tuition for underwriting courses that their trainees complete; some also offer salary incentives. Independent-study programmes for experienced property and casualty underwriters are available as well. The Insurance Institute of America offers both a programme called "Introduction to Underwriting" for beginning underwriters and the specialty designation of Associate in Commercial Underwriting (ACU), a formal step in developing a career in underwriting business insurance policies. Those interested in developing a career underwriting personal insurance policies may earn the Associate in Personal Insurance (API) designation. To earn either the ACU or API designation, underwriters complete a series of courses and examinations that generally last 1 to 2 years.

The American Institute for Chartered Property Casualty Underwriters (AICPCU) awards the Chartered Property and Casualty Underwriter (CPCU) designation, the final stage of development for an underwriter. Earning the CPCU designation requires passing 10 exams, meeting a requirement of at least

3 years of insurance experience and abiding by the AICPCU's code of professional ethics. Exams cover risk management; insurance operations and regulations, business and insurance law and financial management and financial institutions. In conjunction with the Insurance Institute of America, the AICPCU offers 22 insurance-related educational programmes, including associate designation programmes in claims underwriting, risk management and reinsurance. The American College offers the Chartered Life Underwriter (CLU) designation and the Registered Health Underwriter (RHU) designation for all life and health insurance professionals.

Experienced underwriters who complete courses of study may advance to senior underwriter or underwriting manager positions. Some underwriting managers are promoted to senior managerial jobs. Some employers require a master's degree to achieve this level. Other underwriters are attracted to the earnings potential of sales and, therefore, obtain State licenses to sell insurance and related financial products as agents or brokers.

Employment: Insurance underwriters held about 101,000 jobs in 2004. Approximately 2 out of 3 underwriters work for insurance carriers. Most of the remaining underwriters work in insurance agencies or for organizations that offer insurance services to insurance companies and policyholders. A small number of underwriters work in agencies owned and operated by banks, mortgage companies and real estate firms.

Most underwriters are based in the insurance company's home office, but some, mainly in the property and casualty area, work out of regional branch offices of the insurance company. These underwriters usually have the authority to underwrite most risks and determine an appropriate rating without consulting the home office.

Job Outlook: Employment of underwriters is expected to grow more slowly than average for all occupations through 2014. Underwriting software will continue to make workers more productive; however, because computer software does not do away with the need for human skills, employment will increase as economic and population growth result in increased insurance needs by businesses and individuals. Job opportunities should be best for those with a background in finance and strong computer and communication skills. In addition to openings arising from some job growth, openings will be created by the need to replace underwriters who transfer to another job or leave the occupation. Insurance carriers always are assessing new risks and offering policies to meet changing circumstances. Underwriters are needed particularly in the area of product development, where they assess risks and set the premiums for new lines of insurance. One new line of insurance being offered by life insurance carriers that may provide job opportunities for underwriters is long-term care insurance.

Demand for underwriters also is expected to improve as insurance carriers try to restore profitability to make up for an unusually large number of underwriting losses in recent years. As the carriers' returns on their investments have declined, insurers are placing more emphasis on underwriting to generate revenues. This renewed interest in underwriting should result in job opportunities for underwriters. Because insurance is considered a necessity for people and businesses, there will always be a need for underwriters—a profession that is less subject to recession and layoffs than other fields.

Earnings: Median annual earnings of insurance underwriters were $48,550 in May 2004. The middle 50 percent earned between $37,490 and $65,450 a year. The lowest 10 percent earned less than $30,410, while the highest 10 percent earned more than $86,110. Median annual earnings of underwriters working with insurance carriers were $49,280, while earnings of these in agencies, brokerages and other insurance related activities were $46,750.

Insurance companies usually provide better-than-average benefits, including retirement plans and employer-financed group life and health insurance.

Claims Investigators

Significant Points: Adjusters and examiners investigate insurance claims, negotiate settlements and authorize payments; appraisers assess the cost or value of an insured item; investigators deal with claims about which there is a question of liability and where fraud or criminal activity is suspected.

Licensing and continuing education requirements vary by State. College graduates have the best opportunities; competition will be keen for jobs as investigators, because this occupation attracts many qualified people.

Nature of the Work: Individuals and businesses purchase insurance policies to protect against monetary losses. In the event of a loss, policyholders submit claims, or requests for payment, seeking compensation for their loss. Adjusters, appraisers, examiners and investigators work primarily for property and casualty insurance companies, for whom they handle a wide variety of claims alleging property damage, liability, or bodily injury. Their main role is to investigate the claims, negotiate settlements and authorize payments to claimants, all the while mindful not to violate the claimant's rights under Federal and State privacy laws. They must determine whether the customer's insurance policy covers the loss and how much of the loss should be paid to the claimant. Although many adjusters, appraisers, examiners and investigators have overlapping functions and may even perform the same job, the insurance industry generally assigns specific roles to each of these claims workers.

Adjusters plan and schedule the work required to process a claim that would follow, for example, an automobile accident or damage to one's home caused by a storm. They investigate claims by interviewing the claimant and witnesses, consulting police and hospital records and inspecting property damage to determine the extent of the company's liability. Adjusters may consult with other professionals, such as accountants, architects, construction workers, engineers, lawyers and physicians, who can offer a more expert evaluation of a claim. The information gathered, including photographs and written or audio-taped or video-taped statements, is set down in a report that is then used to evaluate the associated claim. When the policyholder's claim is legitimate, the claims adjuster negotiates with the claimant and settles the claim. When claims are contested, adjusters will work with attorneys and expert witnesses to defend the insurer's position.

Many companies centralize claims adjustment in a claims centre, where the cost of repair is determined and a check is issued immediately. More complex cases, usually involving bodily injury, are referred to senior adjusters. Some adjusters work with multiple types of insurance; however, most specialize in homeowner claims, business losses, automotive damage, or workers' compensation.

Claimants can opt not to rely on the services of their insurance company's adjuster and may instead choose to hire a public adjuster. These workers assist clients in preparing and presenting claims to insurance companies and in trying to negotiate a fair settlement. They perform the same services as adjusters who work directly for companies; however, they work in the best interests of the client, rather than the insurance company.

Claims examiners within property and casualty insurance firms may have duties similar to those of an adjuster, but often their primary job is to review the claims submitted in order to ensure that proper guidelines have been followed. They may assist adjusters with complex and complicated claims or when a disaster suddenly greatly increases the volume of claims. Most claims examiners work for life or health insurance companies. In health insurance companies, examiners review health-related claims to see whether costs are reasonable on the basis of the diagnosis.

The examiners are provided with guides that supply information on the average period of disability, the expected treatments and the average hospital stay, for patients with the various ailments for which a claim may be submitted. Examiners check claim applications for completeness and accuracy, interview medical specialists and consult policy files to verify the information reported in a claim. Examiners will then either authorize the appropriate payment or refer the claim to an investigator for a more thorough review. Claims examiners usually specialize in group or individual insurance plans and in hospital, dental, or prescription drug claims.

In life insurance, claims examiners review the causes of death, particularly in the case of an accident, because most life insurance policies pay additional benefits if a death is accidental. Claims examiners also may review new applications for life insurance to make sure that the applicants have no serious illnesses that would make them a high risk to insure and thus disqualify them from obtaining insurance.

Another occupation that plays an important role in the accurate settlement of claims is that of the *appraiser*, whose role is to assess the cost or value of an insured item. The majority of appraisers employed by insurance companies and independent adjusting firms are *auto damage appraisers*. These appraisers inspect damaged vehicles after an accident and estimate the cost of repairs. This information is then relayed to the adjuster, who incorporates the appraisal into the settlement. Auto damage appraisers are valued by insurance companies because they can provide an unbiased judgment of repair costs. Otherwise, the companies would have to rely on auto mechanics' estimates, which might be unreasonably high.

Many claims adjusters and auto damage appraisers are equipped with laptop computers from which they can download the necessary forms and files from insurance company databases. Many adjusters and appraisers use digital cameras, which allow photographs of the damage to be sent to the company via the Internet. Many also input information about the damage directly into their computers, where software programmes produce estimates of damage on standard forms. These new technologies allow for faster and more efficient processing of claims.

When adjusters or examiners suspect fraud, they refer the claim to an investigator. *Insurance investigators* in an insurance company's special investigative unit handle claims in which the company suspects fraudulent or criminal activity, such as arson, falsified workers' disability claims, staged accidents, or unnecessary medical treatments. The severity of insurance fraud cases can vary greatly, from claimants simply overstating the damage to a vehicle to complicated fraud rings responsible for many claimants and supported by dishonest doctors, lawyers and even insurance personnel.

Investigators usually start with a database search to obtain background information on claimants and witnesses. Investigators can access certain personal information and identify Social Security numbers, aliases, driver's license numbers, addresses, phone numbers, criminal records and past claims histories to establish whether a claimant has ever attempted insurance fraud. Then, investigators may visit claimants and witnesses to obtain a recorded statement, take photographs and inspect facilities, such as doctors' offices, to determine whether the doctors have a proper license. Investigators often consult with legal counsel and can be expert witnesses in court cases.

Often, investigators also perform surveillance work. For example, in a case involving fraudulent workers' compensation claims, an investigator may covertly observe the claimant for several days or even weeks. If the investigator observes the subject performing an activity that is ruled out by injuries stated in a workers' compensation claim, the investigator will take video or still photographs to document the activity and report it to the insurance company.

Working Conditions: Working environments of claims adjusters, appraisers, examiners and investigators vary greatly. Most claims examiners employed by life and health insurance companies work a standard 5-day, 40-hour week in a typical office environment. Many claims adjusters and auto damage appraisers, however, often work outside the office, inspecting damaged buildings and automobiles. Adjusters who inspect damaged buildings must be wary of potential hazards such as collapsed roofs and floors, as well as weakened structures.

In general, adjusters are able to arrange their work schedules to accommodate evening and weekend appointments with clients. This accommodation sometimes results in adjusters working irregular schedules or more than 40 hours a week, especially when they have a lot of claims to investigate. Some report to the office every morning to get their assignments, while others simply call in from home and spend their days travelling to claim sites. New technology, such as laptop computers and cellular telephones, is making telecommuting easier for claims adjusters and auto damage appraisers. Many adjusters work inside their office only a few hours a week, while others conduct their business entirely out of their home and automobile.

Occasionally, experienced adjusters must be away from home for days—for example, when they travel to the scene of a disaster such as a tornado, hurricane, or flood—to work with local adjusters and government officials. Adjusters often are called to work in the event of such emergencies and may have to work 50 or 60 hours a week until all claims are resolved.

Insurance investigators often work irregular hours because of the need to conduct surveillance and contact people who are not available during normal working hours. Early morning, evening and weekend work is common. Some days, investigators will spend all day in the office, searching databases, making telephone calls and writing reports. Other times, they may be away, performing surveillance activities or interviewing witnesses. Some of the work can involve confrontation with claimants and others involved in a case, so the job can be stressful and dangerous.

Training, Other Qualifications and Advancement: Training and entry requirements vary widely for claims adjusters, appraisers, examiners and investigators. Although many in these occupations do not have a college degree, most companies prefer to hire college graduates. No specific college major is recommended, but a variety of backgrounds can be an asset. A claims adjuster who, for example, has a business or an accounting background might specialize in claims of financial loss due to strikes, breakdowns of equipment, or damage to merchandise.

College training in architecture or engineering is helpful in adjusting industrial claims, such as those involving damage from fires or other accidents. Some claims adjusters and examiners apply expertise acquired through specialized professional training to adjust claims. A legal background can be beneficial to someone handling workers' compensation and product liability cases. A medical background is useful for those examiners working on medical and life insurance claims.

Because they often work closely with claimants, witnesses and other insurance professionals, claims adjusters and examiners must be able to communicate effectively with others. Knowledge of computer applications also is extremely helpful. In addition, a valid driver's license and a good driving record are required for workers for whom travel is an important aspect of their job. Some companies require applicants to pass a series of written aptitude tests designed to measure their communication, analytical and general mathematical skills.

Licensing requirements for these workers vary by State. Some States have very few requirements, while others require either the completion of pre-licensing education or a satisfactory score on a licensing exam. Fulfilling the requirements for earning a voluntary professional designation may, in some cases, be substituted for completing the exam. In some States, claims adjusters employed by insurance companies can work under the company license and need not become licensed themselves. Separate or additional requirements may apply for public adjusters. For example, some States require public adjusters to file a surety bond.

Continuing education in claims is very important for claims adjusters, appraisers, examiners and investigators, because Federal and State laws and court decisions affect how claims are handled or who is covered by insurance policies. Also, examiners working on life and health claims must be familiar with new medical procedures and prescription drugs. Some States that require licensing also require a certain number of continuing education credits per year in order to renew the license. These credits can be obtained from a number of sources. Many companies offer training sessions to inform their employees of industry changes. A number of schools and associations give courses and seminars on various topics having to with claims. Correspondence courses via the Internet are making long-distance learning possible. Workers also can earn continuing education credits by writing articles for claims publications or by giving lectures and presentations. In addition, numerous adjusters and examiners choose to earn professional certifications and designations for independent recognition of their professional expertise. Although requirements for these designations vary, many entail at least 5 to 10 years of experience in the claims field and the successful completion of an examination; in addition, a certain number of continuing education credits must be earned each year to retain the designation.

For auto damage appraiser jobs, insurance companies and independent adjusting firms typically prefer to hire persons with experience as an estimator for, or manager of, an auto body repair shop. An appraiser must know how to repair vehicles in order to identify and estimate damage and technical skills are essential. While auto damage appraisers do not require a college education, most companies prefer to hire persons with formal training. Many vocational colleges offer 2-year programmes in auto body repair on how to estimate and repair damaged vehicles. Some States require auto damage appraisers to be licensed and certification also may be required or preferred. Basic computer skills are an important qualification for many auto damage appraiser positions. As with adjusters and examiners, continuing education is important because of the continual introduction of new car models and repair techniques.

Most insurance companies prefer to hire former law enforcement officers or private investigators as insurance investigators. Many experienced claims adjusters or examiners also become investigators. Licensing requirements vary among States. Most employers look for individuals with ingenuity who are persistent and assertive. Investigators should not be afraid of confrontation, should communicate well and should be able to think on their feet. Good interviewing and interrogation skills also are important and usually are acquired in earlier careers in law enforcement.

Beginning claims adjusters, appraisers, examiners and investigators work on small claims under the supervision of an experienced worker. As they learn more about claims investigation and settlement, they are assigned larger, more complex claims. Trainees are promoted as they demonstrate competence in handling assignments and progress in their coursework. Employees who demonstrate competence in claims work or administrative skills may be promoted to more responsible managerial or administrative jobs. Similarly, claims investigators may rise to supervisor or manager of the investigations department. Once they achieve a certain level of expertise, many choose to start their own independent adjusting or auto damage appraising firms.

Employment: Adjusters, appraisers, examiners and investigators held about 263,000 jobs in 2004. Only 5 percent of these jobs were held by auto damage insurance appraisers. Insurance carriers, agencies, brokerages and related industries, such as private claims adjusting companies, employed more than 8 out of 10 claims adjusters, appraisers, examiners and investigators. Relatively few adjusters, appraisers, examiners and investigators were self-employed.

Job Outlook: Employment of claims adjusters, appraisers, examiners and investigators is expected to grow about as fast as average for all occupations over the 2004–14 period. College graduates have the best opportunities. Numerous job openings also will result from the need to replace workers who transfer to other occupations or leave the labour force.

Many insurance carriers are downsizing their claims staff in an effort to contain costs. Larger companies are relying more on customer service representatives in call centres to handle the recording of the necessary details of the claim, allowing adjusters to spend more of their time investigating claims. New technology is reducing the amount of time it takes for an adjuster to complete a claim, thereby increasing the number of claims that one adjuster can handle. However, as long as more insurance policies are being sold to accommodate a growing population, there will be a need for adjusters, appraisers, examiners and investigators. Further, as the elderly population increases, there will be a greater need for health care, resulting in more health insurance claims.

Despite recent gains in productivity resulting from technological advances, these jobs are not easily automated.

Adjusters still are needed to contact policyholders, inspect damaged property and consult with experts. Although the number of claims in litigation and the number and complexity of insurance fraud cases are expected to increase over the next decade, demand for insurance investigators is not expected to grow significantly, because technology such as the Internet, which reduces the amount of time it takes to perform background checks, will allow investigators to handle more cases. Competition for investigator jobs will remain keen because the occupation attracts many qualified people, including retirees from law enforcement and military careers, as well as experienced claims adjusters and examiners who choose to get their investigator license.

As with claims adjusters, examiners and investigators, employment of auto damage appraisers should grow about as fast as the average for all occupations. Insurance companies and agents continue to sell growing numbers of auto insurance policies, leading to more claims being filed that require the attention of an auto damage appraiser.

The work of this occupation is not easily automated, because most appraisals require an onsite inspection. However, employment growth will be limited by downsizing in the insurance industry and by the implementation of new technology that is making auto damage appraisers more efficient. In addition, some insurance companies are opening their own repair facilities, which may reduce the need for auto damage appraisers.

Earnings: Earnings of claims adjusters, appraisers, examiners and investigators vary significantly. Median annual earnings were $44,220 in May 2004. The middle 50 percent earned between $33,900 and $57,410. The lowest 10 percent earned less than $27,220 and the highest 10 percent earned more than $72,620.

Many claims adjusters, especially those who work for insurance companies, receive additional bonuses or benefits as part of their job. Adjusters often are furnished a laptop computer, a cellular telephone and a company car or are reimbursed for the use of their own vehicle for business purposes.

Median annual earnings of auto damage insurance appraisers were $45,330 in May 2004. The middle 50 percent earned between $37,210 and $54,280. The lowest 10 percent earned less than $29,550 and the highest 10 percent earned more than $63,220.

Insurance Sales Agents

Significant Points: Agents increasingly offer comprehensive financial planning services, including retirement and estate planning; as a result, in addition to offering insurance policies, agents sell mutual funds, annuities and securities.

Agents must obtain a license in the States where they plan to do their selling.

Despite slower than average growth, job opportunities should be good for college graduates who have sales ability, excellent interpersonal skills and expertise in a wide range of insurance and financial services.

Successful agents often have high earnings, but many beginning agents fail to earn enough from commissions to meet their income goals and eventually transfer to other careers.

Nature of the Work: Most people have their first contact with an insurance company through an insurance sales agent. These workers help individuals, families and businesses select insurance policies that provide the best protection for their lives, health and property. Insurance sales agents who work exclusively for one insurance company are referred to as captive agents. Independent insurance agents, or brokers, represent several companies and place insurance policies for their clients with the company that offers the best rate and coverage. In either case, agents prepare reports, maintain records, seek out new clients and, in the event of a loss, help policyholders settle their insurance claims. Increasingly, some are also offering their clients financial analysis or advice on ways the clients can minimize risk.

Insurance sales agents, commonly referred to as "producers" in the insurance industry, sell one or more types of insurance, such as property and casualty, life, health, disability and long-term care. Property and casualty insurance agents sell policies that protect individuals and businesses from financial loss resulting from automobile accidents, fire, theft, storms and other events that can damage property. For businesses, property and casualty insurance can also cover injured workers' compensation, product liability claims, or medical malpractice claims.

Life insurance agents specialize in selling policies that pay beneficiaries when a policyholder dies. Depending on the policyholder's circumstances, a cash-value policy can be designed to provide retirement income, funds for the education of children, or other benefits. Life insurance agents also sell annuities that promise a retirement income. Health insurance agents sell health insurance policies that cover the costs of medical care and loss of income due to illness or injury. They also may sell dental insurance and short-term and long-term-disability insurance policies.

An increasing number of insurance sales agents are offering comprehensive financial planning services to their clients, such as retirement planning, estate planning, or assistance in setting up pension plans for businesses. As a result, many insurance agents are involved in "cross-selling" or "total account development." Besides offering insurance, these agents may become licensed to sell mutual funds, variable annuities and other securities. This practice is most common with life insurance agents who already sell annuities; however, property and casualty agents also sell financial products.

Technology has greatly affected the insurance agency, making it much more efficient and giving the agent the ability to take on more clients. Agents' computers are now linked directly to the insurance carriers via the Internet, making the tasks of obtaining price quotes and processing applications and service requests faster and easier. Computers also allow agents to be better informed about new products that the insurance carriers may be offering.

The growth of the Internet in the insurance industry is gradually altering the relationship between agent and client. In the past, agents devoted much of their time to marketing and selling products to new clients, a practice that is now changing. Increasingly, clients are obtaining insurance quotes from a company's Web site and then contacting the company directly to purchase policies. This interaction gives the client a more active role in selecting a policy at the best price, while reducing the amount of time agents spend actively seeking new clients. Because insurance sales agents also obtain many new accounts through referrals, it is important that they maintain regular contact with their clients to ensure that the clients' financial needs are being met. Developing a satisfied clientele that will recommend an agent's services to other potential customers is a key to success in this field.

Increasing competition in the insurance industry has spurred carriers and agents to find new ways to keep their clients satisfied. One solution is to increase the use of call centres, which usually are accessible to clients 24 hours a day, 7 days a week. Insurance carriers and sales agents also are hiring customer service representatives to handle routine tasks such as answering questions, making changes in policies, processing claims and selling more products to clients. The opportunity to cross-sell new products to clients will help agents' businesses grow. The use of call centres also allows agents to concentrate their efforts on seeking out new clients and maintaining relationships with old ones.

Working Conditions: Most insurance sales agents are based in small offices, from which they contact clients and provide information on the policies they sell. However, much of their time may be spent outside their offices, travelling locally to meet with clients, close sales, or investigate claims. Agents usually determine their own hours of work and often schedule evening and weekend appointments for the convenience of clients. Although most agents work a 40-hour week, some work 60 hours a week or longer. Commercial sales agents, in particular, may meet with clients during business hours and then spend evenings doing paperwork and preparing presentations to prospective clients.

Training, Other Qualifications and Advancement: For insurance sales agent jobs, most companies and independent agencies prefer to hire college graduates—especially those who have majored in business or economics. High school graduates are occasionally hired if they have proven sales ability or have been successful in other types of work. In fact, many entrants to insurance sales agent jobs transfer from other occupations. In selling commercial insurance, technical experience in a particular field can help sell policies to those in the same profession. As a result, new agents tend to be older than entrants in many other occupations.

College training may help agents grasp the technical aspects of insurance policies and the fundamentals and procedures of selling insurance. Many colleges and universities offer courses in insurance and a few schools offer a bachelor's degree in the field. College courses in finance, mathematics, accounting, economics, business law, marketing and business administration enable insurance sales agents to understand how social and economic conditions relate to the insurance industry. Courses in psychology, sociology and public speaking can prove useful in improving sales techniques. In addition, because computers provide instantaneous information on a wide variety of financial products and greatly improve agents' efficiency, familiarity with computers and popular software packages has become very important.

Insurance sales agents must obtain a license in the States where they plan to do their selling. Separate licenses are required for agents to sell life and health insurance and property and casualty insurance. In most States, licenses are issued only to applicants who complete specified pre-licensing courses and who pass State examinations covering insurance fundamentals and State insurance laws. The insurance industry is increasingly moving toward uniform State licensing standards and reciprocal licensing, allowing agents who earn a license in one State to become licensed in other States upon passing the appropriate courses and examination.

A number of organizations offer professional designation programmes that certify one's expertise in specialties such as life, health and property and casualty insurance, as well as financial consulting. For example, The National Alliance for Education and Research offers a wide variety of courses in health, life and property and casualty insurance for independent insurance agents. Although voluntary, such programmes assure clients and employers that an agent has a thorough understanding of the relevant specialty. Agents are usually required to complete a specified number of hours of continuing education to retain their designation.

Employers also are placing greater emphasis on continuing professional education as the diversity of financial products sold by insurance agents increases. It is important for insurance agents to keep up to date on issues concerning clients. Changes in tax laws, government benefits programmes and other State and Federal regulations can affect the insurance needs of clients and the way in which agents conduct business.

Agents can enhance their selling skills and broaden their knowledge of insurance and other financial services by taking courses at colleges and universities and by attending institutes, conferences and seminars sponsored by insurance organizations. Most State licensing authorities also have mandatory continuing education requirements focusing on insurance laws, consumer protection and the technical details of various insurance policies.

As the demand for financial products and financial planning increases, many insurance agents are choosing to gain the proper licensing and certification to sell securities and other financial products. Doing so, however, requires substantial study and passing an additional examination—either the Series 6 or Series 7 licensing exam, both of which are administered by the National Association of Securities Dealers (NASD). The Series 6 exam is for individuals who wish to sell only mutual funds and variable annuities, whereas the Series 7 exam is the main NASD series license that qualifies agents as general securities sales representatives.

In addition, to further demonstrate competency in the area of financial planning, many agents find it worthwhile to earn the certified financial planner or chartered financial consultant designation. The Certified Financial Planner credential issued by the Certified Financial Planner Board of Standards, requires relevant experience, completion of education requirements, passing a comprehensive examination and adherence to an enforceable code of ethics. The CFP exams test the candidate's knowledge of the financial planning process, insurance and risk management, employee benefits planning, taxes and retirement planning and investment and estate planning. The Chartered Financial Consultant (ChFC) designation, issued by the American College in Bryn Mawr, Pennsylvania, which requires experience and the completion of an eight-course programme of study. The CFP and ChFC designation and other professional designations have continuing education requirements.

Insurance sales agents should be flexible, enthusiastic, confident, disciplined, hard working and willing to solve problems. They should communicate effectively and inspire customer confidence. Because they usually work without supervision, sales agents must be able to plan their time well and have the initiative to locate new clients.

An insurance sales agent who shows ability and leadership may become a sales manager in a local office. A few advance to agency superintendent or executive positions. However, many who have built up a good clientele prefer to remain in sales work. Some—particularly in the property and casualty field—establish their own independent agencies or brokerage firms.

Employment: Insurance sales agents held about 400,000 jobs in 2004. Most insurance sales agents employed in wage and salary positions work for insurance agencies and brokerages. A decreasing number work directly for insurance carriers. Although most insurance agents specialize in life and health insurance or property and casualty insurance, a growing number of "multiline" agents sell all lines of insurance. A small number of agents work for banks and securities brokerages as a result of the increasing integration of finance and insurance industries. Approximately 1 out of 4 insurance sales agents is self-employed.

Insurance sales agents are employed throughout the country, but most work in or near large urban centres. Some are employed in the headquarters of insurance companies, but the majority work out of local offices or independent agencies.

Job Outlook: Although employment of insurance sales agents is expected to grow more slowly than average for all occupations through 2014, opportunities will be favourable for college graduates who have sales ability, excellent interpersonal skills and expertise in a wide range of insurance and financial services. Multilingual agents also should be in high demand because they can serve a wider range of customers.

Insurance language tends to be quite technical, so it is important for insurance sales agents to have a firm understanding of relevant technical and legal terms. Many beginning agents fail to earn enough from commissions to meet their income goals and eventually transfer to other careers. Most job openings are likely to result from the need to replace agents who leave the occupation or retire. A large number of agents are expected to retire over the next decade.

Future demand for insurance sales agents depends largely on the volume of sales of insurance and other financial products. Sales of health insurance and long-term-care insurance are expected to rise sharply as the population ages. In addition, a growing population will increase demand for insurance for automobiles, homes and high-priced valuables and equipment. As new businesses emerge and existing firms expand their insurance coverage, sales of commercial insurance also should increase, including coverage such as product liability, workers' compensation, employee benefits and pollution liability insurance. Employment of agents will not keep up with the rising level of insurance sales, however. Many insurance carriers are trying to contain costs. As a result, many are shedding their captive agents—those agents working directly for insurance carriers—and are relying more on independent agents or direct marketing through the mail, by phone, or on the Internet.

Agents who incorporate new technology into their existing businesses will remain competitive. Agents who use the Internet to market their products will reach a broader client base and expand their businesses, but because most clients value their relationship with their agent, the Internet should not threaten jobs, given that many individuals still prefer discussing their policies directly with their agents, rather than through a computer. Also, the automation of policy and claims processing is allowing insurance agents to take on more clients.

Agents may face increased competition from traditional securities brokers and bankers as they begin to sell insurance policies. Because of increasing consolidation among insurance companies, banks and brokerage firms and due to increasing demands from clients for more comprehensive financial planning, insurance sales agents will need to expand the products and services they offer.

Agents who offer better customer service also will remain competitive. Call centres are another important way carriers and agents are offering better service to customers, because such centres provide greater access to their policies and more prompt services.

Insurance and investments are becoming more complex and many people and businesses lack the time and expertise to buy insurance without the advice of an agent. Moreover, most individuals and businesses consider insurance a necessity, regardless of economic conditions. Therefore, agents are not likely to face unemployment because of a recession.

Earnings: The median annual earnings of wage and salary insurance sales agents were $41,720 in May 2004. The middle 50 percent earned between $29,980 and $66,160. The lowest 10 percent had earnings of $23,170 or less, while the highest 10 percent earned more than $108,800. Median annual earnings in May 2004 in the two industries employing the largest number of insurance sales agents were $42,010 for insurance carriers and $41,840 for agencies, brokerages and other insurance related activities.

Many independent agents are paid by commission only, whereas sales workers who are employees of an agency or an insurance carrier may be paid in one of three ways—salary only, salary plus commission, or salary plus bonus. In general, commissions are the most common form of compensation, especially for experienced agents. The amount of the commission depends on the type and amount of insurance sold and on whether the transaction is a new policy or a renewal. Bonuses usually are awarded when agents meet their sales goals or when an agency meets its profit goals. Some agents involved with financial planning receive a fee for their services, rather than a commission. Company-paid benefits to insurance sales agents usually include continuing education, training to qualify for licensing, group insurance plans, office space and clerical support services. Some companies also may pay for automobile and transportation expenses, attendance at conventions and meetings, promotion and marketing expenses and retirement plans. Independent agents working for insurance agencies receive fewer benefits, but their commissions may be higher to help them pay for marketing and other expenses.

Insurance Broker

Insurance brokers are independent advisers, helping clients to choose the insurance product or products most appropriate to their present and/or future needs. Also known as intermediaries, they are the link between insurance companies and customers. Brokers use their knowledge and experience to assess a client's risk profile and find appropriate policies from over several hundred insurers in the industry, searching for the most comprehensive cover at the most competitive price.

Brokers deal with a great range of cases, from simple ones, such as car insurance, where an immediate quotation can be given, to relatively complex cases. In the case of commercial insurance, they may need to provide reports to insurance underwriters, carry out surveys and negotiate with underwriters for cover. This is a highly regulated industry and insurance brokers are required to put the interests of their client first. They may also help clients resolve claims, processing paperwork and negotiating settlements with the insurer. This can lead into a specialised role as a claims broker.

Entry Level: People join broking firms with a variety of different academic backgrounds. Many organisations prefer two A levels/three H grades plus two GCSEs/S grades (A-C/1-3) in English and maths, although there are no formal entry requirements for insurance brokers. Greater emphasis is placed on individual characteristics, particularly communication.

If you choose to take a degree, one of the following subjects might increase your chances: accounting/finance, business/ management, economics, mathematics or statistics.

Making the Grade: Training is usually undertaken on the job, with trainees working under the supervision of a senior broker or team leader. Large brokers have structured training schemes, giving new entrants experience of different areas of work over a period of 18 months to two years. Working as a Lloyd's broker requires passing the Lloyd's Introductory Test within 15 months of starting work. Study can be undertaken in-house or by public courses.

The Chartered Insurance Institute (CII) and British Insurance Brokers Association run courses in insurance broking and other relevant subjects, such as information technology and marketing, some of which may be linked to qualifications at NVQ/SVQ Levels 2 and 3. The CII courses have been carefully designed to provide insurance brokers with a recognised qualification - from the most basic level through to Fellowship of the Institute. Studying is provided through day release, evening classes or distance learning.

The Institute of Financial Services provides additional qualifications, including the Certificate of Regulated General Insurance. As a your career develops, progression might be possible into a managerial position, managing a team of brokers or even several branches of a division.

Personal Qualities: Personal attributes are important for a career in insurance broking. Some employers prefer applicants to be more mature with relevant experience, as this is a service driven industry.

To succeed as an insurance broker, you must be scrupulously honest and discreet, both with clients and with other professionals. You would need excellent communication and IT skills, together with the ability to gather and absorb information quickly.

You must be numerate in order to understand and work with statistics and you must keep up to date with changes in the insurance market.

Looking Ahead: Broking firms vary widely in size and type. The largest brokers tend to be international companies, negotiating cover on a global basis. Their clients can range from individuals to small businesses, right up to multinational companies with global offices and assets worth millions of pounds.

The larger brokers generally have different divisions with teams specialising in different risks, including commercial property, marine, aviation, political risks and casualty. Smaller brokers often require a more general knowledge of products and services, enabling them to act as a surveyor, loss adjuster, underwriter, negotiator and sales adviser. Some also service dedicated sectors, such as charities or the public sector.

Insurance broking can be quite a volatile sector of employment, evolving constantly through acquisitions and mergers. Legislative developments and changes in the economy can place specialist brokers in high demand, particularly in areas like political risk, construction, claims and commercial property insurance.

Currently, there is a greater need for specialisation and technical competence, creating better opportunities for graduates with the required skills.

Employment with the larger brokers tends to be centred near investment institutions in the larger cities, although brokers are also employed in regional offices. Smaller practices are spread countrywide. Prospects are good for those keen to advance, although competition for graduate placements can be high.

Insurance Agent

Insurance agents sell insurance packages to the public. They visit potential clients in their homes to sell life assurance and general or fire insurance policies. They collect premium payments as they fall due and deal with any enquiries.

Work Activities: Insurance provides a service to customers who wish to be protected from loss caused by events such as fire, theft, accident or illness. The customer pays a regular premium and receives a written policy that sets out the conditions under which an insurance company pays compensation.

Insurance agents sell insurance packages direct to the public. They operate as home service agents, direct selling representatives or financial advisers. Home service agents visit potential clients in their homes to sell general or fire insurance packages. The agent identifies the client's insurance needs, explains policy terms and conditions and tries to sell a policy. The agent collects premium payments as they fall due and deals with any queries. Financial advisers must be registered by their companies with the Financial Services Authority to sell life assurance or other financial packages. Direct selling representatives sell packages by telephone or post or through call-centre operations.

An insurance agent may also act as a new business or agency inspector linking an insurance company with brokers, estate agents and building societies who also promote and sell their policies.

Personal Qualities and Skills: To become an agent you would usually have experience of office based insurance work. Knowledge of insurance is mostly gained on the job. Skills of persuasion are important as most agents depend on commission to supplement their salaries.

Inspectors have experience of work in an insurance office and must obtain the Chartered Insurance Institute's (CII) Associateship qualification as they also need to be knowledgeable about financial planning, estate duty and taxation. Financial advisers must pass the Financial Planning Certificate examinations of the CII.

Pay and Opportunities: Salaries vary widely and some agents work on commission only or basic pay plus commission. The pay rates given below are approximate. Insurance agents with relevant qualifications earn in the range of £16,500 - £18,500 a year, rising to £30,000 - £39,500. Higher earners can make around £43,000 a year.

Working hours may be during the day, in the evening and at weekends to meet clients' needs.

Employers are life assurance companies throughout the UK. Some agents are self-employed.

The following information is sourced from government statistics. The government's definition of types of job is slightly different to that used in this programme. For this type of job, the most relevant Government-defined occupation is 'Finance and investment analysts/advisers'.

In 2001 there were 10,400 people working as 'Finance and investment analysts/advisers' in Scotland. 48 in every 10,000 employees working in Scotland were employed as 'Finance and investment analysts/advisers'.

Entry Routes and Training: You can enter the insurance business from a wide variety of backgrounds. Most employers prefer to recruit older applicants with relevant work experience, in particular in office based insurance work. Graduates of all types enter the industry, but it is also open to non-graduates.

Degrees in Finance are available. Some Business Studies degree courses offer options in insurance. Some institutions offer degree courses in Financial Management or Money, Banking and Finance.

The Chartered Institute of Insurance (CII) offers qualifications in general insurance. These include the Introductory Award in Insurance, Certificate in Insurance, Diploma in Insurance, Advanced Diploma in Insurance and the Fellowship of the CII. These can be studied by day or block release classes, evening classes or through distance learning.

There is an SVQ Insurance General and Intermediaries at level 3.

Qualifications: A good standard of literacy and numeracy are needed for this career. Standard Grades in English and Maths are an advantage. It is usual to have some experience, for example, in office based insurance work.

Adult Opportunities: Most insurance agents and direct selling staff are at least in their mid-to-late 30s. Applicants with relevant experience, for example, in office-based insurance work, have an advantage.

Previous retail experience, either shop-based, by telephone or door-to-door is advantageous. Other customer service work experience, especially dealing with financial products, is useful.

- 20% of people in occupations such as insurance sales adviser are self-employed.
- 9% work part-time.
- 13% have flexible hours.

Insurance Claims Inspector

Insurance claims inspectors are employed by insurance underwriters to investigate claims made by policy holders. They check that each claim is covered by the terms and conditions of the policy and investigate the cause of loss or damage.

Work Activities: Insurance provides a service to customers who wish to be protected from loss caused by events such as fire, theft, accident or illness. The customer pays a regular premium and receives a written policy that sets out the conditions under which an insurance company pays compensation.

Insurance claims assessors, sometimes known as claims inspectors or officials, work for insurance underwriters and are responsible for investigating claims submitted by policyholders. They check that each claim is covered by the terms and conditions of the policy and investigate the cause of loss or damage. The assessor might have to interview claimants who will be upset, shocked or distressed, especially if death or injury are involved. Consequently the assessor must be tactful, sympathetic and patient.

The assessor may need to inspect damaged buildings or vehicles in order to gather the evidence needed to determine a settlement. They may find evidence in more complicated cases by talking to solicitors, the police and eye-witnesses. In straightforward claims, agreement between an insurance company and a claimant may be reached quickly.

However, even after they have decided whether the insurance company should pay out, it can take a long time to decide what the settlement sum should be. Throughout their investigations, assessors must be aware that the claim could be fraudulent.

Very complicated claims require the intervention of an independent loss adjuster who acts as an intermediary between insurer and claimant. A loss adjuster performs the same function as an insurance claims assessor but is employed by a company of loss adjusters rather than an insurance company.

Claims are submitted as a result of personal accident, loss of goods in transit, theft, loss of profits, fire, flood and storm damage. Large scale disasters such as floods generate a huge number of claims, all requiring prompt attention. Some insurance firms and many assessors and loss adjusters specialise in a particular type of insurance such as aviation, motor or marine.

Personal Qualities and Skills: To be a claims assessor you need to be thorough and methodical. Communication skills are essential as assessors advise and interview claimants and negotiate appropriate settlements. Integrity and trustworthiness are necessary to win the confidence of claimants. When interviewing claimants who are upset, shocked or distressed you must show tact, sympathy and patience.

Pay and Opportunities: The pay rates given below are approximate. Insurance claims inspectors earn in the range of £18,000 - £23,000 a year, rising to around £30,500 - £43,000. Higher earners can make around £65,000 a year. Other benefits may include low-rate mortgages, medical insurance and life and pension cover.

Assessors usually work 35 hours Monday to Friday. Occasional evening/weekend work may be required.

Opportunities occur with insurance companies throughout the UK. The following information is sourced from government statistics. The government's definition of types of job is slightly different to that used in this programme. For this type of job, the most relevant Government-defined occupation is 'Estimators, valuers and assessors'.

In 2001 there were 4,600 people working as 'Estimators, valuers and assessors' in Scotland. 21 in every 10,000 employees working in Scotland were employed as 'Estimators, valuers and assessors'.

Entry Routes and Training: Insurance claims assessors may study for the professional examinations of the Chartered Insurance Institute or the Chartered Institute of Loss Adjusters. Many prospective assessors start training after Highers or Higher National Certificate/Higher National Diploma qualifications and, with these qualifications, you can register for the Chartered Insurance Institute's Advanced Diploma qualifications and become an Associate member of the CII. Most employers also recruit graduates from a wide range of academic subjects.

Degrees in insurance studies are available. Some degree and HND/HNC Business Studies courses include insurance options.

A number of Insurance SVQs are available at levels 2 and 3. Modern Apprenticeships, leading to SVQ level 3, may be available in your area.

Qualifications: There are no set entry requirements for this job, as requirements vary from employer to employer. Entry is possible at several levels.

For direct entry to the Chartered Insurance Institute (CII) Advanced Diploma qualification the minimum requirement is 3 Highers (A-C) plus Standard Grades in 2 other subjects, including English and Maths. Applicants with appropriate equivalent qualifications are also considered.

Entry to the Diploma in Insurance requires 4 Standard Grades or equivalent qualifications if you are under 21 years of age.

Entry to this job is also common for those with higher qualifications such as Higher National Certificates/Higher National Diplomas or degrees.

Adult Opportunities: A background in financial or business-related work is an advantage. A clean current driving licence is usually necessary.

Suitable applicants aged 21 or over may do a college or university Access course. No formal qualifications are required to enter an Access course, but you should check individual course details. They lead to relevant degree/HND courses.

Some employers recruit graduates with a business-related (including insurance) or numerate degree.

The Chartered Insurance Institute (CII) may relax the usual academic entrance requirements for adults who wish to take their exams.

Distance learning is available from the CII for professional qualifications.

- 8% of people in occupations such as insurance claims inspector work part-time.
- 22% have flexible hours.

Insurance Clerk

Insurance clerks carry out routine clerical duties in an insurance office. In small offices they perform a range of duties, while in larger offices they may specialise.

Work Activities: Insurance provides a service to customers who wish to be protected from loss caused by events such as fire, theft, accident or illness. The customer pays a regular premium and receives a written policy that sets out the conditions under which an insurance company pays compensation. Insurance clerks carry out clerical duties such as filing, recording and checking information within insurance companies. In a small, high street office they carry out a range of clerical tasks, including dealing with the public over the telephone or face-to-face at a counter. In large organisations clerks may specialise in one area after their initial training. Wherever they work, the job is likely to involve paperwork and the use of computers.

Clerks may work in any department of an insurance company. The underwriting department deals with the terms and conditions of insurance policies. The claims department checks that claims are valid. The broking department assesses clients' insurance requirements. Finally, the processing department issues policies and collects premiums arranged by underwriters.

Personal Qualities and Skills: You'll need good communication skills to be an insurance clerk, as well as accuracy in the use of numbers and a methodical approach to work. You'll also need organisational skills and must be prepared to use computers, calculators, photocopiers and other types of electronic office equipment.

Pay and Opportunities: The pay rates given below are approximate. Insurance clerks earn in the range of £12,000 - £14,500 a year, rising to £17,000 - £23,500 a year. Other benefits may include low-rate mortgages, medical insurance and life and pension cover.

Insurance clerks usually work 35 hours Monday to Friday. Opportunities occur with insurance companies throughout the UK. The following information is sourced from government statistics. The government's definition of types of job is slightly different to that used in this programme. For this type of job, the most relevant Government-defined occupation is 'Pensions and insurance clerks'.

In 2001 there were 8,400 people working as 'Pensions and insurance clerks' in Scotland. 39 in every 10,000 employees working in Scotland were employed as 'Pensions and insurance clerks'.

Entry Routes and Training: Training is carried out on-the-job. Career progression is possible through the professional examinations of the Chartered Insurance Institute (CII). These include the CII Insurance Foundation Certificate and the Certificate of Insurance Practice.

An SVQ in Insurance General and Intermediaries is available at level 3. Modern Apprenticeships, leading to SVQ level 3, may be available in your area.

Qualifications: Most employers require a good general education and some Standard Grades are usually an advantage—English and Maths are useful subjects.

Adult Opportunities: Applicants with previous experience of financial or clerical work, for example, in a finance or accounts department, have an advantage.

Modern Apprenticeships may be available in some areas.

Distance learning is available from the Chartered Institute of Insurance for the Certificate in Insurance Practice.

- 16% of people in occupations such as insurance administration assistant work part-time.
- 27% have flexible hours.
- 3% of employees work on a temporary basis.

Insurance Loss Adjuster

Insurance loss adjusters are responsible for investigating claims submitted by policy holders. They usually become involved in complicated claims and act as a negotiator between insurers and claimants.

Work Activities: Insurance provides a service to customers who wish to be protected from loss caused by events such as fire, theft, accident or illness. The customer pays a regular premium and receives a written policy that sets out the conditions under which an insurance company pays compensation.

Insurance loss adjusters investigate claims submitted by policyholders as a result of personal accident, loss of goods in transit, theft, fire, flood and storm damage. They usually become involved in the investigation of particularly complicated claims and act as an intermediary between insurers and claimants. A large-scale incident such as a flood may generate a sudden rush of claims, all requiring prompt action. Many loss adjusters specialise in a particular type of insurance, such as property or motor insurance, for example.

Loss adjusters check that the terms and conditions of the policy cover each claim and investigate the cause of loss or damage. They may occasionally need to interview claimants who are distressed or upset.

A loss adjuster presents a report to insurers who then agree a suitable settlement with the claimant. Should either party dispute the findings of the report, negotiations continue until a settlement is reached.

If a loss adjuster suspects a claim is fraudulent, they may have to carry out a further detailed investigation. In some cases this might require the involvement of the police, private investigators and, in exceptional cases, forensic experts.

Personal Qualities and Skills: You'll need to be tactful, sympathetic and patient to work as a loss adjuster. You must also be thorough, observant and methodical. Communication skills are important as you will advise and interview claimants and negotiate settlements. Integrity is important and loss adjusters should also be fair and unbiased when dealing with claims.

Good written skills are necessary for report writing. A basic knowledge of accounts and book-keeping is also helpful.

Pay and Opportunities: Salaries for loss adjusters depend on qualifications and experience. The pay rates given below are approximate. Loss adjusters earn in the range of £18,000 - £23,000 a year, rising to around £30,500 - £43,000. Higher earners can make around £65,000 a year.

Loss adjusters usually work 35 hours, Monday to Friday, but often work late and at weekends in response to call-outs.

Employment is with specialist loss adjusting firms throughout the UK. Some work independently as consultants. Work in other countries is possible.

The following information is sourced from government statistics. The government's definition of types of job is slightly different to that used in this programme. For this type of job, the most relevant Government-defined occupation is 'Estimators, valuers and assessors'.

In 2001 there were 4,600 people working as 'Estimators, valuers and assessors' in Scotland. 21 in every 10,000 employees working in Scotland were employed as 'Estimators, valuers and assessors'.

Entry Routes and Training: If you are registering as a student member of the Chartered Institute of Loss Adjusters (CILA), you will need to have a professional qualification in a relevant subject. Examples are insurance, accountancy, law, engineering or surveying. You'll also need to have two years' experience with a firm of chartered loss adjusters before being eligible to sit the Institute's examinations.

The majority of entrants have professional qualifications and relevant work experience, although some do enter directly from school or college with Highers (or equivalent) or a degree. To enter without a relevant qualification you would generally begin work with a company of loss adjusters and study for the qualifications of the Chartered Insurance Institute (CII). Students who pass the CII's examinations may go on to study for the CILA's qualifications.

Training is usually provided on the job. Those with professional qualifications take three to four years to study for CILA's examinations. But it can take up to six or seven years to qualify. Subjects include principles and practice of insurance in connection to loss adjusting, property claims, accident and liability claims and commercial claims.

It is also possible to start working in an insurance company as a clerk and study for further qualifications. Once these have been gained, you may move onto a loss adjusting firm.

A number of Insurance SVQs are available at levels 2 and 3.

Qualifications: For direct entry to the Chartered Insurance Institute (CII) Associateship examinations, the minimum requirement is 3 Highers plus 2 Standard Grades. English is required at either level.

Entry to this job is also common for those with higher qualifications such as Higher National Diplomas or degrees.

Applicants with relevant equivalent qualifications are also considered. Candidates with a professional qualification in a relevant subject such as Accountancy, Law or Engineering may register directly with the Chartered Institute of Loss Adjusters.

Adult Opportunities: Applicants with a background in surveying, engineering, law or accountancy plus professional qualifications have an advantage.

Previous experience in insurance, for example, in administration, is useful. A clean current driving licence is often necessary.

Relevant distance learning courses are available from The Chartered Insurance Institute (CII), which may relax the normal academic requirements for adults who wish to take their exams.

- 11% of people in occupations such as insurance loss adjuster are self-employed.
- 8% work part-time.
- 22% have flexible hours.

Insurance Surveyor

Insurance surveyors provide underwriters with detailed technical reports on the risks involved in a request for insurance cover. Reports outline any aspects which might affect the insurance premium.

Work Activities: Insurance provides a service to customers who wish to be protected from loss caused by events such as fire, theft, accident or illness. The customer pays a regular premium and receives a written policy that sets out the conditions under which an insurance company pays compensation.

Most insurance surveyors work for insurance companies, providing underwriters with detailed technical reports on the risks involved in a particular request for insurance cover. Surveyors normally inspect premises to obtain information on factors such as the construction of buildings or the work processes that take place in a location. They may also look at factors such as the condition of machinery, the possibility of fire or flood damage and the current extent of safety precautions.

An insurance surveyor's report outlines any aspects that may affect the insurance premium charged by an underwriter. A surveyor's report may also suggest ways in which risks can be minimised and unsatisfactory factors improved. This could involve installing smoke detectors and sprinkler systems in case of fire and burglar alarms in case of theft.

The insurance surveyor recommends whether insurers should accept any risk and offer insurance cover and whether any conditions should be attached to that cover. Surveyors can specialise in different areas, for example engineering or liability.

Personal Qualities and Skills: As an insurance surveyor you'll need good information gathering and report writing skills. You need a methodical approach to work and a high level of technical expertise. Insurance surveyors need to have a current driving licence.

Pay and Opportunities: Salaries for insurance surveyors vary depending on qualifications and experience. The pay rates given below are approximate. Insurance surveyors earn in the range of £24,000 - £32,500 a year, rising to £45,000 - £72,500 a year. Higher earners can make around £105,000 a year

Surveyors normally work 35 hours Monday to Friday. However, depending on the post, they may work flexible hours, evenings and weekends.

Opportunities occur with insurance companies throughout the UK and with specialist engineering insurance companies. There may be opportunities to work in other countries, for example, for a UK insurer.

The following information is sourced from government statistics. The government's definition of types of job is slightly different to that used in this programme. For this type of job, the most relevant Government-defined occupation is 'Estimators, valuers and assessors'.

In 2001 there were 4,600 people working as 'Estimators, valuers and assessors' in Scotland. 21 in every 10,000 employees working in Scotland were employed as 'Estimators, valuers and assessors'.

Entry Routes and Training: Insurance surveyors are often appointed from the ranks of experienced insurance staff who have developed an interest in this field.

Insurance surveyors are qualify as an Associate of the Chartered Insurance Institute (ACII), by studying for the Advanced Diploma in Insurance. This can be through day or block release, evening classes or by distance learning.

The Institute of Risk Management offers the Certificate and Diploma in Risk Management through distance learning.

Employers also recruit graduates, particularly if your degree is in science or engineering. There are a number of degrees and postgraduate courses in risk management available.

An SVQ in Insurance General and Intermediaries is available at level 3.

Modern Apprenticeships, leading to SVQ level 3, may be available in your area.

Qualifications: It is usual to have experience in a related area, for example in insurance underwriting, engineering, architecture or science.

Most employers would prefer candidates to have at least 3 Highers and 2 Standard Grades, including English and Maths, or equivalent qualifications.

Many employers prefer to recruit those who have a degree. No specific degree subject is required, but degrees in science or technology, insurance or risk management may be particularly helpful. Candidates who hope to specialise in engineering surveying may have to have an engineering degree. To enter a degree course you need to have a minimum of 3 Highers and 2 Standard Grades, including English and maths. Many courses will ask for higher entry qualifications than the minimum.

Adult Opportunities: Entry is unlikely before the age of about 25.

Many insurance surveyors are recruited internally from staff in underwriting departments.

Adults with qualifications such as those in engineering, civil engineering, architecture or science can enter specialist areas of insurance surveying.

Suitable applicants aged 21 or over may do a college or university Access course. No formal qualifications are required to enter an Access course, but you should check individual course details. They lead to relevant degree/HND courses.

Some employers recruit graduates, especially those with a science, engineering or other numerate degree.

The Chartered Insurance Institute may relax the usual academic entrance requirement for adults who wish to take their exams.

- 7% of people in occupations such as insurance surveyor are self-employed.
- 8% work part-time.
- 22% have flexible hours.

Bibliography

Albarran, Alan B. and Gregory G. Pitts: *The Radio Broadcasting Industry*, Boston, Allyn and Bacon, 2001.

Albrecht, Ulrich: *A Short Research Guide on Arms and Armed Forces*, New York, Facts on File, 1980.

Alexander, James: *Internships in Communications, Ames*, Iowa State University Press, 1995.

Allman, Paul: *Careers in Video and Digital Video*, New York: Rosen, 2001.

Anders, Peter: *Envisioning Cyberspace*, New York, McGraw-Hill, 1999.

Arkin, William M.: *Research Guide to Current Military and Strategic Affairs*, Washington, Institute for Policy Studies, 1981.

Baehr, H. and Gary A.: *Turning In On: A Reader in Women and Media*, London, Arnold, 1996.

Ball, Victoria Kloss: *Opportunities in Interior Design and Decorating Careers*, Chicago, VGM Career Horizons, 2002.

Barnouw, Erik: *A Tower in Babel: the History of Broadcasting in the United States to 1933*, New York, Oxford University Press, 1966.

Baucom, Alfred H.: *Hospitality Design for the Graying Generation: Meeting the Needs of a Growing Market*, New York, Wiley, 1996.

Baxter, John: *Australian Cinema*, Sydney, Pacific Books, 1970.

Beaman, Jim: *Interviewing for Radio*, New York, Routledge, 2000.

Berkowitz, Ira: *Vault Career Guide to Advertising*, New York, Vault, 2004.

Bertrand, Ina and Diane Collins: *Government and Film in Australia*, Sydney, Currency Press, 1981.

Bliss, Edward and James L. Hoyt: *Writing News for Broadcast*, New York, Columbia University Press, 1994.

Boella, Michael John: *Principles of Hospitality Law*, London, Cassell, 1999.

Bone, Jan, & Ana Fernandez: *Opportunities in Film Careers*, New York, VGM Career Books, 2004.

Bowers, C. A.: *The Cultural Dimension of Educational Computing: Understanding the Non-neutrality of Technology*, New York, Teachers' College Press; 1988.

Boyd, Andrew: *Broadcast Journalism: Techniques of Radio and TV News*, Woburn, Focal Press, 2001.

Brown, Douglas Robert: *The Restaurant Managers Handbook: How to Set Up, Operate, and Manage a Financially Successful Restaurant.* Lauderhill, Atlantic Pub., 1991.

Brown, James and Quaal Ward: *Radio-Television-Cable Management*, New York, McGraw Hill, 1998.

Bryant, Jennings: *Television and the American Family*, Hillsdale, Lawrence Erlbaum, 1990.

Buckingham, David: *Young People and the Media*, New York, Manchester University Press, 1993.

Buckner, Robert W.: *Site Selection: New Advancements in Methods and Technology*, New York, Lebhar-Friedman Books, 1998.

Caldwell, J. T.: *Electronic Media and Technoculture*, New Brusnwick, Rutgers University Press, 2000.

Careers in Focus: *Photography*, New York, Ferguson, 2004.

Carmouche, Rita: *Behavioural Studies in Hospitality Management*, New York, Chapman & Hall, 1995.

Carroll, Victoria: *Writing News for Television*, Ames, Iowa State University Press, 1997.

Cassiday, Doris, and Bruce Cassiday: *Careers in the Beauty Industry*, New York, Franklin Watts, 1978.

Clark, Mona: *Interpersonal Skills for Hospitality Managers*, London, Chapman Hill, 1995.

Clark, Roy Peter: *A Journalist Teaches Young Writers*, Portsmouth, Heinemann, 1987.

Cockburn, C. and Ormrod, S.: *Gender and Technology in the Making*, London, Sage, 1993.

Cohler, David Keith: *Broadcast Newswriting*, Englewood Cliffs, Prentice Hall, 1990.

Cracknell, H. L.: *Escoffier: The Complete Guide to the Art of Modern Cookery*, New York, John Wiley, 1979.

Craig, James: *Graphic Design Career Guide*, New York, Watson-Guptill, 1992.

Crawford, Tad: *Starting Your Career As a Freelance Photographer*, New York, Allworth Press, 2003.

Crouse, Chuck: *Reporting for Radio*, Chicago, Bonus Books, 1998.

Davidson, M. J. and Cooper, C. L.: *Women and Information Technology*, New York, John Wiley & Sons, 1987.

Delaney, Chuck: *Photography Your Way*, New York, Allworth Press, 2005.

Dennis, Everette E. and Edward C. Pease: *Children and the Media*, New Brunswick, Transaction Publishers, 1996.

Diamond, S. Taylor's Way: *Women, Cultures and Technology*, New York: Routledge; 1997.

Donald, Ralph and Thomas Spann: *Fundamentals of Television Production*, Ames, Iowa State University Press, 2000.

Dornenburg, Andrew: *Culinary Artistry*, New York, John Wiley & Sons, 1996.

Douglas, George H.: *The Early Days of Radio Broadcasting*, Jefferson, NC: McFarland, 1987.

Easlea, B.: *Fathering the Unthinkable: Masculinity, Scientists and the Nuclear Arms Race*, London, Pluto Press, 1982.

Ellis, Elmo: *Opportunities in Broadcasting Careers*, Chicago, VGM Career Books, 2005.

Faulkner, W. and Arnold, E.: *Smothered by Invention: Technology in Women's Lives*, London, Pluto Press, 1985.

Fensch, Thomas: *Television News Anchors*, Jefferson, McFarland, 1993.

Field, Shelly: *Career Opportunities in Advertising and Public Relations*, New York, Ferguson, 2006.

Foster, Timothy R. V.: *How to Succeed As an Independent Consultant*, London: Kogan, Page, 2002.

Fox Keller, E.: *Reflections on Gender and Science*, New Haven, Yale University Press, 1985.

Gardner, Garth: *Careers in Computer Graphics and Animation*, Fairfax, GGC, 2001.

Gibbs, Jenny: *Interior Design*, New York, H. N. Abrams, 2005.

Go, Frank M.: *Human Resource Management in the Hospitality Industry*, New York, Wiley, 1996.

Goldfarb, Roz: *Careers by Design*, New York, Allworth Press, 2001.

Gordon, Sandra R.: *Great Jobs for Film Majors*, Chicago, VGM Career Books, 2004.

Graham, Duane: *The Remarkable Story of Otto Graham*, Wayne, Immortal Investments Publishing, 2004.

Green, E. and Adam, A. Virtual Gender: *Technology, Consumption, and Identity*, New York, Routledge, 2001.

Greenman, Robert: *The Adviser's Companion*, New York, Columbia Scholastic Press Association, 1991.

Griffiths, D.: *The Exclusion of Women from Technology*, London, Pluto Press, 1985.

Hall, Ken G.: *Australian Film: the Inside Story*, Sydney, Summit Books, 1980.

Hewitt, John: *Airwords: Writing for Broadcast News, Mountain View*, Oxford, Mayfield Pub. Company, 2002.

Higham, Robin: *A Guide to the Sources of United States Military History*, Hamden, Archon Books, 1975.

Hilliard, Robert L. and Michael C. Keith: *The Broadcast Century and Beyond*, Boston: Focal Press, 2001.

Hinkin, Timothy R.: *Cases in Hospitality Management: A Critical Incident Approach*, New York, Wiley, 1995.

Holloway, J. C. : *Towards a Core Curriculum for Tourism: A Discussion Paper*, London, The National Liaison Group for Higher Education in Tourism, 1995.

Horstede, G.: *Cultures and Organizations: Software of the Mind*, London, McGraw-Hill Book Company, 1991.

Hungerland, Buff: *Marketing Your Creative Portfolio*, Upper Saddle River, Prentice Hall, 2003

Jain, S. C.: *Women and Technology*, Jaipur, Rawat Publications, 1985.

Jefferson, Michael: *Breaking into Graphic Design*, New York, Allworth Press, 2005.

Jensen, Clayne R.: *Opportunities in Recreation and Leisure Careers*, Lincolnwood, VGM Career Horizons, 2000.

Jones, Sue Jenklyn: *Fashion Design*, New York, Watson-Guptill, 2002.

Kieffer, John: *The Photographer's Assistant*, New York, Allworth, 2001.

Kirkham, P.: *The Gendered Object*, Manchester, Manchester University Press, 1996.

Kissane, Sharon F.: *Career Success for People with Physical Disabilities*, Lincolnwood, VGM Career Horizons, 1997.

Kring, Robin: *Party Creations: Book of Theme Event Design*, Denver, Clear Creek Pub., 1993.

Kurzweil, R.: *The Age of Spiritual Machines*, New York, Viking, 1999.

Lavery, P.: *Tourism Marketing and Management Handbook*, New York, Prentice Hall, 1989.

Lewis, Robert C.: *Cases in Hospitality Marketing and Management*, New York, John Wiley, 1997.

MacCloskey, Monro: *How to Qualify for the Service Academies*, New York, Richards Rosen Press, 1964.

Maclay, Edgar Stanton: *A History of the United States Navy 1771-1893*, New York, Appleton Co., 1894.

Mauro, Lucia: *Careers for Fashion Plates and Other Trendsetters*, Chicago, VGM Career Horizons, 2003.

McGuire-Lytle, Erin: *Careers in Graphic Arts and Computer Graphics*, New York, Rosen, 1999.

Miller, Samuel D.: *An Aerospace Bibliography*, Washington. Office of Air Force History, 1978.

Mitchell, Leslie Scott: *Freelancing for Television and Radio*, London; Routledge, 2005.

Mogel, Leonard: *Creating Your Career in Communications and Entertainment*, Sewickley, GATF Press, 1998.

Noronha, Shonan F. R.: *Opportunities in Television and Video Careers*, Chicago: VGM Career Books, 2003.

Orlik, Peter B.: *Career Perspectives in Electronic Media*, Ames, Blackwell Pub., 2004.

Packard, Sidney: *The Fashion Business: Dynamics and Careers*, New York, Holt, Rinehart, and Winston, 1983.

Parks, Peggy J.: *The News Media*, San Diego, Lucent Books, 2002.

Paullin, C.O.: *The Navy of the American Revolution*, Cleveland, The Burrows Brothers Co., 1906.

Perna, Rita: *Fashion Forecasting*, New York, Fairchild Publications, 1987.

Rachlis, Eugene: *The Story of the U.S. Coast Guard*, New York, Random House, 1961.

Reis, Ronald A.: *Careers in Art and Graphic Design*, Hauppage, Barrons, 2001.

Rocha, Tony L.: *Careers in Magazine Publishing*, New York, Rosen, 2001.

Rubinstein, Donna: *The Modeling Life*, New York, Berkeley Publishing Group, 1998.

Satterthwaite, Frank: *The Career Portfolio Workbook*, New York, McGraw-Hill, 2003.

Seguin, James: *Media Career Guide*, Boston, St. Martin's, 2006.

Sones, Melissa: *Getting into Fashion: A Career Guide*, New York, Ballantine, 1984.

Vogt, Peter: *Career Opportunities in the Fashion Industry*, New York, Facts on File, 2002.

Wilson, Wayne: *Careers in Publishing and Communications*, Bear, Mitchell Lane, 2002.

Yager, Fred, & Jan Yager: *Career Opportunities in the Film Industry*, New York, Ferguson, 2003.

Zahler, Karen Gantz.: *Superchefs: Signature Recipes From America's New Royalty*, New York, John Wiley & Sons, 1996.

Index

J

L

M

N

O

P

R

❑❑❑